The

The Body in Late-Capitalist USA

Donald M. Lowe

DUKE UNIVERSITY PRESS   *Durham and London 1995*

© 1995 Duke University Press

Printed in the United States of America on acid-free paper ∞

Typeset in Minion by Keystone Typesetting, Inc.

Library of Congress Cataloging-in-Publication Data
appear on the last printed page of this book.

for Tani

"Social life is essentially *practical*. All mysteries which mislead theory into mysticism find their rational solution in human practice and in the comprehension of this practice."—Marx, "Eighth Thesis on Feuerbach"

"But life involves before everything else eating and drinking, a habitation, clothing, and many other things. The first historical act is thus the production of the means to satisfy these needs, the production of material life itself. . . . The second fundamental point is that as soon as a need is satisfied new needs are made. . . ."—Marx and Engels, *The German Ideology*

"In culture every entity can become a semiotic phenomenon. The laws of signification are the laws of culture. For this reason culture allows a continuous process of communicative exchanges, in so far as it subsists as a system of systems of signification."—Eco, *A Theory of Semiotics*

"The incomplete character of every totality necessarily leads us to abandon, as a terrain of analysis, the premise of 'society' as a sutured and self-defined totality. 'Society' is not a valid object of discourse. There is no single underlying principle fixing—and hence constituting—the whole field of differences."—Laclau and Mouffe, *Hegemony and Socialist Strategy*

Contents

Acknowledgments

I wish to thank Tani Barlow, Jeff Escoffier, and Steve Martinot for critical reading of an earlier draft of the manuscript, especially Tani who helped me revise it several times; Ava Baron and Aihwa Ong for reading lists on gender construction; Richard Busacca for a discussion on exchange theory; Gilles Deleuze and Felix Guattari for the stimulation of *Anti-Oedipus;* Judith Farquhar for leads on schizophrenia; Donna Haraway for inspiration on the cyborg body; Thomas Laqueur who alerted me to Barbara Duden's bibliography; John Miller for a lead on political economy; Ilene Philipson and Jeff Escoffier for readings on mental health professions; Scott Sereno for materials on advertising; members of the former Bay Area reading group on Marxism and semiotics; my former students at San Francisco State University; the undersupported History Department of that underfinanced university, for giving me some release time for researching and writing the book; the interlibrary loan service at the San Francisco State University Library; and Ken Wissoker for shepherding the manuscript through the review process.

Introduction: Language, Body Practices, and the Social

In this work, I argue that the body in contemporary USA is socially constructed by the work we do, the commodities we consume, the ways we procreate and socialize the next generation, the politics of gender and sexuality, and the promised healing of impaired bodies by psychoanalysts and psychotherapists. These phenomena are what I term respectively production practices, consumption practices, social reproduction practices, practices of sexuality and gender construction, and practices of psychopathology. These practices define the limits and prospects of our bodily lives; changes in them change our bodily lives.

The work therefore is not about the body as that term is usually understood. In other words, it is not about literary representation or photo image of the body. Body image is currently ubiquitous, from the ever-youthful, aerobic image of the middle-aged Jane Fonda to the scan of the fetus swimming about in a woman's womb. And there are increasing numbers of books and articles on body image. To some extent, the way in which the body is represented and imaged deeply affects our lives, but representation and image do not directly reflect the actual conditions of the lived body. I reject any equivalence between body image/representation and the lived body.

On the other hand, academic disciplines such as sociology, psychology, and biology provide for compartmentalized studies of "society," "the psyche," and "organic life." Given this division of scholarship, any subsequent attempt to seek connection among the social, the psychical, and the organic is beyond the bounds of academia's societal, behavioral, and organismic paradigms, and will inevitably fail. Thus the lived body is equally missing from academic knowledge.

In the stead of traditional academics, I propose to undertake a synchronic study of the body by means of a Marxism informed by discourse theory, systems analysis, and semiotics. My study not only goes beyond the schismatic contradiction between mere body representation/image and specialized, compartmentalized knowledge of the body, but also takes into account that body representation and disciplinary studies of the body are also integral aspects of the social construction of bodily life in late-capitalist USA.

As living beings, we are more than body and mind, more than the representations and images of our bodies. We lead a bodily life in the world. Bodily life generates needs, some of which we must satisfy in order to survive, and others that are extraneous despite our fervent beliefs to the contrary. Needs, in other words, are not stable, unchanging universals. They vary not only from person to person, but also across social strata and historical moments. Thus, the needs of a homeless person are very different from those of an upscale yuppie; correspondingly, the range of needs in late capitalism is quite different from those in industrial capitalism. Furthermore, the very acts we undertake in order to satisfy our needs are seldom freely selected or invented. Always, there exists an ensemble of precedented practices that delineate existing needs and delimit the satisfaction of those needs, thus predetermining how we should devise specific acts. These are what I call body practices.

The ensemble of ongoing practices, in other words, code and construct the body. In late-capitalist USA, the practices of production and consumption, social reproduction, gender construction and sexuality, and psychopathology code and construct our bodily needs and their satisfactions. (Other worlds have different configurations of practices.) However, I shall argue, with the expansion and acceleration of late-capitalist production and consumption, two problems have ensued. All body practices—not just production and consumption, but social reproduction, gender construction and sexuality, and even psychopathology— have become commodified to such an extent, that the satisfaction of our diverse bodily needs is reconfigured by the requirements of flexible accumulation. Not only do late-capitalist body practices cut across terrains, these practices as such can no longer be analyzed as just structural. We need to re-analyze their very constitution.

To penetrate beneath body images, my study requires a reflexive understanding of the relations between language and bodily life in the world. Language grids and operates in the world. There is always more of the world and of ourselves than language can comprehend and represent. Nevertheless, language frames the transmission and continuance of body practices to satisfy our needs. Since we now realize how crucial language is in bodily lives, the methodological issue becomes one of clarification rather than the reduction of the central importance of language in the world. In order to address this issue, I shall refer to three important epistemic positions already staked out in the study of the body, namely Marxism, semiotics, and postmodernism.

Marxists usually assume that language is not a problem, and that within language we can realistically conceptualize the social relations or structures which code our bodily needs. Until recently, most Marxists believe that a one-to-one equivalence exists between concepts and their referents. Nevertheless, this realism was already questioned within the Marxist tradition by the Soviet semiotician V. N. Voloshinov, whose *Marxism and the Philosophy of Language* criticized the naive language realism of Marxism. The second epistemic position is that of the Swiss structural linguist Ferdinand de Saussure, whose *Course in General Linguistics* pointed to the existence of linguistic structure or system as the necessary synchronic order through which we interact and live in the world. The structuralism stemming from this position assumes a fundamental distinction between the sign and the referent. However, structuralism is only concerned with the workings of the signs, and does not deal with the referents of signs. The third, most recent position is that of postmodernism, which takes into account the central importance of language and communication in actively transforming the contemporary social reality. For example, Jean Baudrillard, the French sociologist who is a leading proponent of this view, has gone so far as to argue in *Simulations* that there is only a simulatory reality in the contemporary world, an order without stable referents. Nevertheless, Fredric Jameson, the American Marxist critic, insists that postmodernist culture is an integral part of a late, consumer capitalism.

This work takes into account the Marxist problematic of the reality of practices which code bodily needs, the structuralist and poststructuralist distinction between the sign and its referent, and the postmodernist concern with the new simulatory, semiotic reality. It differs from my earlier work on the history of bourgeois perception, which relied on a combination of Marxism and phenomenology. (Lowe 1982) In that work, I drew heavily from Merleau-Ponty's phenomenology of perception. The major difference between that work and the present one is that a phenomenology of perception presupposes an embodied existential being, and describes social reality from the standpoint of that embodied existence, while contemporary Marxism and poststructuralist semiotics propose a new problematic which questions the very possibility of a Logos of social phenomena to establish embodied being. The body has become problematical, a construction of changing social practices. I base the present study on three axiomatic concepts, *language, body practices,* and *the Social.* The three are neither commensurable nor co-equal, but rather intersect each other. These concepts are, I propose, the necessary axioms that render possible a study of the reality of body practices in the world, axioms that do not avoid the crucial importance of language. Or to put it the other way around, it is at the intersection of the three concepts of *language, body practices,* and *the Social* that I locate the reality of a lived body.

I use the term *language* not in the sense of the English as opposed to the Chinese language, nor the spoken as opposed to the written. What I mean by language is, as structuralists and poststructuralists suggest, that language as a system or structure is the categorical ordering of social reality. Language is a system or structure of signs. And a sign is a correlation of a signified and a signifier. (de Saussure 1966, p. 66) The signified is a concept which refers to something; the signifier is the sound-image conveying the signified; and the referent is what the sign refers to. Often, the referent of a sign may not be a real object or subject, but the signified or signifier of another sign. Thus, according to Umberto Eco, the Italian semiotician, the signified (a content) or the signifier (an expression) of one sign correlate can, in turn, be either the signifier (expression) or signified (content) of another sign correlate. Signification is therefore a *juxtaposition of signs.* There is never an equivalence between one signified and another, between one signifier and another, between a sign and its referent.

The concept of language as system or structure is necessarily synchronic, in the sense that the analytical framework here is spatial rather than temporal. All the signs in a moment cohere as a spatial order. They do not all necessarily persist together across time, nor change according to uniform laws. Yet practices based upon language go beyond its synchronic order to interact with existing, sedimented practices in the world; and the world is transformed across time. The consequences of practices in the world transcend the synchronic order of language; language then has to recoup them. It is in this sense that the study of diachronic change resembles, in its limitations, Eadweard Muybridge's effort at capturing the body in motion by means of a series of successively static photos intercepting an actual lived body in motion.

Body practices are the social practices which code the body. We can never know an actual lived body in the world. There is always an unbridgeable gap between the concept (a signified) of a body, and its referent (what the signified or concept refers to), which is the lived body in the world. The actual lived body is therefore the referent of the signified (or concept), what I call the body referent. However, in this case, unlike all other referents of signifieds, the body referent is our own body. This body referent, the actual, lived body in the world, i.e., our own body, is coded and realized by language, yet concurrently and in spite of that it is nevertheless always more than any concept, image or representation of it.

The body referent, our lived body, is not one half of a Cartesian body/mind dualism, nor even a psycho-bio-physiological unity. These are second-degree, social scientific conceptualizations of the body referent. Nor is there an actual body-in-itself without the world. The body referent as a human body living in the world already utilizes language for the sake of living, is already coded by the social practices in the world. Language thus infiltrates and frames the world. But there is more to the actual lived body than language, than what language can comprehend. The actual lived body undertakes practices by means of language. From the standpoints of both post-Kantian epistemology and poststructuralism, we cannot conceive of a body-in-itself. But we can study body practices, i.e., the social practices in the world which code, construct, and contextualize the body.

If language is synchronic, the concept of body practices is thoroughly temporal. The concept of body practices locate the body in its lived context by analyzing the actions and interactions which are necessary to satisfy its needs. Language plays a crucial role in these practices, for practices are transacted, passed on, revised and overcome by means of language. Nevertheless, I shall insist that practice is more than language, since it is an activity undertaken in the world. Moreover, there is never any single practice by itself. Practices are not undertaken *de novo*. They are a continuum of action and interaction. New practice is always undertaken against a background of precedented, sedimented practices. Precedented practices constitute a terrain within which new practices, whether conformist or innovating, become possible. Practices therefore are at once synchronically coded and temporally open-ended. Coded, in that existing practices establish the context or terrain for new practice; open-ended, in that new practice whether innovative or preservative will cumulatively change the context or terrain. The concept of body practices seeks to approximate the language-mediated practices undertaken by the lived body in the world to satisfy its needs.

The Social is an empty, abstract sign. It is the naming of the world, in order to avoid the functional, rationalist assumptions implicit in such existing categorical terms as "society" or "totality." The world is not necessarily functional, rational, or even orderly, as these two terms imply. The Social is more than language, since language exists and operates within it. Thus, the Social is beyond the conceptualization of language. It is in this sense that I agree with the post-Marxist political theorists, Ernesto Laclau and Chantal Mouffe, when they argued:

> The incomplete character of every totality necessarily leads us to abandon, as a terrain of analysis, the premise of "society" as a sutured and self-defined totality. "Society" is not a valid object of discourse. There is not a single underlying principle fixing—and hence constituting—the whole field of differences." (1985, p. 111)

In this work, I propose that production and consumption, social reproduction, gender construction and sexuality, and psychopathology constitute different terrains or contexts of body practices in late capitalism. These terrains of practices are contending, overlapping, and contradictory, in that the demands of practices within one terrain conflict with the demands of another. The demands of production and consumption practices, already at odds among themselves, conflict with the demands of social-reproduction practices, gender construction and sexuality, and psychopathology. There is neither social equilibrium nor functional rationality in the world, despite the attempts of social scientists to impose such rationalistic frameworks on the "societies" that they study.

I will argue in this work that the terrain of production and consumption practices has so expanded and accelerated in late-capitalist USA (chapters 1 and 2) as to valorize the practices of social reproduction, gender construction and sexuality, and psychopathology. In other words, exchangist, capital-accumulationist practices have by now become hegemonic (chapter 3). And from the standpoint of the practices which code the body, the commodified needs delineated and satisfied by social reproduction, gender construction and sexuality, and psychopathology have now become means or signifiers for the accumulation of exchange value (chapters 4, 5, and 6).

Practices code, construct, and determine the satisfaction of bodily needs. But how do we conceptualize and analyze body practices? Specifically, are late-capitalist body practices *structural* (in the Marxian, not the linguistic, sense), *discursive* (in the Foucaultian sense), *systematic* (in the sense of cybernetic systems with feedback mechanisms), or *semiotic* (at once signifying and communicative, as Eco would define it)? Or are they varying, differential combinations, in different locations and specific instances? Structure, discourse, systems, and semiotics are not equal, distinct, comparable entities. They combine and recombine in actual practices. (I assume that the analytics of practices in other social formations require other combinations of paradigms.)

Marx proposed that the social relations of production (what I would call production practices) constituted the economic structure of society, the real foundation on which a legal and political superstructure rose, and to which definite forms of social consciousness corresponded. (1859 "Preface" to *A Contribution to the Critique of Political Economy*) But, in the "Introduction" to his *Grundrisse,* he considered production and consumption to be a connected, dynamic circuit, with production ending in consumption, and consumption leading to another round of production. Nevertheless, "production is the real point of departure and hence also the predominant moment" of the circuit. (1973, p. 94) And, in *Capital,* Marx assumed that the reproduction of labor, or social reproduction, though necessary for the reproduction of capital, needed to be only minimally financed, since industrial capitalism had not yet commodified it. "The capitalist may safely leave its fulfillment to the laborer's instinct of self-preservation and of propagation." (1906, vol. I, 627)

For Marx, the terrain of capitalist production and consumption was ordered as a "structure." This structure has its outer limits, namely superstructure and forms of social consciousness—both being beyond the terrain of production and consumption, and reflecting that substructural terrain. This terrain is structured by a series of related sign correlates, which converge on the production of commodity as exchange value (a quantity) and its consumption as use value (a quality or specific utility). A commodity, according to Marx, is a mysterious thing, being at once the embodiment of exchange value and use value. But there can be no exchange value without use value, no quantity without quality, no production without consumption, nor reproduction of capital without the reproduction of labor. The relation between each set of correlates constitutes semiotically a sign function. Thus, within the structure of capitalist production, quality is the signifier for the development of quantity; use value the signifier for the development of exchange value; consumption the signifier for the development of production; and the reproduction of labor (or social reproduction) the signifier for the reproduction of capital. Marx's argument is that production, exchange value and the reproduction of capital constituted the problematic for industrial capitalism, while consumption, use value, and the reproduction of labor, though slow to change, were not problematical.

Marx's paradigm of structure broke important new ground in nineteenth-century social analysis. However, from the standpoint of the structuration of late capitalism, we see two problems in the Marxist paradigm. First, does this structural paradigm correspond to the reality of late capitalism? I shall argue that all the signifiers used as a means for the production of exchange value—consumption, use value, the reproduction of labor—are now dynamically developed in an expanded hegemonic terrain of production and consumption, thus also becoming problematical. Second, Michel Foucault's paradigm of discourse/power unearthed a complex of discursive practices in the nineteenth century which disputes the structural determination of the Marxist paradigm.

According to the French poststructuralist, discursive knowledge generates a field of micro-power; in turn, power is activated and sustained by discourse. The two implicate each other. There is no discourse without power, nor power without discourse. Discourse/power, a practice, disciplines the body. And subjectivity is the effect of discourse/power on the body. Foucault's work is a critique of the Marxist paradigm of structure. Discourse/power replaces the structure of production in the analysis of social practices. To Foucault, the needs of the body are delineated and satisfied by discursive practices. Instead of structure, he proposes discursivity as the paradigmatic ordering of the Social. Furthermore, Foucault does not believe in historical continuity. His genealogical method posits a past so different from the present, that we, from the standpoint of our present, cannot trace the continuous development of any concept or institution across time. (Foucault 1977) Knowledge, therefore, is not only discursive, but genealogical.

With neither structure nor linear history, Foucaultian discourse/power thus appears free-floating. But is there nothing besides discourse/power and the disciplined body? In *Discipline and Punish*, Foucault considered the discursive disciplining of the body "bound up, in accordance with complex reciprocal relations, with its economic use. . . . "

In fact, the two processes—the accumulation of men and the accumulation of capital—cannot be separated; it would not have been possible to solve the problem of the accumulation of men without the growth of an apparatus of production capable of both sustaining them and using them; conversely, the techniques that made the cumulative multiplicity of men useful accelerated the accumulation of capital. (1978a, pp. 25–26, 221)

Yet, since both discourse and production are processes, what are the differences and the connections between them? On this Foucault remained resoundingly silent.

Discourse, an analytical paradigm, cannot by itself explain the generation and circulation of micro-power. And in his preoccupation with discourse/power, Foucault was repeatedly forced to enlarge upon the meaning of discourse, supplementing it with other, non-discursive elements. In *Discipline and Punish,* he spoke of a "political technology" of the body. This technology is "diffuse, rarely formulated in continuous, systematic discourse; it is often made up of bits and pieces; it implements a disparate set of tools or methods. . . . Moreover, it cannot be localized in a particular type of institution or state apparatus." (1978a, p. 26) In *The History of Sexuality,* vol. I, he reformulated this political technology of the body as "bio-power." (1978b, pp. 139–40)

Foucault also used the term "*dispositif*" (translated into English as "apparatus") to denote the interplay of knowledge and power. "*Dispositif,*" he explained in an interview, is

firstly, a thoroughly heterogeneous ensemble consisting of discourses, laws, administrative measures, scientific statements, philosophical, moral and philanthropic propositions. . . . Secondly, . . . between these elements, whether discursive and non-discursive, there is a sort of interplay of shifts of position and modifications of function which can also vary very widely. Thirdly, I understand by the term 'apparatus' a sort of formation which has as its major function at a given historical moment that of responding to an *urgent need.* The apparatus thus has a dominant strategic function. (1981, pp. 194–95)

But Foucault admitted that he found himself "in a difficulty" that he could not get out of, since "*dispositif,*" with its heterogeneous elements, "is both discursive and non-discursive." (pp. 196–97)

I propose that the implicit other to Foucaultian discourse is the Marxist paradigm of structure. Foucault upended the Marxist hierarchy between structure *and* forms of social consciousness, and replaced forms of social consciousness with a poststructuralist concept of discourse. Thus, instead of forms of social consciousness as the explicit opposite to the Marxist economic structure, the Marxist structure has become the unstated opposite to Foucaultian discourse/power. Nevertheless, there is no structure without discourse, for structure as social relations is a cumulative, sedimented ordering of practices, and practices necessarily involve discourse. Nor is there discourse without structure, since discourse as practice is always undertaken against the background of prior discourses now established as social relations, i.e., structure. Structure and discourse are not two parallel, reciprocal processes. They supplement each other, in the sense that each analytical paradigm intersects from a different temporal perspective the workings of body practices in the Social. There ought to be a place for discourse within structure; and discourse always operates to confirm, modify, or transform existing structure. If Foucaultian discourse generates a field of micro-power from the bodies, then Marxist structure transforms this available power into the production of exchange value.

Furthermore, I believe, even the combination of Marxist structure and Foucaultian discourse is not sufficient to analyze the transformations of bodily practices in late capitalism. Marx considered technology as a part of the material forces of production. And Foucaultian discourse never dealt with semiotics. But, in late capitalism, the practices of technology (specifically cyberneticized systems analysis) and of semiotics (the signification of image and sign by communications media) have transformed structural and discursive practices beyond the recognitions of Marx and Foucault. We need therefore to analyze late-capitalist practices not only in terms of structure and discourse, but also from the standpoints of systems analysis and semiotics. For late-capitalist body practices are a complex combination and recombination of these four components.

Cybernetic systems are the new technology of late capitalism. Originating as a technique to target enemy aircraft and submarines, in World War II, they were introduced as "systems analysis" to large US corporations in the 1950s, and to the federal government in the 1960s. In the last two decades, with the coming of the micro-electronic revolution, the promises of cybernetic systems are finally becoming a reality; however, cybernetic systems are not neutral. Not only are they used for the sake of capital accumulation, but in the process they have subverted the knowledge and beliefs we inherited from the nineteenth century regarding the "natural," "stable," and "universal" oppositions between object and subject, individual and society, humans and machines.

Computer design, as Winograd and Flores point out, "has added a new dimension—the design of mechanisms that can carry out complex sequences of symbolic manipulations automatically, according to a fixed set of rules." (1986, p. 175) And as we work in this systematic domain, "we develop patterns of language and action that reflect [these] assumptions. These carry over into our understanding of ourselves and the way we conduct our lives." (p. 178) Katherine Hayles sees this as leading to an opposition between decontextualized, quantifiable information and natural language in context. According to Hayles, Claude Shannon's mathematical theory of information which underlies cybernetic practice is able to overcome the problem of contextual meanings in ordinary language, by defining information in purely quantitative terms. Instead of text dependent on context, information as a quantitative text is able to transcend, and therefore decontextualize, all contexts. "Never before in human history had the cultural context itself been constituted through a technology that makes it possible to fragment, manipulate, and reconstitute informational texts at will." (1987, p. 26) One application of this is the construction of a "military information society." (Cf., Levidow and Robins, eds., 1989)

A system is defined against its environment as the background. The boundary separating a system and its environment is flexible, depending on the purposes and goals of those in control of the system. Within the system, all information is quantifiable. And the system has feedback mechanisms to correct its workings. Thus, the system is able to subsume both humans and machines as quantities of information. The systematic equivalence between humans and machines has yielded a new science— ergonomics or human factors engineering. Ergonomists design systems which include and take into account the necessarily slower and less reliable human responses within them. This is true not only for human space flights, but also for any large, complex operation.

A new epistemic order underlies the practice of cybernetic systems. Twenty years ago, Foucault suggested that representation of identity and difference in space was the episteme of the seventeenth and eighteenth centuries, and temporal development in terms of analogy and succession that of the nineteenth century. (Foucault 1970) In my earlier work, I suggested systems of differences without identity as the episteme of the present century. The new synchronic order is unbounded by absolute space or time, since space and time have themselves become elements of a system. Elements of a system are interchangeable, since none possesses intrinsic value or stability. The new episteme emerged during the perceptual revolution of 1905–15. (1982, pp. 11, 117) But only in the second half of this century did the practice of cybernetic systems succeed in generating a new currency of power.

The practice of cybernetic systems presupposes and enhances differences without identity. With "information," "noise," "communication," "feedback," "interface," "simulation," "optimization," "replication," "boundary," and "environment," systems knowledge can supersede all binary oppositions. As Donna Haraway, the historian of science and postfeminist philosopher, puts it,

> modern regulation works by statistical control of least elements, not by a microcontrol or microtherapeutics of coherent individual bodies. Modern control is about stress engineering analysis of possibly overloaded systems; modern productive control is about rapid assembly, disassembly, and reassembly of all system components— biotic or otherwise. Females, bodies, and factories are all subject to these logics. Modern control is about the rates of information flows across boundaries; much is permissible within statistically well-policed boundaries. . . . It's all a question of rates and their management. (1984, p. 224)

Marx argued that the exchange value accumulated by capitalist production is mere quantity, not quality. I propose that the epistemic order of differences without identities in the late twentieth century finally confirms and facilitates the expanded, accelerated production of exchange value—a quantitative production no longer hindered by qualitative distinctions. This is the distinctly new possibility of late-capitalist accumulation.

Finally, late-capitalist body practices are not just structural, discursive and systematic, but also semiotic. And the crucial characteristic of contemporary semiotic practices is the superimposition of the image over the sign. (Throughout this work, I shall follow Eco's distinction between visual image and linguistic sign.) The result is a postmodernist culture of simulation, as opposed to the typographic culture based upon mechanical reproduction of the sign.

I accept Eco's argument that the sign (including the visual image) is not a fixed, physical entity, but a correlation between an expression (a signifier or sign vehicle) and a content (a signified or meaning). "Signs are the provisional result of coding rules which establish *transitory* correlations of elements, each of these elements being entitled to enter . . . into another correlation and thus form a new sign." Thus semiotics is at once communication—the physical production of expression for practical purposes, *and* signification—the generation of content or meaning by means of codes. Furthermore, Eco makes a fundamental distinction between the visual image and the linguistic sign. According to him, it is not that the image is iconic (similar to its referent), as Charles Peirce had proposed. The similarity is not between the content of the image and its referent, but "between the image and a previously culturalized content." Our belief in the seeming iconicity of the image is a cultural convention, based upon a set of codes which are much more complex than the codes for linguistic signs. "Similitude is *produced* and must be *learned*." (1976, pp. 49, 204, 200)

The codes of the image, I suggest, provide an extra level of signification, beyond the codes of linguistic signs. Not only does the image have a signified, a concept or a meaning, like the linguistic sign; the codes of the image work on us perceptually, to convince us that the image is exactly like its referent, that is the image is an icon, *when in fact it is not.* This is what makes an image more powerful than a linguistic sign. (Think for a moment of advertising image, which I shall elaborate on in chapter 2, sec. *b.*) Twentieth-century semiotics is meta-communication, by means of the juxtaposition of disembodied (i.e., non-perspectival, disproportionate) sights and sounds to facilitate the transfer of meanings from one sign to another. (Lowe 1982, pp. 134–39)

In *Simulation,* Baudrillard does not make a distinction between sign and image. But his simulatory sign works very much like the image. Baudrillard's argument is that simulatory signs no longer possess stable referents. Signs have lost their representational role. They refer, instead, to each other to signify a hyperreality. Within this simulated reality, accordingly, it is no longer possible to ascertain what is real, nor even to ask, "who is the addresser?" Baudrillard does admit, in passing, the existence of "a neo-capitalist cybernetic order that aims now at total control." But this order of simulation "puts an end to the myth of its origin and to all the referential values it has itself secreted along the way." (1983, pp. 111–12)

I agree with Baudrillard's notion of simulation, or the destabilization of referents. But I find his exclusive preoccupation with it insufficient. I accept that the signified of a sign refers to, but never is, its referent. The referent of a sign may, in its turn, become the signified or signifier of another sign. It is in this juxtaposition of signs, via electrical and electronic meta-communication of linguistic signs and visual images, that referents are destabilized in late capitalism.

However, I suggest, there still remains one referent apart from all the other destabilized referents, whose presence cannot be denied, and that is the body referent, our very own lived body. This body referent is in fact the referent of all referents, in the sense that ultimately all signifieds, values, or meanings refer to the delineation and satisfaction of the needs of the body. Precisely because all other referents are now destabilized, the body referent, our own body, has emerged as a problem. It is this problematic that Baudrillard does not acknowledge.

In "Postmodernism, or, The Cultural Logic of Late Capitalism," Fredric Jameson criticizes Baudrillard without mentioning him by name. Unlike Baudrillard, Jameson seeks to locate postmodernism in a late-capitalist political economy. The features of the postmodern culture as succinctly described by Jameson are

> a new depthlessness, which finds its prolongation both in contemporary 'theory' and in a whole new culture of the image of the simulacrum; a consequent weakening of historicity, both in our relationship to public History and in the new forms of our private temporality . . . ; a whole new type of emotional ground tone . . . [or] intensities which can best be grasped by a return to older theories of the sublime. . . . (1984, p. 58)

All this, Jameson argues, has "deep constitutive relationships . . . to a whole new technology, which is itself a figure for a whole new economic world system." Jameson follows Ernest Mandel in arguing that the third technological revolution, typified by cybernetic systems, is the correlate of a "late or multinational or consumer capitalism" which has led to "a prodigious expansion of capital into hitherto noncommodified areas." The result is that "aesthetic production today has become integrated into commodity production generally. . . . " Instead of being a Baudrillardian hyperreality unto itself, or even a relatively autonomous culture, postmodernism is an integral aspect of the workings of late capitalism. (pp. 58, 78, 56) I agree that postmodernism is no longer a relatively autonomous culture, but an integral aspect of late capitalism. However, I would like to extend this argument further, by delineating the workings of an expanded and accelerated production/consumption, beyond the paradigm of production structure.

I argue in this work that, in late capitalism, consumption as well as production are changing dynamically. Use value as a relatively stable quality has also become problematical. Expanded and accelerated production/consumption, with no stable point of reference, now characterize the new hegemonic terrain. The expansion and acceleration of production/consumption practices have eroded the relative autonomy of other practices, where non-exchangist practices, based upon distinct, qualitative values, once prevailed—not just social reproduction, but also gender construction and sexuality, even psychopathology. In the process, combinations and recombinations of discursive, systematic, and semiotic practices are dismantling what we formerly ordered as structure. With the hegemony of exchangist practices in late-capitalist USA, rapidly and constantly changing needs have propelled the body as a new problematic. The problematic is embodied existence in a world where all aspects of our lives, the environment we live in, and everything in between, have become means, or signifiers, of exchange value.

1 Production Practices

We live bodily lives within a changing social/historical world, beginning with the work we do and the goods and services, i.e., commodities, we consume, although politics, culture, religion, and personal aspirations provide extra meanings to life. Production and consumption practices are fundamental in the "social" construction of the body. (The "social" is a generic term, which I propose consists of structural, discursive, systematic, and semiotic components.) In this chapter, I argue that production practices have changed a great deal in the past two decades. Specifically, I single out three aspects of late-capitalist production practices in the coding and disciplining of the laboring body—flexible accumulation and the labor market, cybernetic systems and the labor process, and the discipline of neoclassical economics. I hope to accomplish two tasks here: to illustrate how under new production practices the laboring bodies are placed in new, different, and, I would hazard, greater jeopardies and stresses; and to present evidence that these new production practices consist of varying, differential combinations of structural, discursive, systematic, and semiotic components. In the next chapter, I shall discuss the equally important changes in consumption practices.

a. Flexible Accumulation and the Labor Market

Beneath statistical figures, changing labor market practices sort out and discipline laboring bodies along class, gender, and racial lines. Since the end of World War II, capital accumulation in the USA has gone through two phases. In the 1950s, gross domestic product grew at an average annual rate of 3.3 percent; in the 1960s, it reached 3.8 percent per annum. By the 1970s, the average annual rate of growth fell to 2.8 percent; in the 1980s, it was 2.6 percent. In the earlier period, labor costs were low, factory productivity grew apace with Germany's and Japan's, and the cost of capital was more equitable. However, in the more recent period, investment became anemic, real wages stagnated, and the economy's debt burden increased. If the first phase was characterized by a growth that trickled down to the lower classes and minorities, the second has been one of crises and a redistribution of wealth in favor of the wealthy few.

The two phases in US economy were demarcated by the decline in American productivity and growth, and the challenge of revived German and Japanese economies in the late 1960s, followed by the monetary crisis and the recession of the early 1970s. As the growth of the US economy slowed, the country became more dependent on foreign trade. That trade's share in the US economy increased from 9.4 percent in 1960 to 22.8 percent by 1991. (All figures from *Business Week: Reinventing America 1992*, pp. 22–23, 54) However, the increasing dependence on foreign trade occurred at the very time when the USA's share of the world exports of manufactures dropped from 25.3 percent in 1960 to 18.3 percent in 1980. (*SAUS 1982–83*, p. 781) The situation has not improved since then. As we all know, US merchandise trade balance became increasingly unfavorable, with exports increasing faster than imports. The balance dropped from +$4.9 billion in 1960 to +2.6 billion in 1970. It became −$25.5 billion in 1980, and worsened to −$108.1 billion in 1990. (*SAUS 1992*, pp. 746, 784)

In the two decades after the end of World War II, the USA was uniquely advantaged by its military and nuclear, as well as financial, industrial, and technological superiority, in dominating the non-socialist world. The USA's postwar hegemony was due as much to the wartime devastation of its allies and enemies as to its own strength, so that immediately after the war, American corporations could harvest the rewards with little competition. That hegemony was the foundation for the convertibility of the dollar into gold, an instrument which steadied capitalist investment calculation and therefore accumulation through growth. As Howard Wachtel observes, historically the world economy has grown faster when there is a pre-eminent economic power that writes the rules for the game, enforces their acceptance, and underwrites the risks. (1986, p. 33)

By the late sixties and early seventies, the Vietnam War, the collapse of the gold standard and the free-floating currency exchange, the economic challenges of Germany and Japan, and the imbalance in foreign trade put an end to that hegemony. The situation worsened with the explosion of the US national debt in the 1980s. Though still "number one," the USA could no longer prevail over the rest of the world. Concurrently, the world economy moved from crisis to crisis. Thus, the *New York Times* reported on December 17, 1986 that duplication and competition among national industries, as well as automation and technological improvement in production, resulted in over-production capacity and a persistently high level of unemployment. Dozens of industries throughout the world—such as steel, petrochemical, auto, aircraft, semiconductor, television, glass, apparel, shoe, toy—could not find sufficient markets for their products. By then, manufacturing and mining in the USA were operating at only 79.3 percent of capacity, as compared with more than 86 percent in the late 1970s. Overcapacity in production was reflected in a continuously high level of unemployment, both abroad and at home. The rate of unemployment for all of Western Europe rose from an average of 3.4 percent in 1970 to 12 percent in 1986. And in the USA, unemployment rose from 4.9 percent in 1970 to 7 percent in 1986.

Accumulation in a slower growing, less stable, more competitive capitalist world economy fundamentally differs from that in the faster growing, postwar capitalist economy under US hegemony. David Harvey has characterized the period since the early 1970s as one of *flexible accumulation*, necessitated by the crisis in the postwar pattern of capital accumulation. Instead of one based on the mass production and mass consumption of standardized products which relied on economies of scale, the new pattern favors the production and consumption of a variety of rapidly changing, specialized products targeted at specific market segments. Now, production can and has to be more flexible, utilizing the new machinery technology in small batch production. Flexible production implies not only new products and new consumption patterns, but also changes in managerial organization, capital investment, labor force, and labor market segmentation, as well as different roles for the nation state. Ultimately, according to Harvey, flexible accumulation entails "a new round of . . . 'time-space compression' in the capitalist world—the time horizons of both private and public decision-making have shrunk, while satellite communication and declining transport costs have made it increasingly possible to spread those decisions immediately over an ever wider and variegated space." (1989, p. 147)

Space has always been important in Marxist analysis. Dependency theory, underdevelopment theory, and world systems theory, with their emphasis on core/periphery relation, all emphasize spatial distribution in capitalist production and reproduction. From a different perspective, the French Marxist Henri Lefebvre wrote *The Production of Space* (1974), which concerns the urban spatial development that favors the reproduction of the social relations of capital production. Harvey himself has done extensive work on the built environment. In *The Condition of Postmodernity* (1989) he extends the analysis of late-capitalist space to discuss how new technology and communications enable finance capital to overcome spatial distance, and multinational corporations to transfer stages of their activities to different geographic locations. (chapter 11) And from a non-, though not necessarily anti-Marxist perspective, Edward Soja (1989) has argued for a postmodern geography which utilizes the category of space in analyzing the world economy.

Harvey also discussed the acceleration in the turnover time of the production and consumption of products, so that the half-life of a product is cut down. Quite independently, Juliet Schor has shown how American workers are caught in a time squeeze, putting in more hours and more days on the job, and having less leisure time. Between 1969 and 1987, she estimates, the annual hours of paid employment for male workers increased 98 percent, and for female workers 305 percent. Women's working hours increased even more than men's, because the former are now more likely to work full time and to take less time off for childbirth and child care. Wages have deteriorated in the last two decades, forcing men and women to resort to working overtime and holding more than one job at a time, in order to defray the higher costs of living. The situation is doubly burdensome for women employed full time who, after more than forty hours of paid work, have to do anywhere from twenty-five to forty-five extra hours of work around the house. This, despite the fact that, in married couple households, some husbands are helping more in domestic chores than before. (1991, pp. 29–31, 103–4)

I will return to Harvey's concept of "time-space compression" in flexible accumulation again, in chapter 3. But more immediately, I want to discuss here how flexible production has led to a resegmented and more flexible labor market in sorting out laboring bodies.

The employment of the labor force occurs not in a freely competitive market, but in a segmented labor market, reflecting the diverse demands of the different sectors of the economy. Edwards (1979), and Gordon, Edwards, and Reich (1982) have shown two dimensions of segmentation which resulted in a tripartite division of the postwar labor market. One dimension was the distinction between primary and secondary jobs.

Primary jobs were defined and organized by the large core corporations that controlled key industrial sectors, whereas secondary jobs laid outside of core corporate control, mostly in the smaller firms and in the peripheral industries. The other dimension was the division within the primary sector between the non-union, independent jobs which required education in general skills, and the subordinate jobs which required mostly on-the-job training and were negotiated by collective bargaining with trade unions. Thus, the postwar labor market was divided into the independent primary, the subordinate primary, and the secondary segments.

The independent primary segment included middle-level corporate employees, skilled craft workers, and professionals in both the corporate and public sectors. Independent primary jobs in both the corporate and public sectors had professional standards governing work performances. The workers here usually obtained formal skills at the college level, internalized the formal objectives of their firms, and were usually given greater discretion in their work situations. In return for education, responsibility, and experience, they could usually expect greater returns, high job ladders, and greater job mobility both within and between firms.

The subordinate primary segment included industrial workers, lower-level unionized sales, clerical, and administrative workers, and production-type workers in large transportation, retail and wholesale, and utility industries. These were semi-skilled, blue-collar, and white-collar union jobs. The work was usually routinize, typically machine-operated, with repetitive tasks governed by specific supervision and work rules. Workers here needed some formal education, but acquired most of the necessary skills on the job, within the firm. Controlled by company rules and union regulations, subordinate primary workers often lacked job mobility, but have job ladders, advancement, and security.

The secondary segment consisted of the non-union jobs in the peripheral industries. They included low-skill workers in the non-union and smaller firms, in the services, in retail and wholesale trades, as well as the lowest-level clerical workers, and migrant farm workers. Unlike primary jobs, these jobs were casual and dead-end, requiring little formal education, lacking stable employment, opportunity for job advancement, and security. Workers in the secondary segment typically earned, for comparable work, from two-thirds to four-fifths of the wages in the primary segments.

In 1970, the independent primary segment accounted for a third of the total nonagricultural employment of 68.2 million workers, the subordinate primary segment for a little less than a third, and the secondary segment for a little more than a third. Forty-three percent of working males were in the independent primary segment, 25 percent in the subordinate primary, and 32 percent in the secondary segment. On the other hand, only 18 percent of women were in the independent primary segment, while 40 percent were in the subordinate primary, and 42 percent in the secondary segment. As for minorities, 60 percent of all African-American workers and 50 percent of all Hispanic workers, both male and female, were in the secondary segment. Thus, women and minorities were under-represented in both of the primary segments, and over-represented in the secondary segment. In 1970, 95 percent of all women were employed in the lower-paying jobs in the peripheral manufacturing industries, retail trade, clerical occupations, and the health and educational sectors. (Gordon, Edwards, and Reich 1982, pp. 211–12, 204–10; Edwards 1979, pp. 167–70)

The postwar segmented labor market was based upon a revision of the capital-labor accord developed between management and unions in the mid-1930s, under the sponsorship of the New Deal. That revision, as Bowles, Gordon, and Weisskopf pointed out, included a purge of militant union leaders and the passage of the Taft-Hartley Act in 1947. The result ensured US management's control over mass production, technology, plant location, investment, and marketing. In return, and as long as they did not challenge these managerial controls, unions could bargain for the workers' immediate economic interests. In effect, "unions would help maintain an orderly and disciplined labor force while corporations would reward workers with a share of the income gains made possible by rising productivity, with greater employment security, and with improved working conditions." (1983, p. 73) In this way, the real value of the spendable hourly earnings of production workers rose at an average of 2.1 percent yearly from 1948 to 1966; workers' job security improved; and working conditions improved, with industrial accident rate, declining by nearly one-third between 1948 and the early 1960s; and aggregate unemployment rates dropped officially to 3.8 percent by 1966.

However, by the late 1960s, signs appeared to indicate problems in the existing postwar pattern of capital accumulation—a pattern based upon mass production and mass consumption, with the revised capital-labor accord and the welfare state playing important supporting roles. The growth of US productivity, which averaged 3.2 percent per annum between 1948 and 1965, slowed to an average of 2.4 percent yearly between 1965 and 1973. By the mid-1960s, Western European and Japanese economies began to grow faster than America's. (Reich 1983, p. 118) And as James O'Connor already pointed out in 1973, capital accumulation in postwar USA required increased support of the state in social investment and social consumption; but growth in that necessary support has resulted in the fiscal crisis of the state. (pp. 7–9)

The economic crisis of the 1970s accompanied and worsened the fiscal crisis of the state. In the last two decades, corporations had to learn to move away from mass production to flexible production. And the Reagan-Bush administrations tried to help by dismantling the capital-labor accord, deregulating industries, and privatizing certain governmental services.

The domestic labor market has been very much affected by the international competition in non-union labor supply, and the promise of special tariff reduction and tax write-offs. With advances in cybernetic systems and information technology, transnational corporations are able to rediscipline American workers with the threat of overseas manufacturing. They have dismantled the New Deal capital-labor accord by asking union workers in the subordinate primary segment to give back wages and fringe benefits, and to invest union pensions in the company. In addition, they are closing union plants, subcontracting more in the cheaper secondary labor segment, and employing greater numbers of temporary workers. Finally, corporations are consolidating and eliminating some independent primary jobs, especially the more expensive, middle-level managerial positions.

Instead of a segmented labor market, the new labor market conforms much more to the *Flexible Patterns of Work* characterized by the London-based Institute of Personnel Management. (1986, quoted in Harvey 1989, pp. 150–51) A core of primary jobs with full-time, permanent status, central to the long-term future of the corporate organization, is shrinking. Besides this core are two peripheral groups. One group consists of clerical, secretarial, routine, and lesser skilled manual jobs. Workers for these jobs are readily and cheaply available. They can be easily hired and discharged in tune with the needs of the company. The second group consists of the even cheaper, less secure, part-time, casual, temporary, fixed-term contract, subcontract, and publicly subsidized trainee jobs. This new pattern destructures the segmented labor market, enabling capital to adjust more flexibly to changing, new economic demands.

Three trends characterize changes in employment from the postwar to the more recent pattern of capital accumulation. Between 1970 and 1990, total employment increased from 78.7 million to 117.9 million. Agricultural jobs declined slightly from 3.5 million to 3.2 million. In 1970, these jobs represented 4.4 percent of total employment; by 1990, only 2.7 percent of the total. Manufacturing jobs grew slightly from 20.7 million to 21.2 million, but as a percentage of total employment, they declined from 26.4 percent in 1970, to 18 percent in 1990. On the other hand, services jobs of all kinds jumped from 49.1 million to 85.1 million. The former number represented 62.4 percent of total employment in 1970, whereas the latter was 72.2 percent of the 1990 total.

Total employment between 1970 and 1990 increased 49.9 percent, but services jobs of all types grew by 73.3 percent. Different types of services jobs grew at different rates. Employment in transportation, communication, and other public utilities grew by 52.9 percent; wholesale and retail trade by 61.7 percent—somewhat higher than the rate of growth of total employment, but below the average rate of growth for services as a whole. Higher growth rates within services occurred in *business-related services* such as advertising, building maintenance, personal management and consulting, computer and data processing, detective and protection services, and automobile maintenance (by 91.7 percent); *professional services* such as health, education, social, and legal services (by 96.3 percent); and *finance, insurance, and real estate* (by 103.3 percent). On the other hand, *public*, i.e., government, services increased by only 25.3 percent. Thus, between 1970 and 1990, above-average growth in jobs occurred mainly in business-related services, professional services, and financial services.

In terms of the actual number of jobs available, in decreasing order, professional services offered 12.4 million more jobs in 1990 than in 1970 (from 12.9 to 25.3 million); wholesale and retail 9.3 million more jobs (from 15 to 24.3 million); finance, insurance, and real estate 4.1 million more jobs (from 3.9 to 8 million); business-related services 3.9 million more jobs (from 1.4 to 5.3 million); transportation, communication, and public utilities 2.8 million more jobs (from 5.3 to 8.1 million); and public services 1.1 million more jobs (from 4.5 to 5.6 million). (*SAUS 1992*, p. 396) Most of the new jobs are necessary to the servicing of late-capitalist production and social reproduction, rather than production *per se*, i.e., manufacture or agriculture.

And these jobs pay more poorly. The US Bureau of Labor Statistics announced in 1987 that, over the last seven years, 83 percent of the jobs created have been in the lowest paying sectors of the US economy—retail trade and health and business services. Average weekly wages in these categories are $174 and $270 respectively, well below the poverty line for a family of four. The impact of the low-wage and part-time jobs being created in the economy is evident in the decline in average weekly earnings of American workers in real terms of over 9 percent in the last 10 years. (*New York Times*, June 20, 1987) Average hourly earnings in private industry groups have declined from $8.03 in 1970 to $7.53 in 1990 (in 1982 constant dollars). Within the group, this is true for manufacturing, construction, wholesale and retail trade, finance, insurance, and real estate, though it is not true for mining, transportation, public utilities, and services. However, in the entire twenty-year span, the total number of jobs in mining, transportation, and public utilities increased by only three million. (*SAUS 1992*, pp. 410, 396) Services jobs, which increased by 18.7 million between 1970 and 1990, are more at the lower pay scale, though there is debate as to whether these jobs are inherently unequal, or their inequality is a part of the general decline in productivity. (Levy 1987, chapter 5) Most recently, Kevin Lang and Bill Dickenson have found that service-producing industries have on the average a lower proportion of good jobs and a higher proportion of bad jobs than manufacturing industries. Furthermore, there are five times as many jobs in the former than in the latter. (*New York Times*, December 29, 1992)

From the standpoint of the gender and ethnic composition of the labor force that fill these jobs, the outstanding feature has been the steadily increasing participation of women, and more recently of non-black minorities, as the total employment grew from 78.7 million in 1970 to 117.9 million in 1990. In 1960, two thirds of those in civilian employment were male, one third female. By 1990, 54.6 percent male, 45.4 percent female. In 1960, 35.5 percent of women over the age of 16 were employed; by 1990, 54.3 percent. In 1980, 9.4 percent of the actively employed were African Americans; in 1990, 10.1 percent. In 1980, 5.6 percent of the workforce was Hispanic; by 1990, 7.5 percent. Nevertheless, over the decades, even with the increasing entry of females into the labor force, males are more likely to be employed than females; whites more likely than African Americans, and white males more likely than African-American males. But, at the bottom of the ladder, African-American females are more likely to work than white females. (*SAUS 1992*, pp. 381–83) Women and minorities continue to be over-represented at the bottom, and under-represented at the top of the labor force. In

1984, white women who worked full time earned an average of 35 percent less than white men. In that same year, nearly a quarter of all black men between the ages of twenty-five to fifty-five reported incomes of less than $5,000 per year! (Levy 1987, p. 141)

As the economy became more unstable and competitive, corporations have resorted to overtime work, part-time work, temporary work, and subcontracting work. *Business Week* (Dec. 15, 1986) reports a doubling of the number of "contingent employees" since 1980, mostly females who work at home, jobbing for outside contractors or involuntarily working part-time. This labor force presently constitutes nearly 17 percent of all workers. Contingent work is growing most rapidly in the services; here part-timers have accounted for 40 percent of the retail industry's job growth over the past twelve years, and in 1985, more than one-third of all retail employees were part-time employees. Typically, 3.8 million part-timers wanted full-time work, but could not find it. Part-timers earn $4.17 per hour on the average, whereas full-time workers earn $7.05 per hour. Furthermore, 70 percent of part-timers have no employer-provided retirement plan, and 42 percent have no health insurance coverage whatever. On March 16, 1988, *The New York Times* reported that anywhere from one to three million of the ten million jobs created in the USA since 1982 are temporary full-time jobs, where workers put in at least thirty-five hours of work each week. Temporaries are paid less and receive fewer benefits, and can be fired at will. Many full-time temporary employees are clerical workers, or in low-level jobs in health care, computer operations, and other such fields. On March 15, 1993, the *New York Times* estimated "about half of the jobs people have been getting in [1992] are part-time or temporary or involve other unconventional arrangements."

Beyond and below the active labor force is a reserve army of un-, under-, non-, and temporarily employed. This reservoir of labor is difficult to assess, since government figures for the unemployed surrealistically include only those "unemployed" who are actively looking for jobs, but not the discouraged, permanently "non-employed." Nor are formerly unemployed and presently active part-time, underemployed workers who need full-time work included in the government count of the "unemployed." Altogether, Leggett and Cervinka calculated, this reserve army might be anywhere from two to three times the official unemployment figure kept by the government. (1979; also Gordon ed. 1977, pp. 70–75)

By using these considerably deflated figures, we can still discern trends, even though actual conditions must be considerably worse. In 1970, with the general unemployment rate officially at 4.9 percent, the breakdowns were 4.5 percent for whites, 4.4 percent for males, and 5.9 percent for females. No figures were available for African Americans and Hispanics. In 1980, with the general unemployment rate at 7.1 percent, the breakdowns were 6.3 percent for whites, 14.3 percent for African Americans, and 10.1 percent for Hispanics; 6.9 percent for males, and 7.4 percent for females. By 1991, with the general unemployment rate at 6.7 percent, the breakdowns were 6 percent for whites, 12.4 percent for African Americans, and 9.9 percent for Hispanic; 7 percent for males, and 6.3 percent for females. (*SAUS 1992*, p. 383) In other words, white workers suffer less from unemployment than minorities, with African Americans twice as likely to be unemployed as whites, and Hispanics faring somewhat better than African Americans. Women used to be more likely to be unemployed than men, but with more women working at lower wages, men became more likely to be unemployed in the recession year of 1991.

The threat of unemployment disciplines the labor force. A Congressional study in 1986 reported that it was not the rise of single-parent households, but unemployment and falling wages that mostly accounted for the seven million increase in the number of poor Americans since 1979. Households headed by married couples accounted for 44.9 percent of the increase in poverty since 1979. By contrast, persons in single-parent, female-headed families accounted for 31.5 percent of the new poverty over the same period. Weak trends in employment and wages were also important factors in the growth of poverty, notably among workers earning the minimum wage. The poverty rate seemed to rise and fall in lock step with the unemployment rate. The US Census Bureau reported that, in 1985, 33.1 million Americans, or 14 percent of the population, lived in poverty. (*New York Times*, December 22, 1986)

The social consequences of the economic and political readjustments to the demands of flexible accumulation in the last twenty years are a more unequal America, with the rich (a slightly increasing number) getting richer, the poor (a much larger increase in number) getting poorer, and the middle shrinking in number. The *New York Times* reported, on February 23, 1989, a "widening" gap between the nation's rich and poor. New Congressional data show that, taking inflation into account, the average family income of the poorest fifth of the population declined by 6.1 percent from 1979 to 1987, while the highest-paid family income rose 11.1 percent during the same period. To some extent, the rise among those in the upper income levels is due to the increasing number of working women in two-income families. The poor, on the other hand, take up the many jobs paying only poverty level wages or below that. In 1972, the richest 1 percent of American families owned 27 percent of the nation's wealth. By 1987, they were approaching the 36 percent peak share attained in 1929. (*New York Times,* June 21, 1987) Breaking this figure down along racial lines, *Business Week* reported on September 25, 1989, that the white median household income stood at $27,427 in 1987, while African Americans earned only 56 percent of that. Back in 1969, the median African-American household income was 60 percent of white income. Cutbacks in welfare disbursements and the loss of high-paying manufacturing jobs help to explain the worsening income position of African Americans.

b. Cybernetic Systems and the Labor Process

Cybernetic systems are not neutral. They are always controlled, used, and promoted to reinforce and revise an existing labor process. I shall in this section argue that systems analysis using cybernetic automation and microelectronics have, in the last two decades, so transformed the labor process that the laboring bodies, already sorted out in the resegmented labor market, are recoded and redisciplined at the new workplaces.

Labor process as a concept is helpful in providing a contextual approach to the issue of technology. At the heart of the concept is its emphasis on the combination of human labor and technology in the production of capital accumulation. From the standpoint of capital accumulation, the calculation of the cost and benefit of technological innovation in reducing labor cost requires management to maintain hierarchical control in the labor process. Hierarchical control is fundamental. In other words, efficiency is never an end in itself, but always at the service of hierarchical control. Such is the case with the latest technology, i.e., cybernetic systems.

In the late 1970s and early 1980s, the debate over the labor process centered on Harry Braverman's *Labor and Monopoly Capital* (1974). The thesis of that work is summarized in its subtitle, "the degradation of work in the twentieth century." Braverman associated skill with the tradition of craft mastery, which was based on a combination of knowledge and manual dexterities in a specific branch of production.

The breakup of craft skills and the reconstruction of production as a collective or social process have destroyed the traditional concept of skill and opened up only one way for mastery over the labor process to develop: in and through scientific, technical, and engineering knowledge. But the extreme concentration of this knowledge in the hands of management and its closely associated staff organizations have closed this avenue to the working population. What is left to workers is a reinterpreted and woefully inadequate concept of skill: a specific dexterity, a limited and repetitious operation, "speed as skill," etc. (pp. 443–44)

This deskilling of workers, according to Braverman, occurs not only on the assembly line, but also with the more recent automation of office work.

Three kinds of criticisms have been directed at Braverman's deskilling thesis. First, it erects a romantic vision of craft skill, against which it proposes that specialized work processes have broken up the skill or mastery of craftwork. Second, it does not admit the possibility that some jobs may be reskilled, while others deskilled. And third, it overlooks how management obtains labor cooperation by negotiating with workers about their work organization. (Blackburn, Coombs, and Green 1985, p. 89)

Thus, Richard Edwards (1979) in modifying Braverman's deskilling thesis, distinguished three successive types of hierarchical control of work: Simple, personal control in the small firm; technical control of the physical labor process in the large corporate firm, as epitomized in assembly-line production and time-and-motion study; and bureaucratic control embedded in the system of social relations of the large firm. In type three, i.e., bureaucratic control, hierarchical power is routinized through rules and procedures to direct work, evaluate performance, and exercise sanctions and rewards. Work in the corporation is highly stratified, with each job given its distinct title and control, and impersonal rules governing promotion. Bureaucratic control emerged in the postwar era as the organizing principle in both production and nonproduction jobs in many large firms. It "institutionalized the exercise of capitalist power, making power appear to emanate from the formal organization itself." (p. 145)

These three types of hierarchical control, according to Edwards, emerged successively in the history of the capitalist enterprise. But presently, they exist as stratified layers of management strategies for different types of firms in the different sectors of the political economy. Combining his typology of management control with the segmented labor market, Edwards shows that most jobs in the secondary segment, such as small manufacturing, service, retail sales, temporary, and typing-pool office work, are under simple control; while most jobs in the subordinate primary segment, such as auto and steel plant, assembly-line production, and machine-paced clerical work, are under technical control; and most jobs in the independent primary segment, such as those at the multi-unit business enterprise, craft work and nonproduction staff level, are under bureaucratic control. (p. 179)

Michael Burawoy, in his study of assembly-line manufacturing, criticized the concept of labor process as a structure. He adds a political contest between management and labor to the labor process, and distinguishes between the labor process conceived as a particular organization of tasks *and* the political apparatuses of production conceived as labor's mode of regulation in late capitalism. (1985, pp. 7–8) Thus, the labor process is a contested terrain between management and labor. The contest is carried out beyond the bargaining table, occurring daily on the shop floor. Social and ideological conflicts outside the workplace are also reflected in the day-to-day politics of production. Finally, this specific labor process was fostered and mediated, in the initial postwar decades of prosperity, by a state-sponsored capital-labor accord which encouraged collective bargaining.

Braverman's thesis assumes an assembly-line model of production. Yet assembly-line manufacture never provided more than a third of the jobs throughout twentieth-century USA. And the real growth in post-World War II jobs has occurred in the services. Of course, the argument can be made that the assembly-line model is the locomotive which sets the norm. Even so, the labor process has by now far exceeded the perimeter of the debate set by Braverman.

During the late fifties and early sixties, with advances in computer technology and prospects of its likely applications in industry, business, and government, discussion surfaced over the economic and social impacts of computer technology. Nevertheless, despite that anticipation, the much-heralded computerization of the world did not immediately materialize, and the public's interest soon waned. However, the invention of miniaturized, low-cost microprocessors and sensor-scanning machines in the 1970s spread the use of microelectronic automation, from industrial robotics and self-regulated instruments for spacecraft control and guidance, to automatic bankteller machines and programmable household appliances. (cf., Forester 1981 ed.)

By August 3, 1981, *Business Week* reported that the speed of automation had led to a radical restructuring of work, including the devaluation of current work skills and the creation of new ones at an ever-increasing rate, so that 45 percent of the total labor force had already been affected. In April 25, 1983, the same magazine reported a new era of management, in which offices and factories were computerized, and data transmitted directly from the shop floor to the executive suite, thus making many middle managers redundant. "Companies will be leaner, more fluid, with fewer levels of management and more direct communication." And in October 14, 1985, *Business Week* crowed that computerized information power would now provide an edge in the highly competitive business world, which no corporation can afford to ignore.

Thus, at the very start of the Braverman debate, in the mid-1970s, production practices had, under the impact of automation and microelectronics revolution, already begun to shift away from the assembly-line model. Specifically, management's application of systems analysis and microelectronic automation calls into question Braverman's reference to the pre-cybernetic science of industrial management, Edwards's distinction between technical control in the subordinate primary segment and bureaucratic control in the independent primary segment, and Burawoy's generalization in regard to the politics of production in the subordinate primary segment. We need, instead, to look at the impact of automation and microelectronics in the labor process—not only in manufacturing, but also in the services.

Harley Shaiken, in *Work Transformed* (1984), argues that what computers and microelectronics have done is to automate the collection, transfer, and control of information. This is true not only in the factory, but also in the office. Although he never uses the term labor process nor mentions Braverman by name, Shaiken very much follows the argument of labor process that corporations maintain capital accumulation by means of hierarchical control. According to him, automation based upon computer and microelectronics, as compared with previous technologies, provides greater flexibility, has wider applicability, and accelerates the rate of change. Theoretically, the new technology provides a number of new choices, ranging from a greater degree of worker autonomy to greater managerial authority, more skills to fewer skills. But "management's central criterion for production is maximizing profitability." And in its drive for profitability "management's development of new machines and systems reflects the desire to increase control over production, over the activities of workers as well as over the movement of materials." It is not technically nor economically feasible to eliminate the worker on the job entirely. Instead, new computer-based designs seek to "reduce skill requirements, transfer decision-making off the shop floor, and exert tighter control over the workers who remain. The result can be more boring and stressful work in a more tightly controlled work environment." (pp. 4, 5) Feldberg and Glenn (1983) confirm Shaiken's thesis that computerization has sped up work and increased the rationalization of the work force. This is true not just on the assembly line. Monitoring systems are built into office computer equipment to check and speed up work pace.

Blackburn, Coombs, and Green, in their study (1985) of the link between technological developments in the labor process *and* long waves in capitalist economic growth, see three aspects to the computer-based automation. The first is *technological* development in control mechanization, which weakens the link between mechanization and economy of scale. This flexible form permits increased variability in products and processes at higher levels of mechanization. The second is *organizational* change in favor of the adoption of work roles, rather than individual repetitive tasks organized on a hierarchical basis. The third is *informational* infrastructure, which integrate different productive sub-units— such as semi-autonomous groups, machining centers, or different interdependent, geographically separated production units—with control of materials flow, stock control, and production planning. (pp. 104–5) Blackburn, Coombs, and Green then examine the development and use, among small-batch engineering industries, of numerically controlled and computer-controlled machine tools in cellular systems which ultimately link together in computer-aided manufacturing systems.

They conclude that "rather than a centralized, highly mechanized system, the result is likely to take the form of tighter organizational control over production, with workers exercising a relatively high degree of autonomy and skill at a local level." (pp. 144–45) As for the many different services, "the integration of separate pieces of office equipment, within and between offices, and their diffusion . . . will permit all sorts of 'information workers' to perform a wider array of non-standardized tasks at higher productivity levels." (pp. 170–71) Nevertheless, as the authors do point out, other areas of clerical work are more resistant to computerization.

However, from the standpoint of work content, Cavestro (1989) argues that "automation and computerization bring a new diversity of tasks as a result of a general transformation of working activities, skills and areas of competence." (p. 219) He sees several characteristic trends emerging with the automation of industrial processes. First, the growing complexity and variety of technologies mean that workers have to cope with increasingly difficult information systems. Second, workers have to learn how to anticipate and resolve new and different breakdowns, unforeseen incidents and errors which inevitably and repeatedly occur in such highly formalized work processes. And third, workers have to gather data and construct hypotheses and strategies to resolve these problems in a coded language. Thus,

> the operators work increasingly from a symbolic representation of the [work] process, in coded language form. A symbolic system of data representation is set up between the operators and the automated installation. The operators must learn how to code and decode the data which is part of their stock of knowledge. They are confronted by several types of information—visual, aural, symbolic—which accentuate the intellectual dimension of their work. (pp. 226–27)

The point Cavestro raised regarding the content of knowledge resulting from the new technology is reconfirmed by Winograd and Flores. According to them, computer design "regards language as a system of symbols that are composed into patterns that stand for things in the world. Sentences can represent the world truly or falsely, coherently or incoherently, but the ultimate grounding is their *correspondence* with the affairs they represent." (1986, p. 17) Computer design promotes the mathematical analysis of decision making and the related behavioral analysis of human conduct. Here, "decision making is regarded as the central task of management and is characterized by a process of information gathering and processing. Rational behavior is seen as a consequence of choosing among alternatives according to an evaluation of outcomes." (p. 20) Finally, computer design seeks to unify theories of human thought and language under a new discipline of cognitive science, which analogizes cognitive systems to programmed computers. The result is "artificial intelligence—the design and testing of computer programs that carry out activities patterned after human thought and language. These programs are then taken as theories of the corresponding human behavior." (pp. 25–26) The danger, argue Winograd and

Flores, is that this highly rationalistic approach tends to reduce human understanding and the intersubjective world to the level of computer rationality.

Also, Zuboff (1988) discovers that workers formerly had to have "action-centered skills," which were sentient, action-dependent, context-dependent and personal. (1988, p. 61) But cybernetic computerization requires "intellectual skills," which utilize abstract rather than physical clues, emphasizing inferential reasoning and procedural systematic thinking. Such skill "works through the problem of symbolic meaning at two levels. First, it establishes the referential power of symbols and thus provides them with legitimacy. Second, it uses the symbolic medium to ascertain the condition of 'reality' in ways that cannot be reduced to correspondence with physical objects." (pp. 95–96) Though new skills require education, and have the potential to erode the hierarchical power of managers, Zuboff finds management so far has refused to reorganize in response to the new intellectual skills. Instead, it has turned to cybernetic computerization as a sort of "information panopticon" over its workers, to enhance its own hierarchical control.

In effect, management science and microelectronic automation create some high-paying professional, managerial jobs, but create many more low-paying, deskilled blue-collar and white-collar jobs. The few will need general education, while the majority will need only limited, specialized data processing skills. The labor force as a whole is being polarized into a mildly expanding top echelon, a shrinking middle, and an enlarged bottom. Because of the imbedded discrimination against women and minorities in the resegmented and more flexible labor market, the present polarizing trend between the managerial, professional elite and the majority of specialized technical workers will increase the already high proportion of women and minorities in low-paying, dead-end, insecure jobs. (Levitan and Johnson 1982, pp. 135–40; Schwartz and Neikirk 1983, chapter 5)

Furthermore, computerization has led to jobs loss. In 1985, the US Labor Department reported that growth rate for clerical jobs has begun to decline for the first time in more than two decades; and "9 to 5," the Association of Working Women, has said that the Midwest was already losing clerical jobs due to automation. (*New York Times*, October 7, 1985) Those displaced have a tough time finding other jobs, and often are not retrained in other skills. And many of the middle-level management jobs eliminated in the most recent "recession" of 1991 are not expected to be restored.

Laboring bodies suffer specific hazards and stresses on the job. These hazards extract physical, physiological, and psychological tolls beyond the alienation of labor power. Hazards and stresses are built into the workplace as part of the labor process, but usually are over-looked for the sake of capital accumulation. The labor market sorts out bodies in terms of class, gender, and ethnicity, then channels them into various types of work, which inflict a plethora of hazards and stresses on them. Thus, laboring bodies suffer specific hazards and stresses in accordance with class, gender, and ethnicity.

Clerical workers, not usually confronted with immediately fatal or overwhelming hazards, suffer from excessive sitting, muscular and mental fatigue, noise, muscle strain, and various kinds of air contaminants in the workplace. Blue-collar, manual workers, including some service workers, tend to suffer higher incidences of bodily injury and illness than white-collar and professional, managerial workers.

Women and minority workers are over-represented in clerical and blue-collar work, and under-represented in managerial, white-collar work. These workers suffer a double jeopardy, particularly African-American workers, who sustain heavy occupational hazards and stresses. The US Bureau of Labor Statistics shows that, among thirty industries with the highest percentages of non-white workers, non-whites are concentrated primarily in manufacturing and service industries, two sectors of the economy with high rates of occupational disease. Not only are minority workers concentrated in the most dangerous sectors of the economy, they are also over-represented in the more dangerous occupations within these industries. Government statistics do not report the number of minority workers in specific job classifications. Nevertheless, one independent study estimated that African-American workers have a 37 percent greater chance than white workers of having an occupational injury or illness and a 24 percent greater chance of dying from one. (Davis and Rowland 1983, pp. 418, 420)

New work brings new dangers. Automation and computerization have enhanced control of workers, robbed them of any remaining job autonomy, and increased the physical hazard and psychological stress. Also, the distinctions between white-collar and blue-collar jobs are lessening, since both categories of workers now operate video display terminals. Field studies of VDT operators, according to Howard (1985), show symptoms of blurred vision, irritated eyes, and other signs of ocular discomfort; chronic pains in the back, neck, and shoulders; and frequent headaches. The more time spent working at the terminals, the greater the frequency of complaints. At the same time, reports of psychological indications of stress—insomnia, feelings of fatigue, nervousness, and depression—are also unusually common among VDT workers.

The Labor Department reported in 1989 that computer technology has contributed to a sharp increase in workplace injuries caused by repetitive motion. Repetitive motion disorders accounted for 18 percent of occupational illnesses and injuries in 1981, 38 percent in 1987, and 48 percent in 1988. Furthermore, full-time workers spent more time out of work or doing limited work due to illnesses or injuries in 1988, than in any year since the Bureau of Labor Statistics started to gather these data in 1972. "We seem to be asking people to do their jobs faster and in smaller, more finely defined tasks," said the head of the Occupational Safety and Health Administration (OSHA). (*New York Times*, Nov. 16, 1989) This is true for both blue- and white-collar workers. "In factories, new machines divide work into small tasks repeated thousands of times a day. In offices, employees can make more than 10,000 keystrokes an hour on video display terminals." All of these cause painful nerve injuries arising from the accumulated effects of making the same movement over and over again. (January 30, 1989)

And job stress is on the rise. In California, stress claim filings by workers increased sixfold in nine years in the 1980s, with the real totals possibly four times higher, according to the California Workers' Compensation Institute. Stress claims occur primarily in white-collar jobs, with more women filing than men. There are many reasons for the increase, including greater awareness of the option to file a stress claim. But one reason for the increase in stress claims is the pressure of computerization. (*San Francisco Chronicle*, July 22, 1990)

c. The Discipline of Neoclassical Economics

Neoclassical economics is a Foucaultian discourse, at once an academic knowledge and a body discipline. I argue in this section that the shift from neo-Keynesian economics to neoclassical economics, in the 1970s, is a change in the deployment of discourse/power. The change at once justifies and obfuscates the transformation of late-capitalist production practices in the USA, to adversely affect the laboring bodies.

Changes in production practices cannot be simply attributed to the structural and systematic demands of flexible production. Different advanced industrial nations respond to the structural, systematic demands differently. Production practices in late-capitalist USA devaluate the workers much more than in other advanced industrial nations. Lester Thurow estimates that, in the USA, service workers are paid only 67 percent as much as manufacturing workers, whereas in Japan they are paid 93 percent as much, and in Germany 85 percent as much. (*New York Times*, September 4, 1989) Workers in this country get much less paid vacation than their counterparts in Western European nations. (Schor 1991, p. 82) Other advanced industrial nations have maternity leaves, but the USA did not until 1993.

Business Week has long complained about the inadequate investment in the education and training of American workers. (September 19, 1988) Following the most recent recession of 1991, corporations have downsized, dispensing with workers and middle-management personnel. (*Ibid.*, December 28, 1992; *San Francisco Chronicle*, October 26–29, 1992) The magazine reports that American corporations, unlike those in other advanced industrial nations, are currently structured on a high-turnover and low-wage model which deskills workers. For example, in a survey of some four hundred companies, the National Center on Education and the Economy found less than 10 percent of these firms plan to spur output by reorganizing work in a way that calls for employees with broad-based skills and adaptability; less than 30 percent of the companies plan to have special training programs for the women, immigrants, and minority youths that will become the new workers; but over 80 percent are more concerned about workers' attitudes and personalities than about basic skills. (June 25, 1990) Even with the slow, uneven recovery, US corporations are investing more in equipment than the training of workers. (*Ibid.*, January 11, 1993)

Various factors have been identified as explanations for the more stark, less supportive policies toward laboring bodies in this country— such as lower minimum wages, weaker unions, less generous social welfare systems, little emphasis on equality in settling wage levels, and looser labor markets. However, beyond this positivist "causality by identity," corporate as well as Reagan-Bush policies toward labor were justified by the discourse of neoclassical economics. The transformation in late-capitalist production practices is not just structural and systematic, but also discursive.

The discourse of neo-Keynesianism, influential during the Kennedy-Johnson administrations, was somewhat supportive of laboring bodies. Neo-Keynesian economics, unlike neoclassical economics, did not claim to be a self-contained, autonomous science. It assumed an imperfect capitalist market which requires fine-tuning by the state. Thus, in times of high unemployment, fiscal policies could stimulate demands, and in times of inflation, that stimulation would lessen. Underlying this discursive logic is the hypothesis of an inverse correlation between inflation and unemployment, the so-called "Phillips curve." The argument for fiscal policies opened the door to various welfare policies and legislations by the Democratic administrations. However, the "stagflation" of the 1970s, i.e., high unemployment in a stagnant economy accompanied by inflation, destroyed the plausibility of the fiscal policies of neo-Keynesian economics.

Neoclassical economics, in claiming to be a self-contained discipline based upon statistical data and econometric modeling, argues for the autonomy and integrity of the capitalist market. At the core of the new discourse is the belief in the self-correcting, equilibrial mechanism of the market, if it were freed from the interference of fiscal policies and government regulations. Neoclassical economics provided the political rhetoric of the Reagan-Bush administrations, even if some neoclassical economists may not agree with the economic policies of the Republican administrations. I shall evaluate the discourse of neoclassical economics, by first reviewing briefly the conceptual assumptions of the new classical economics, and then examining the concepts of two influential neo-conservative economists from the Chicago school, Gary Becker and Milton Friedman.

The new classical economics of academicians like Robert Lucas, Thomas Sargent, and Robert Townsend rests on three related arguments (even if the emphasis on the three arguments may vary): rational expectations, equilibrium prices, and the neutrality, i.e., long-term ineffectiveness, of government policies. (Klamer 1984, p. 70) The argument of "rational expectations" hypothesizes that individuals and firms make decisions on the basis of their knowledge of the workings of the capitalist market, in order to optimize their own economic gains. The workings of the market are not erratic, and in the long run cannot be distorted by non-economic factors. Since it is self-contained and self-corrective, the market can be econometrically modelled. Thus, the rationality in "rational expectations" is one of economic expectation and the decision-making based on that expectation. Knowledge, Lucas insists, is not a problem. "These things have a lot to do with information. Learning, for example, is a red herring. According to the way I look at things, this is just a question of how you like to think about probabilities. Things that we model which have probability distributions I call 'random variables' and things that don't, 'parameters.' . . . Nothing operational is at stake here." (p. 39)

In the market, aggregate supply and aggregate demand meet in equilibrium, i.e., market clearing. Prices actually reflect that equilibrium, business cycles and unemployment notwithstanding. According to Sargent,

> What we mean by equilibrium is essentially two things. First, we set out to explain data on prices and quantities resulting from the interaction of individual decisions; that's the key thing together with the notion that markets clear in some sense. That doesn't mean everybody has a job every period. The notion of clearing may be much more complicated and may involve lotteries. There are various responses why workers are unemployed. An example would be construction, an industry in which the probability of being thrown out of work for a certain fraction of the year is higher than it is in many other industries. Instead of saying that that's disequilibrium in the construction industry, we would seek reasons why the industry is organized that way. *So the models seek to permit the theory of choice to explain things.* Another thing is that these environments are sufficiently complicated so that it's not automatic that equilibrium is optimal. (Klamer 1984, p. 68, italics added)

It could very well be, continues Sargent, that something which appears like a disequilibrium model is one "in which there are multiple equilibria." Besides, "adjustments don't occur instantaneously. There are lags, but the adjustments occur at about the right rate." (p. 69)

Because rationality and equilibrium pertain to the market, the new classical economics proposes that government policies are in the long run ineffective. Immediately, they may stimulate individual demand. But stimulated demand will lead to inflated prices, which will then restore the equilibrium between supply and demand, though at an inflated level. In the meantime, stimulatory policies may very well generate other unintended consequences. New classical economists differ among themselves regarding the role of the government. The control of money supply is important; some rules and regulations admittedly are necessary, though in varying degrees; but macromanaging is beyond the pale.

Unlike neo-Keynesian economics, the new classical economics is based on systematic analysis and statistical modeling. That is the basis for its claim of being scientific, while countering that neo-Keynesianism, with its political objectives, is not. The scientific claim is more important to new classical economists than any sense of realism, since reality is more complex and not easily quantifiable. As Lucas admits, "we're programming robot imitations of people, and there are real limits on what you can get out of that." (Klamer 1984, p. 49)

What the scientism of the new classical economics proposes is a highly restricted category of the "economy," which it equates to the capitalist market. The discipline claims competence over this market economy. Everything other than the market economy is beyond the disciplinary boundary, and is considered by the new classical economists as exogenous. In the market, supply and demand meet in equilibrium; disequilibrium forces always come from without. By definition, these other factors are not "economic." For the new classical economists, their statistical model approach is the only proper one for the study of the market economy. But they also accept the limitations of their discipline, admitting it is not able to say anything about the non-"economic." The "economic" is quantifiable and amenable to scientific study, the non-"economic" is not quantifiable and therefore not amenable to scientific study.

However, such modesty does not pertain to Gary Becker, of the neo-conservative Chicago school. In *The Economic Approach to Human Behavior* (1976), Becker proposes a somewhat different approach to the study of the market economy than that of the new classical economists. However, the real difference is that, unlike the new classical economists, Becker claims his economic approach is appropriate in studying the non-economic as well. "Indeed, I have come to the position that the economic approach is a comprehensive one that is applicable to all human behavior. . . . "(p. 9)

For Becker, the economic approach assumes maximizing behavior by individual workers, firms, and households, which prices and other instruments of the market make "mutually consistent," "with varying degrees of efficiency." (p. 5) So far, Becker and the new classical economists seem to be in agreement. But they differ in regard to knowledge as the basis for the individual's choice. For the new classical economists, individual knowledge is not a problem, because ultimately all the choices by all the individuals in the market can be determined stochastically. Becker views the knowledge problem differently. He admits the need for "a theory of the optimal or rational accumulation of costly information when undertaking major rather than minor decisions." (pp. 6–7) In other words, knowledge is an economic factor, even if sometimes individuals, i.e., an individual worker, firm, or household, may choose a non-optimal decision, because of psychic costs. But Becker's "knowledge" is narrowed down to choices for market goods and services. It does not include "preferences," which define "fundamental aspects of life, such as health, prestige, sensual pleasure, benevolence, or envy." Preferences, Becker insists, do not change substantially over time, nor are they very different between wealthy and poor persons, or even between persons in different societies and cultures; and they do not bear a stable relation to market goods and services. For him, "the combined assumptions of maximizing behavior, market equilibrium, and stable preferences, used relentlessly and unflinchingly, form the heart of the economic approach." (p. 5) Thus, Becker and the new classical economists disagree in regard to the boundary of the discipline. The "economy" that Becker studies is broader than that delimited by the new classical economics, since his includes information, though excluding preference.

But what really distinguishes Becker's economics from the new classical economics is that, unlike the latter, Becker claims his "economic approach provides a valuable unified framework for understanding *all* human behavior, although I recognize, of course, that much behavior is not yet understood, and that non-economic variables and the techniques and findings from other fields contribute significantly to the understanding of human behavior." He argues that "human behavior is not compartmentalized, sometimes based on maximizing, sometimes not, sometimes motivated by stable preferences, sometimes by volatile ones, sometimes resulting in an optimal accumulation of information, sometimes not. Rather, all human behavior can be viewed as involving participants who maximize their utility from a stable set of preferences and accumulate an optimal amount of information and other inputs in a variety of markets." (p. 14, italics in the original)

To put it very simply, the discipline of new classical economics proposes a category of the "economy," bounded by rational expectations, market equilibrium, and policy neutrality. This economy, it claims, approximates the capitalist market that Adam Smith was talking about. New classical economics sees a rigorous disciplinary relation between its method and the subject matter of its study, the economy. It does not claim competency over anything beyond its own category of the "economy." This economy, which is none other than the capitalist market, is quite apart from the non-economic, and cannot in the long term be affected by the political. Becker, on the other hand, proposes a somewhat different category of the "economy," though it is still the same Smithian capitalist market. His "economy" is bounded by maximizing behavior, market equilibrium, and stable preferences. However, not only does Becker propose that his discipline has competency over the "economy"; it is competent in the study of all human behavior, the non-economic as well as the economic, because maximizing behavior transcends the economic realm. In fact, Becker has studied the economics of education, marriage, and family as market phenomena of maximizing behavior.

Lucas likes Milton Friedman's *Capitalism and Freedom* (1962) a lot, claiming it is really written for economists. In it, Friedman lays down the boundary and the relative importance between the economy and government. According to Friedman, that "economy" is competitive capitalism, and the book's major theme is

> the role of competitive capitalism—the organization of the bulk of economic activity through private enterprise operating in a free market—as a system of economic freedom and a necessary condition for political freedom. Its minor theme is the role that government should play in a society dedicated to freedom and relying primarily on the market to organize economic activity. (p. 4)

Freedom in economic arrangement is fundamental. Not only is it "an end in itself," but "also an indispensable means toward the achievement of political freedom." (p. 8) The former is a guarantee of the latter. Thus the "free man . . . regards government as means, an instrumentality." (p. 2) The scope of this government must be limited, and its power dispersed, not centralized.

The foundation of economic freedom, according to Friedman, is "voluntary co-operation of individuals—the technique of the market place." It "rests on the elementary . . . proposition that both parties to an economic transaction benefit from it, *provided the transaction is bi-laterally voluntary and informed.*" (p. 13) This is only possible "*provided:* (*a*) that enterprises are private, so that the ultimate contracting parties are individuals, and (*b*) that individuals are effectively free to enter or not to enter into any particular exchange, so that every transaction is strictly voluntary." (p. 14) The market organization of economic activity prevents one person from interfering in the activities of another.

The consumer is protected from coercion by the seller because of the presence of other sellers with whom he can deal. The seller is protected from coercion by the consumer because of other consumers to whom he can sell. The employee is protected from coercion by the employer because of other employers for whom he can work, and so on. And the market does this impersonally and without centralized authority. (pp. 14–15)

This is Friedman's concept of economic freedom, and the model for political freedom. In contrast, he insists, political action "tends to require or to enforce substantial conformity." (p. 23)

There are several assumptions underlying Friedman's argument for the need to separate the economy from politics, and maintain the priority of the economic over the political. He assumes that society consists of discrete individuals who can freely enter, contract, and exchange in the economic realm, in order to realize their own interests. Only in the modern economy of what he terms competitive capitalism, burdened by a minimum of government regulations, can the human being realize the ideal of individual freedom. And this economic freedom based upon self-interest is the model for political freedom.

Klamer (1984), Klamer and Colander (1990), and Klamer, McCloskey, and Solow, eds. (1988), in an attempt to overcome positivism, criticize the discipline of economics as "conversation" in its use of rhetoric and metaphor. I do not think their concept of conversation, based on Richard Rorty's pragmatics of knowledge (1982), is critical enough. The scholarly exchanges among academic economists are more than conversation. They are exercises, researches, and contributions to a discipline, which consolidate the discipline's competencies and boundaries, i.e., knowledge claims. Concurrently, they accrue power to those who possess such competency, providing them with the authority to define and guard the boundaries. The published and successfully contested economists can then speak authoritatively on behalf of the discipline, for extra-economic purposes. In effect, the discipline of economics fits exactly Foucault's concept of discourse/power.

Economics, in this case neoclassical economics, is a discipline, not a conversation. But what exactly is a discipline, in the academic sense? I propose that a discipline is an established, enduring, yet changing relation among its method, subject matter, categories, and boundaries. One has to learn its method, subject matter, categories, and boundaries, and to accept the relation among them, in order to qualify and maintain standing as an academician. There are no positivist facts and data in themselves, on which the blank Lockean intellect can then generalize. Nor is there any subject matter prior to a method. But rather, changing method redefines its appropriate subject of study and data.

From the Chicago school of Friedman and Becker to the new classical economics of Lucas, Townsend, and Sargent, we find the boundaries of the discipline more consolidated, as the discipline bases itself more rigorously on statistical methods and data. Friedman makes strong pronouncements on the political, and Becker insists that all of the non-economic can be studied economically. But the new classical economists stick more rigorously to the boundaries demarcated by their statistical method, disclaiming competency over the non-economic. Nevertheless, they all agree on the foundational assumptions of the market economy which they study, namely the equilibrium of the market, the rationality of choice, and the self-interest of the individual, even though they may differ in their understanding of these terms. Furthermore, they all agree that the market should be separate from and only minimally regulated by government, i.e., the *laissez-faire* ideal.

Neoclassical economics is a discipline. The subject matter of the discipline, i.e., its *referent,* is the capitalist market economy. The discipline's study of the market economy is premised upon such categorical concepts as "individual interest," "market equilibrium," and "rational choice." These are categorical concepts, in that they are asserted as true and are foundational to the subject matter, since without them the very concept of the market economy is meaningless and not amenable to disciplinary study. In fact, each categorical concept is highly ideological. Macpherson (1962) had studied the historical class basis of the concept of the individual. Folbre and Hartmann (1988) more recently discussed the discipline's suppression of class and gender considerations, in its conceptualization of a masculinist individualist interest. New classical economists admit the highly restricted understanding of the "rationality" they employ in the discipline. And "equilibrium," as we have seen, is a lens by which the neoclassical economists frame the workings of the market. These categorical concepts are complex and highly composite signs, which enable the discourse of neoclassical economics to propose knowledge of the workings of a market economy. The signs have meanings in relation with each other, within a system, i.e., the market economy. In this sense, they constitute a first-level signification, within an internally consistent discourse.

But there is more to neoclassical economics than that, since it competes with neo-Keynesian economics in formulating the monetary/fiscal policies of the government, and the former was certainly more influential during the Reagan-Bush administration. This is a second-level signification (or meta-communication). The market as a system founded on neoclassical categorical concepts refers to the late-eighteenth-century *laissez-faire* ideal of Adam Smith, not an actual market as it existed in the nineteenth century, although there is usually a slippage between a textual ideal and an idealized past. In other words, the referent of the neoclassical market is the idea of the market as proposed by Smith. Regardless of whether that market actually existed in the nineteenth century, there is no such market in the contemporary world, since neoclassical economists themselves constantly complain how much market forces are tampered with, regulated, and restricted by government policies. However, the referent of the neoclassical market system, i.e., the *laissez-faire* market ideal, is semiotically useful in seeking to reorder aspects of the contemporary political economy in accordance with a late-eighteenth-century ideal.

The second-level signification here is the semiotics of a politics of nostalgia. The signs of "individual interest," "market equilibrium," and "rational choice" have extra-disciplinary meanings in everyday language. When neoclassical economic pronouncements are made to the public at large, people without training in that discipline would translate these signs from the standpoint of their extra-disciplinary meanings. These everyday meanings are a part of our political vocabulary. And if the pronouncements are repeated often enough, people will forget the changing etymology of the signs. Furthermore, these signs are the cornerstones of the idealized *laissez-faire* market of neoclassical economics. If they transcend history, then the neoclassical ideal which they construct, i.e., "the market," becomes a sort of timeless, Platonic paradigm.

What is so remarkable is that the categorical signs of neoclassical economics, in a translation, i.e., a conflation of meaning that often goes unnoticed, become part of current political rhetoric. The conflation, a second-level signification, enables their proponents to argue that the market ideal is the safeguard for the politics of democratic freedom and individual liberty. In other words, the politics of democracy come to depend on the neoclassical ideal of the market. It may be the case that the market ideal and the democratic ideal both came out of the anti-monarchical, anti-aristocratic struggle of the eighteenth-century urban mercantile class. But to insist that the prospect of democratic politics in the late twentieth century depends on the unfettering of the forces of late capitalism—that is to leap a couple of steps in connections. Nostalgia is an investment in objects from the past, so that they become a part of our own present. It is a denial of gaps across time, of changing historical contexts—by surrealistically collapsing signs into images and accepting them as a part of our own environment. I will discuss the new prospect for the politics of nostalgia in chapter 3. But, in the meantime, I want to point out the first- and second-level significations of the discourse of neoclassical economics.

Foucault posits that discourse/power disciplines the body by coding body practices. I propose that neoclassical categorical concepts and the market ideal they establish already discipline the body in contradictory ways.

In the name of science, the discipline bifurcates the terrain of late-capitalist production/consumption into "economy" and "politics." The former possesses rationality, equilibrium; the latter does not. In other words, "economy" is positive and prior, whereas "politics" is the negative other. The discipline then analyzes this "economy" in reference to its late eighteenth-century ideal of the market. Neoclassical study of the "market" in effect obfuscates any understanding of the full working impact of late capitalism. Whatever that does not conform to the market ideal is then attributed to the excesses of the other, i.e., "government."

Furthermore, by arguing that any "well-informed" "individual" can "rationally" and "voluntarily" enter into contracts of exchange on a basis of "equality" with other "individual entities," whether corporate or human, in order to realize "his" "interest" in "the market"—the discipline is reducing all of these signs to narrow economic denotations. It overlooks the unequal power between labor and management, between a human person and a large corporation, and prevents us from dealing with the full human dimensions of economic exchange. The second-level signification of these categorical signs in the non-"economic," i.e., the so-called separate realms of "politics" and "society" *by analogy* prevents any discussion and understanding of the real problems of "individual," "reason," "choice," and "freedom" in a late-capitalist political economy.

There are gaps between the discourse of neoclassical economics and our actual lives. It is not that neoclassical economics is unrealistic, but rather that its signs constrain and discipline our bodies to profit capital. These signs are the discursive underpinnings for the production and accumulation of exchange value in late capitalism.

2 Consumption Practices

In the last chapter, we reviewed some of the major changes in late-capitalist production—a resegmented labor market, an increasingly systematized, cyberneticized labor process, and a discourse of neoclassical economics. In this chapter, we discuss some major changes in late-capitalist consumption. I argue that the commodities, or goods and services, we now consume no longer possess relatively stable, slow-changing, qualitatively distinct use value, as Marx once characterized it. Commodity in late capitalism has instead become a package of changing "product characteristics." Moreover, by means of a relay of juxtaposed images and signs, advertising connects product characteristics with prevailing social and cultural values. As a result, we no longer consume commodities to satisfy relatively stable and specific needs, but to reconstruct ourselves in terms of the lifestyle associated with the consumption of certain commodities. The late-capitalist commodity has, in effect, become a three-level semiotic hybrid of social and cultural values, changing product characteristics, and exchange value. Currently, consumption is developed by the combination and recombination of structural, discursive, cybernetic, and semiotic practices.

Production and consumption are two aspects of a dynamic circuit. Though production is the determining moment of that circuit, consumption is necessary to make possible yet another round of production. Late-capitalist production is different from earlier moments of capitalist production, not only because of the new development we discussed in the last chapter, but because it is much more closely coordinated with the new, dynamic development of consumption we will analyze here.

a. Product Characteristics and Use Value

Marx assumed that the use value of a commodity was relatively stable, though historically changing, and unproblematical. People knew what they needed, and the use value of a commodity would satisfy their perceived needs. But now this is no longer an appropriate assumption. The late-capitalist commodity is not stable and unproblematical. Commodities are now packages of changing product characteristics that obfuscates our needs rather than satisfying them.

In *Capital*, Marx shifted emphasis from the episteme of development-in-time implicit in his theory of historical materialism, to undertake instead a synchronic, systematic analysis of capitalist production. That analysis, I would argue, anticipated the twentieth-century epistemology of differences without identities. In *Capital*, he emphasized the duality of capitalist commodity, at once the embodiment of use value and exchange value.

From the standpoint of consumption, the use value of a commodity is its specific properties capable of satisfying human needs of one sort or another, regardless of whether these needs pertain to the stomach or to the mind.

> The utility of a thing makes it a use-value. . . . Being limited by the physical properties of the commodity, it has no existence apart from that commodity. . . . This property of a commodity is independent of the amount of labor required to appropriate its useful qualities. . . . Use-values become a reality only by use or consumption. . . . (1906, p. 42)

Though socially constructed, use value was relatively stable and changed only gradually. Marx did not consider use value to be a problem of any consequence.

Rather, he concentrated on the problematic of exchange value. From the standpoint of production, a commodity is an embodiment of exchange value. Exchange value is not a quality, but an abstract quantity, being

> the amount of labor socially necessary, or the labor-time socially necessary for its production. . . . The value of one commodity is to the value of any other, as the labor-time necessary for the production of the one is to that necessary for the production of the other. (p. 46)

Exchange value does not pertain specifically to any particular commodity. Instead, all commodities are characterized by different quantities of the same exchange value. "When commodities are exchanged, their exchange value manifests itself as something totally independent of their use value." (p. 45) It is the different quantities of exchange value that make commodities exchangeable with each other. "The total labour-power of society, which is embodied in the sum total of the values of all commodities produced in that society, counts here as one homogeneous mass of human labour-power, composed though it be of innumerable individual units." (p. 46) All the exchange values in a production process, I suggest, constitute a synchronic system of differences without identity.

In Marx's analysis, the central contradiction in the circuit of production and consumption is between the requirements of an ever-expanding production of exchange value *and* the consumption of seemingly stable, qualitatively different use values to satisfy human needs. The contradiction is bounded by the conjoint requirements that capital needs the use value of labor power for production, and workers have to sell their labor power so as to command the use value of other commodities.

There are two aspects to this contradiction. From the standpoint of capitalist accumulation, consumer demands at home and from abroad can never keep up with the realization requirement of ever-expanding production. From the standpoint of human needs, the ever-expanding production of commodities would eventually create a new problematic of the satisfaction of human needs. The two are aspects of the same contradiction, with the problem of the realization of the over-production of exchange value leading, by implication, to the problem of human needs under the pressure of expanding consumption. *Capital*, in its critique of nineteenth-century capitalist production, emphasized the problem of realization of exchange value due to over-production, and gave background to the problem of the satisfaction of human needs. However, in late capitalism, with changes in consumption practices, the problem of the satisfaction of human needs has become as acute as that of the realization of the over-production of exchange value.

Semiotically speaking, the Marxist *structuration* of the terrain of production and consumption was based upon a series of sign correlations— between production and consumption, between exchange value and use value, and between quantity and quality. The two terms in each sign correlate presuppose each other. Thus, there is no production without consumption, no exchange value without use value, no quantity without quality. Furthermore, the first term (i.e., signified or content) in each correlate is dynamic, developmental, and problematical, whereas the second term (i.e., signifier or expression) is relatively stable, seemingly non-developmental, and therefore unproblematical. Thus, the development of production presupposes the seeming non-development of consumption, the development of exchange value presupposes the seeming non-development of use value, and the development of exchange use presupposes the seeming non-development of use value.

But, I propose, this slow-changing, seeming stability of qualitatively distinct use value as the signifier of dynamic, quantitative exchange value in the terrain of production and consumption actually depends on the support of non-exchangist practices in other relatively autonomous terrains, such as social reproduction, laws and politics, and forms of social consciousness. These latter practices are reciprocal and social, but non-exchangist. Though meshed in obligations and power relations, they are not based specifically on consideration of exchange value. Therefore, use value is a double signifier—at once a correlate of the signified, exchange value, within the terrain of production, but also a correlate of the signified, social, cultural values in other relatively autonomous, non-exchangist terrains. Without the maintenance and sustenance by the social, cultural values which relatively autonomous non-exchangist practices generate, the stability and unproblematicity of use value as the signifier for the development of exchange value would collapse.

As a double signifier straddling across exchangist and non-exchangist terrains of practices, use value is a transferent between exchange value and non-exchangist social, cultural values. The development of exchange value must always be at the expense of something, somebody, some resource, some non-exchangist value. Because it is a transferent, use value seemed to be relatively stable and unproblematical, while in actuality the development of exchange value depletes the social and cultural values in other non-exchangist terrains. The terrain of production and consumption in industrial capitalism, therefore, presupposed other relatively autonomous terrains of reciprocal social practices to generate non-exchangist social, cultural values. The problematic of use value in late capitalism, i.e., its destabilization, is due to the collapse of the relatively autonomous non-exchangist practices, with the hegemony of exchangist practices.

Capitalism is the great transformer. (Polanyi 1957) Under industrial capitalism, the development of exchange value and the seeming stability of use value in the terrain of production and consumption actually implied a gradual, continuous depletion of the social and cultural values generated and sustained in other relatively autonomous terrains of non-exchangist practices. Use value was slowly changing, with new commodities produced to satisfy needs in new, different ways. Late capitalism, however, has resorted to the wholesale development and, therefore, destabilization of use values, in an expanded and accelerated terrain of production and consumption.

Eco (1976) provides an excellent example of the destabilization of late-capitalist commodity's use value, its transformation into one of many changing units within an open-ended semiotic system of differences. Up to November 1969, cyclamates were used as a substitute for sugar in the design, packaging, and marketing of diet foods. Under the dietary regime at that time, it was sugar, rather than cyclamates, that was designated as fattening, and therefore held to contribute to death. Cyclamates were preferable to sugar. In November of that year, however, medical researchers discovered that consuming cyclamates could give people cancer, thus eventually causing death. Immediately thereafter, diet foods were redesigned, repackaged, and remarketed without cyclamates, and relabeled "sugar added." In the open-ended system of different dietary values, sugar has become cancer-free, as opposed to cancer-causing cyclamates, therefore sugar is now life-enhancing. (pp. 287–88)

Support for my argument regarding the destabilization of use value comes partly from our common personal experience as consumers of ever-changing late-capitalist commodities (one day cyclamates are healthy, the next carcinogenic), when newly packaged commodities can redirect and redefine *what we think we need*. Experiential evidence is nevertheless confirmed by the analytical studies of Kelvin Lancaster, a mainstream, non-Marxist economist. (Cited in Leiss 1976, pp. 79–81) Lancaster, in a subsequent work, generalized that, in advanced industrial society, goods or products are no longer "entities in a gestalt sense but . . . bundles of properties or characteristics. These characteristics are objective, and the relationship between a good and the characteristics it possesses is a technical one, determined by the design of the good" or even the redesign of agricultural produce. (1979, p. 17) Products have thus become simply a transfer mechanism whereby characteristics are bundled up into packages at the manufacturing end, passing through the distribution and marketing processes as packages, and then, so to speak, opened up to yield their characteristics again at the point of consumption. (pp. 20–21) Physical characteristics such as size, shape, color, smell, chemical composition, ability to perform any one of a variety of functions, etc., are all objective and quantifiable. Goods are designed as preferred characteristics, then quantitatively produced in terms of economy of scale and potential market.

What Lancaster calls products, or goods and services, are what Marxists call commodities. What he refers to as product characteristics are the use values of commodities. The use value of late-capitalist commodities is no longer the slow-changing, seemingly stable quality assumed by Marx. Use value is an ever-changing bundle of product characteristics, designed and produced primarily for the sake of the accumulation of exchange value. An automobile, or any other commodity for that matter, is not just a commodity with stable use value. We don't buy an automobile simply or merely for the sake of transportation. An automobile is a bundle of changing characteristics, designed, produced, and marketed by the manufacturer to appeal to an already profiled buyer. The various, different characteristics that constitute a specific automobile distinguish it from, and enable it to compete with, other makes, brands, and models in an open-ended system of changing, differential characteristics. A specific characteristic, e.g., the cylinder of an auto engine, the speed of acceleration from zero, or the color of an auto body, etc., is not a stable, meaningful identity, but a differential distinction in relation to all other engine cylinders, accelerators, body colors, etc., available in the automobiles being marketed at that moment. These differences are meaningful only in relations among themselves. The introduction of a new engine, accelerator or body color automatically changes the differential relations among all the automobiles available in the market at a particular time.

Lancaster's concept of product characteristics is highly pertinent to the argument of this section. It forces us to rethink the use value of late-capitalist commodity, and recognize it as nothing more or less than a bundle of changing characteristics. Lancaster, however, places his analysis within too narrow an economic framework. That framework is bounded by individual preferences, variety of goods, and economies of scale. According to Lancaster, "the optimum problem involves the *design* of goods as well as their quantities." (p. 21) Individual preference is one of the cornerstones of mainstream economic rationality. He assumes that individuals express rational preferences not for goods, but for collections of characteristics, although he admits that the preference can be influenced by advertising.

What about the problem of the perception of needs and of their satisfaction, when advertising influences individual preference in the marketing of product characteristics? From the standpoint of Lancaster's narrow framework of analysis, that issue is no longer an economic one, and therefore not a part of his *discipline*. Ever-changing product characteristics, as Leiss among others emphasized, lead to the problem of "the fragmentation and 'destabilization' of the categories of needing." (1976, p. 88) While Lancaster's insight is exceedingly valuable, his narrowly economistic framework for analyzing product characteristics is not sufficient to reveal the extent and impact of the practice of design, production, circulation, and consumption of product characteristics.

Leiss, Kline, and Jhally (1988) point out two fundamental aspects constituting the commodity as an unstable collection of characteristics. On the one hand, the commodity is a collection of "physical characteristics" determined by the ingredients that give it distinctive traits. But the commodity is also a collection of "imputed characteristics" determined by the way it is advertised and marketed. When the characteristics of goods change quickly and continuously, the needs through which individuals relate to them must also be in a state of permanent fluidity. When goods are little more than changing collections of characteristics, judgments about the suitability of particular goods for particular needs are, so to speak, "destabilized." (p. 59) Characteristics are distributed and redistributed across previously distinct categories of needs, experiences, and objects. Late capitalism tends to abandon fixed forms of need-satisfaction and to experiment continuously with newly constructed formats. "Each facet of self-presentation has been broken down into component parts, and related in astonishingly varied ways to changing assortments of products and consumption styles." (p. 60)

Therefore, the design and production of late-capitalist commodity as a bundle of changing characteristics requires support and sustenance from a new kind of advertising in order to market these characteristics.

b. Image in Late-Capitalist Advertising

Postwar advertising connects changing product characteristics with non-exchangist social, cultural values, using the latter to sell the former. This is done by means of a relay of juxtaposed visual images and linguistic signs, inducing us to believe that changing product characteristics partake of the meanings of social, cultural values. In this section, I shall analyze postwar advertising as a new semiotic practice.

Leiss, Kline, and Jhally, in their study of advertising in Canadian magazines, observe that after the 1950s the visual frequently stands on its own, undescribed and unexplained. The language of ads becomes condensed, allusive, conversational, or poetic. It is the visual that conveys the story, use, or reason for consumption. By today the assumption is that the audience is capable of very complex visual decoding, that it can construct an understanding of the ad simply from a montage of visual signs for which the text often plays a minor explanatory or sloganeering role, helping only to draw attention to a key ideational element of the ad. (1988, pp. 181–82)

I am assuming that this trend in Canadian magazines since the 1950s is even more pronounced in the USA, home of the Madison-Avenue hype.

Leiss, Kline, and Jhally then go on to say that "metaphor is the very heart of the basic communicative form used in modern advertising." (p. 241) The metaphors of symbol, image, and icon work by analogy and allusion, referring beyond themselves to something else, inviting comparison between two things which appear dissimilar, but which, they suggest, have a shared meaning. However, I would like to analyze the phenomenon of postwar advertising, not from their standpoint of the metaphors of symbol, image, and icon, but from Eco's standpoint of the semiotic distinctions between visual image and linguistic sign, as well as between communication and signification. (1976)

First, let me cite a few examples of the sort of postwar advertising I have in mind. One is the well-known Doyle, Dane, and Bernbach ad that ran very successfully in New York City during the early 1950s. The ad shows the stereotypical image of a Native American or Chinese eating rye bread. This image is sandwiched between the written caption, "You don't have to be Jewish to love Levy's real Jewish rye." The ad does not extol the virtues of Levy's Jewish rye; nor does it show a Hasidic Jew eating Jewish rye. Instead, several juxtapositions and contradictions revolve around the bread as the focal point.

The ad immediately captures attention at the visual level by juxtaposing the image of a Jewish rye sandwich with a stereotypical image of a Native American or Chinese. It then juxtaposes the visual message with the linguistic message. The visual ethnicity of the bread is identified by the linguistic message, "Levy's real Jewish rye." However, the visual stereotyping of the Native American or Chinese is downplayed by the non-specific written category of "you don't have to be Jewish." The ethnicity of the bread is advanced, while the ethnicity of the eater is at once visually stereotyped, but linguistically erased. Thus, Jewish rye, linguistically affirmed as "Levy's real Jewish rye," transcends the visual/linguistic opposition between Jews and non-Jews, to become more valuable than any ethnic identity, whether Jewish, Native American, or Chinese.

The juxtapositions within the image itself, and between the image and the linguistic sign, utilize the accepted codes in social, cultural meanings. However, the choice underlying the linguistic caption is not between a Hasidic Jew or a Native American/Chinese; nor between eating Jewish bread or some Native-American/Chinese food item. Instead, it proposes a pseudo-opposition between Jewish bread (a potentially appetizing item of food) and a Native American or Chinese stereotyped person (an ethnic stereotype imposed by the white majority on members of these minorities). Visually, one doesn't have to be a Native American or Chinese stereotype to eat Jewish rye; but linguistically, one doesn't have to be Jewish to eat Levy's real Jewish rye. The point is that most New Yorkers are neither Native Americans nor Chinese, though quite a number of them are Jewish. The ad effectively utilizes the tension between ethnic stereotypes and the cosmopolitan ideal of New York City. It is Levy's real Jewish rye, and the eating of it can actually be considered "cosmopolitan."

This newer type of "juxtaposition ad" creates a surrealist shock, to arrest the addressee's attention. By juxtaposition, I mean "setting one thing beside the other without connective." (Shattuck 1958, p. 332) Or, in the words of Eco, it is a "transitory correlation" of two functives which breaks conventional "systems of expectations." (1976, pp. 49, 204) Thus, besides the Chinese or Native-American stereotype eating Jewish rye, we see in ads a glass bottle of Chivas Regal attached to an iron chain, a soft-boiled egg exposed in an Orrefors crystal glass, a Talon zipper closing a walnut shell, a carton of king-sized Kent cigarettes on a tray placed adjacent to a natural food item, the woman exposed in public wearing only her Maidenform bra.

A recent example of more complex, multiple juxtapositions is a 1987 Isuzu TV ad, with both image and captioned words visually communicating truthful information about the car, as opposed to a spokesman orally telling lies about the car. By now, the addressee expects advertising to exaggerate and therefore tends to discount its claim. However, because of the outrageousness of the lies told orally in this ad, the addressee is induced to accept the visual information as being truthful, or at least more believable. The juxtaposition of truth/falsehood is reinforced by the disjuncture of visual/oral communication, so that visual communi-

cation is to truth as oral communication is to lies. The dissynchroniza-
tion between sight and sound as well as the binary opposition of truth
and falsehood are combined in this ad, to bring home the message of the
value of the Isuzu automobile.

I propose that Leiss, Kline, and Jhally's concept of metaphor cannot
adequately explain what's happening in these ads, and what make them
different from prewar and other postwar ads. Instead, the analysis must
proceed from the standpoint of Eco's distinction between image and
sign, and between signification and communication.

From the standpoint of *signification*, the image possesses properties
which make it much more pliable and powerful than the linguistic sign.
The image is not an icon. The image does not "naturally" correspond to
its referent. It does not have the same properties as its object, it is not
similar or analogous to its object, nor is it motivated by its object.
Instead, the belief in iconism, according to Eco, actually "covers many
semiotic procedures, many ways of producing signals ordered to a sign-
function, and . . . even though there is something different between the
word /dog/ and the image of a dog, this difference is not the trivial one
between iconic and arbitrary (or 'symbolic') signs." (p. 190) Image as a
visual sign is different from linguistic sign. Any sign is subject to codes of
articulation. But, in the case of images, one can assume that they are
culturally coded "*without* necessarily implying that they are arbitrarily
related to their content and that their expression is discretely analyzable."
(p. 192) The perceived similarity in the visual sign does not concern the
relationship between the image and its object, but between the image
and a previously culturalized content, for we are informed by "a codified
system of expectations which allows us to enter into the semantic world of
the artist or the image-maker." (p. 204)

The referential potential specific to the image is a semiotic property,
and should be studied as such. However, until recently, the assumption
that the image is just like the linguistic sign has been a cause of much
error in the discussion of the image. This has led many critics to neglect
the difference between visual and linguistic signs. Non-semiotic explanations implicit in such adjectives as "unconscious," "archetypical," and
"oneiric" fill the consequent analytic vacuum—claiming, by implication,
that the referential potential of the image is derived from the Freudian
unconscious, the Jungian archetype, or the Pasolinian dream. These
frameworks are non-semiotic and non-hermeneutic. They beg the question of the referential potential of the image, since they attribute that

potential to something beyond the image. They can tell us nothing about the workings of the image itself. The non-semiotic reduction of the image does not constitute a semiotic analysis, and therefore underrates the dynamism of the image.

As Tagg stated so well in *The Burden of Representation*, the photo image is already the product of a highly complex set of conditions in material production, which is then distributed and consumed according to learned schemas, all within specific social and institutional contexts. "The image is therefore to be seen as a composite of signs, more to be compared with a complex sentence than a single word. Its meanings are multiple, concrete and, most important, *constructed*." (1988, p. 187)

The content of any sign, whether visual or linguistic, points to a referent. The sign is not its referent, although in the case of the image, i.e., a visual sign, we are induced to believe that it is equivalent to its referent. The sign, whether visual or linguistic, is structured by systems of abstract, arbitrary codes. The distinction between image and linguistic sign is that the codes of the images not only communicate a content, but do so in such a way as to induce the addressee to overlook the difference between the coded content and its referent, and to believe that the image is not abstract but an icon of its referent. Take, for example, our response to the life-like image of a horse, as opposed to our reading of the linguistic sign "horse." The codes of the linguistic sign communicate a content, but do not induce us to believe there is no difference between the sign and its referent. Thus, the codes of the image work at two levels, in not only signifying a content, but also in simulating the referent, whereas the codes of the linguistic sign work at only one level, to signify a content.

Because of their different codings, image and linguistic sign have different referential potentials. Linguistic sign denotes and connotes by means of abstract, non-simulatory codes. Image in correlation with linguistic sign can also function denotatively and connotatively. However, prior to any superimposition of the sign, the image is already simulated. This is because of the double function of the codes of the image, in not only signifying but also in simulating, leading us to believe that the image is icon-like.

My point is that the image, seeming like its own referent, yet quite different from its referent, is ultimately able to overwhelm its referent. The referent—the original referred to by the image, that which the image seeks to simulate by means of codes—is always located within a specific context. Context changes, but the referent is already grounded. To see the

Parthenon, one has to go to the Acropolis, even though the Parthenon on the Acropolis one sees now is very different from the Parthenon erected there in mid-fifth century B.C. An image, on the other hand, is a coded duplication of the referent, always detachable from the (historically conditioned) context of the referent. One can easily see an *image* of the Parthenon, without having to go all the way to the Acropolis. Freed from the referent's context, yet likened to the referent, the image can then be associated with other images and linguistic signs for signifying purposes. The image of the Parthenon can easily become a vehicle or signifier for "antiquity," "beauty," "classicism," "humanism," "Occidentalism," "Greece," "tourism," "nostalgia," or any number of cultural and changeable meanings. Thus, the image, in becoming a decontextualized "icon"—definitely decontextualized, not really an icon, but perceived as an icon—can be used to signify by juxtaposition, association, correlation. It has more volatility and motility than the opposition of denotation/connotation possessed by the linguistic sign.

I am reminded of the scene in Jean-Luc Godard's "Les Carabiniers" (1963), when the mercenaries returned home with suitcases filled not with loot from abroad but photo images. Images are the new loot, since they are the latest currency. From the standpoint of *communication,* i.e., the physical production of image, the issue is no longer the mechanical reproduction of the original and the loss of the aura of the original, as Walter Benjamin argued so long ago. We have gone far beyond that in late capitalism. For us, the issue has become the decontextualization and recontextualization of the image, by means of its combination and recombination with other images and signs. This is what I would like to call communication of image by means of juxtaposition. Translucent but not innocent, the coded, simulatory image has always been a potentially powerful vehicle for signification. In the twentieth century, the photo snapshot first revealed this potential of the image. Surrealism then juxtaposed images to obtain what Breton called an intimation of grace. But the practices of cinematography, television, and especially advertising have taken advantage of the surrealist potential of the photo image as a vehicle for the linguistic sign. The linguistic sign harnesses the potential of the icon-like image by recontextualizing the latter for the purpose of the former.

Roland Barthes suggested two types of association between photo image and linguistic sign: anchorage and relay. In anchorage, the linguistic message specifies one of the possible meanings of the photo image. The denominative function of words "correspond exactly to an *anchor-*

age of all the possible meanings of the object by recourse to a nomenclature. . . . Anchorage is the most frequent function of the linguistic message and is commonly found in press photographs and advertisements."
(1977, pp. 39–41) On the other hand,

> the function of relay is less common; it can be seen particularly
> in cartoons and comic strips. Here text (most often a snatch of
> dialogue) and image stand in a complementary relationship; the
> words, in the same way as the images, are fragments of a more
> general syntagm and the unity of the message is realized at a higher
> level, that of the story, the anecdote, the diegesis. While rare in the
> fixed image, this relay-text becomes very important in film, where
> dialogue functions not simply as elucidation but really does ad-
> vance the action by setting out, in the sequence of messages, mean-
> ings that are not to be found in the image itself. (p. 41)

While accepting his distinction of the anchored and relayed relations
between photo image and linguistic sign, I disagree with Barthes that
anchorage rather than relay is commonly found in advertising. Quite the
contrary. Until 1949, advertising tended to employ mostly anchored relation between photo image and words. But postwar juxtaposing ads are
relayed, not even in a general but actually in a specific kind of relay, akin
to cinematic montage.

On the other hand, fictional film provides a narrative by means of the
juxtaposition of discontinuous film strips, camera shots, and scenes, all
accompanied by dialogue, musical score, or even sometimes silence. Juxtaposition and discontinuity are fundamental properties of the film. Ever
present within a shot, between shots, between scenes, between the visual
and the acoustic, they are inherent, cinematographic properties that advance the film's narrative, making it different from and much more complex than literary narrative. Eisenstein has argued that we should not try
to smooth over these inherent cinematic properties, but that we should,
instead, exploit them in the making of a film. The practice of using
juxtaposition and discontinuity in film is precisely what he meant by
montage. Montage is more than editing; it is a practice deriving its
information from and culminating in the realization of the fundamental
properties of the film. Montage is conflict, conflict based upon counter-
point, a dialectical approach to film form. (1957, pp. 38ff, 46ff, 72ff)

The montaged relay of juxtaposed, discontinuous images and signs,
unlike either anchorage or even other types of relay, demands the addressee's active participation. Montage presents a plethora of possible

levels for the addressee's delectation. There is the insistently linguistic meaning. There are myriads of visual meanings, a few of which are anchored or relayed by the linguistic message. But there are always more meanings in the images than the signs convey explicitly. In montage, the addressee completes the message by connecting the juxtaposition and discontinuity. And in actively connecting the juxtaposed, discontinuous images and signs, the addressee absorbs more of the visual meanings than in either anchored or other relayed communication of image and sign. The power of montaged relay is that it requires the active, perceptual connection by the addressee.

There is a certain irony in the fact that, though montage as a principle emerged in Soviet cinematography after World War I, its practice became most prevalent in late-capitalist advertising. This may be due to the emergence of television as a popular media, where montage rather than anchorage or other types of relay of images and words proved more suitable. Because of television's smaller screen, the shot necessarily has to focus on the action in the foreground of a scene. The resulting close-ups and details are more juxtaposed and discontinuous than in film. Television with its juxtaposition, according to Sorkin, is like the "exquisite corpse" of surrealism, a composite drawing done by several persons with each not knowing what the others have drawn. (1986, p. 162) Also television, according to Zettl, requires greater perceptual connection on the part of its viewer than film. (1973, p. 113) In recent years, confronted by competition from television, Hollywood has also resorted to montage by accelerating the tension and pace of film. But the most recent example of montage has come from MTV. Since the mid-1980s, reports the *New York Times* (October 9, 1989), TV ads began to use such MTV techniques as "slow motion, split screens, quickcuts, unnaturally bright coloring, and, most prominently, the use of music."

Signification is the result of a transitory correlation between an expression, or sign-vehicle, and a content, or signified. In advertising, non-exchangist social, cultural values are the expression, or signifier, for product characteristics as the content, or signified. The result is that product characteristics as the content of this signification are inflated by the content of the expression, i.e., social, cultural values. Signification in advertising is

$$\frac{\text{social, cultural values (as expressions)}}{\text{product characteristics (as content)}}$$

The Doyle-Dane-Bernbach ad uses the social, cultural value of a New York cosmopolitanism based upon ethnic diversity, as the expression for Levy's Jewish rye. Elsewhere, Barthes (1975), Langholz-Leymore (1975) and Williamson (1978) have shown how contemporary advertising utilizes each and every cultural value to promote the consumption of commodities. "Beauty," "sexuality," "love," "nature," "culture," "science," "progress," "innovation," "the future," "the past," "parents," "youth," "wisdom," "patriotism," "nativism," "internationalism," "cosmopolitanism," "primitivism," "celebrity," etc.—these social, cultural values have become signifiers for the signification of commodity. Thus, to buy an American commodity is "patriotic" in an era of intensified multinational corporate competition, whereas to buy a technologically advanced Japanese commodity is "cosmopolitan." "Patriotism" and its opposite, "cosmopolitanism," have both become signifiers for the advertising of commodities.

Signification by means of the transitory correlation between social, cultural values and product characteristics is not new in advertising. However, the production of this signification by means of a montaged relay of juxtaposed images and signs is new. Thus, the juxtaposition of the Native American or Chinese eating a rye bread sandwich in the image, and between that image and the linguistic sign "you don't have to be Jewish to love Levy's real Jewish rye" *is* the communicational basis for the signification to connect the eating of Jewish rye with the cultural value of New York cosmopolitanism. It is the communication by means of montaged juxtaposition within the image and between image and sign that makes the new advertising much more powerful.

There is no signification without communication. Changes in communication transform signification. The montaged relay of juxtaposed images and signs destabilizes them by detaching them from their referents. We have evidences of communication using social, cultural values as signifiers from all sides, whether from our own everyday life, or from scholarly analysis. An extreme example here would be the case already introduced—that of sugar in the diet food advertising which Eco analyzed. (1976, pp. 287–88) Vestergaard and Schroeder have also shown how advertising uses different social, cultural values, in strategically addressing men and women, as well as different classes of people. (1985, chapter 4) Westbrook (1983) has shown the recent transformation of electoral politics in the USA by advertising. And Silverman (1986), in studying the revival of Francophilia and chinoiserie in the early 1980s, proposed a close personal connection as well as a mutual ideological reinforcement between elitist consumption of culture on the one hand, and Ronald Reagan's politics of nostalgia on the other. At the personal level, we have all experienced Reagan's politics of nostalgia, in which popular mythic values are skillfully communicated so that the presidential image comes to embody these values.

Social, cultural values are transacted and sustained by non-exchangist reciprocal practices. Nonetheless, when non-exchangist social, cultural values are encapsulated in images and used as signifiers for changing product characteristics, they are destabilized. Once activated, this process is cumulative. By now, because of the new montaged relay of juxtaposed images and signs, the entire realm of social, cultural values have become simulatory images. We live in a world of images which encapsulate and signify "beauty," "nature," "love," "sexuality," "the past," "the future," "motherhood," "purity," "masculinity," "femininity," "youth," "war," "peace," "terrorism," "nuclear holocaust," "a higher authority," and what-have-you—all for the sake of the marketing of product characteristics.

c. The Consumption of Lifestyle

Since the mid-1960s, marketing research has emphasized the segmentation of the consumer market, providing information on the consumption preferences, the lifestyle attitudes, and the media use of different groups of the population; and advertising has shifted accordingly to a lifestyle format. (Leiss, Kline, and Jhally, 1988, pp. 125, 210) I shall argue, in this section, that market segmentation and lifestyle advertising, together with changing product characteristics, have produced the unprecedented phenomenon of the consumption of lifestyle. With the development of consumption in late capitalism, *lifestyle* as the new social relations of consumption has overshadowed *class* as the social relations of production.

Lifestyle is a new key word in the postwar era. Before the war, Alfred Adler used the term to denote a person's basic character, established in early childhood, and governing subsequent reactions and behavior. Max Weber used lifestyle as a characteristic of status groups, in opposition to economic classes. But it was only in the postwar era that the term became popular. In 1946, George Orwell described Arthur Koestler as being "true to his life style"; and in 1947, Marshall McLuhan wrote of certain people having a "life style of their own." *The Guardian* claimed, in 1961, that the mass media "continually tell their audience what lifestyles are 'modern' and 'smart.'" (1976 supplement to the *OED*) In the 1960s, "alternative lifestyle" emerged, to denote a way of life based upon one's own choice, rather than on psychological or status principles. Claudia Dreifus's *Radical Lifestyles* illustrated such distinct 1960s cultures as "hip, political, academic, drop-out, black militant, Indian, Chicano, Puerto Rican, women's liberationist, gay, radical professional, *straight*." Together, she argued, these cultures have broken up "the monolithic lifestyle of America." (1971, p. 13)

In the 1970s, market research went beyond the existing conceptualizations of motivational research and mass culture, to analyze lifestyle in terms of demography, geography, personality traits, tastes, and buying habits. In this way, the consumer market was segmented into aggregate groups of different lifestyles. Information about lifestyle aggregates is useful both in the design and production of product characteristics, as well as in the targeting and positioning of commodities in the market. (Leiss, Kline, and Jhally 1988, pp. 255–56)

A good example of market segmentation research is that of Arnold Mitchell and his associates, who employed the concept of "values and lifestyle" to sort out *The Nine American Lifestyles* (1983). By values, they meant "the entire constellations of a person's attitudes, beliefs, opinions, hopes, fears, prejudices, needs, desires, and aspirations that, taken together, govern how one behaves." In addition, "one's entire set of values—numerous, complex, overlapping, and contradictory though they are—finds holistic expression in a lifestyle." (p. vii)

The nine lifestyles, according to Mitchell and associates, are "the survivors," "the sustainers," "the belongers," "the emulators," "the achievers," "the I-Am-Me," "the experiential," "the societally conscious," and "the integrated." Each lifestyle has its own demographics, attitudes, financial status, activity patterns, and consumption patterns: The "survivors," representing some 4 percent of adult Americans, are old, poor, fearful, and far removed from the cultural mainstream. The "sustainers," representing 7 percent of the population, live on the edge of poverty, and are angry, resentful, street-wise, and involved in the underground economy. These two poor lifestyles are need-driven.

Twenty-five percent of American adults are "belongers": aging, conventional, intensely patriotic, and traditional. The "emulators" constitute 9 percent of the population, and are young, ambitious, and flashy, trying to break into the system. The "achievers," 22 percent, are middle-aged, prosperous, self-assured, the leaders and builders of the American dream. These three groups, constituting two-thirds of the total adult population, are outer-directed.

On the other hand, the next three groups are smaller in size and inner-directed. The "I-Am-Me," 5 percent, are very young, narcissistic, impulsive, exhibitionist, and in transition to inner growth. The "experiential," 7 percent, are youthful, artistic, seeking direct experience, and oriented to inner growth. And the "societally conscious," 9 percent, are well-educated, prosperous, politically liberal, and motivated by social ideals. Lastly, the "integrated," 2 percent, are tolerant and flexible, and have succeeded in combining inner with outer direction.

Let us take a look specifically at the consumption patterns of the "survivors" and the "achievers," to show how producers would find market segmentation research useful. According to Mitchell and associates, survivors purchase high levels of used cars and meatless meals; pain relievers, decaffeinated coffee, and margarine; various household cleaners and personal deodorants; and "canned dog and cat food despite low indices of pet ownership." (p. 70) On the other hand, achievers have above-average ownership of luxury and midsize cars; more appliances than average—substantially so for dishwashers, food processors, garbage disposals, and microwave ovens; above average ownership of all types of recreational equipments (except motorcycles), home electronic products, and photographic equipment. Achievers show a traditional and conservative approach to clothing, and they are disproportionately high users of wines and champagne, most kinds of liquor, and domestic beer. (p. 109)

Another example of market segmentation research is the ACORN Market Segmentation System produced by the Market Analysis Division of CACI. (ACORN is an acronym for "A Classification of Residential Neighborhoods.") ACORN claims it can transform "household, survey respondents, sales records, and subscribers into vivid social portraits for *precise target marketing*. The ACORN market segmentation system has many uses. [It] will tell a retailer what kind of people live around a proposed new store site. [It] can describe the media preferences of a neighborhood for successful marketing campaigns." And it can be used "to boost response rates of mailing lists and to enhance customer information files." In sum, "ACORN is used to profile current customers and to target prospective customers." (1988, p. i, italics added) The ACORN system divides the entire country into some 260,000 blocks of neighborhoods, each block consisting on the average of 340 households. A block is analyzed and sorted by some forty-nine characteristics, including household income, job occupations, age distribution, education, age of the housing stock, and other key determinants of neighborhood purchasing power. Blocks are then recombined under forty-four distinct market segments. The forty-four segments are themselves reconstituted into thirteen groups. The thirteen groups are characteristically entitled

Wealthy metropolitan communities
Trend setting, suburban neighborhoods
Apartment house and college communities
Big city urban neighborhoods
Hispanic and multi-racial neighborhoods
Black neighborhoods
Young middle-class families
Blue-collar families in small towns
Mature adults in stable neighborhoods
Seasonal and mobile home communities
Agriculturally oriented communities
Older, depressed rural towns
Special populations

For instance, "wealthy metropolitan communities" consist of such market segments as old money, conspicuous consumers, and cosmopolitan wealth; "black neighborhoods" consist of mainstream family homeowners, trend conscious families, and low-income families; "older, depressed rural towns" consist of low-income retirees and youth, rural displaced workers, factory worker families, and poor young families; and "special populations" consist of military base families and residents and staff of institutions.

Each segment is analyzed in terms of demographic, socioeconomic housing characteristics, geographic location, and lifestyle and marketing implications. And each reveals high, medium, or low preferences for specific types of "media," "entertainment and leisure," "shopping styles," "major household purchases," "travel activities," "major financial products," "investment products," and "shopping baskets." At last, the segment is described in one key sentence. For example, the cosmopolitan wealth segment, following analysis in terms of its characteristics, is finally described as those consumers who would "go to considerable expense to maintain their possessions and to enhance their leisure time."

(p. 9) On the other hand, the low-income black families are enjoying "low-cost entertainment, especially music, and spend[ing] to enhance their homelives." (p. 28)

According to Leiss, Kline, and Jhally, lifestyle advertising as a format emerged after the 1950s. Formerly, ads directly informed buyers about the product, then linked the product with social, cultural values by means of images, or personalized the product's use. But the lifestyle ad format depicts a leisure activity, such as entertaining, going out, going on holiday, or relaxing, with the consumption of the advertised product linked to the depicted activity. For example, the image of a bottle of Michelob beer is juxtaposed with a scene of tennis players relaxing with drinks, reinforced by the caption: "Weekends were made for Michelob." "In lifestyle ads, the dimension of consumption that provides the unifying framework of interpretation is action or behavior appropriate to or typical of a social group or situation, rather than use, satisfaction, or utility." (1988, p. 215) The characteristics of the product partake of the social, cultural meanings associated with the activities.

I propose that we have gone far beyond the use of market segmentation to design and produce product characteristics, *and* beyond even the use of the lifestyle ad format to target the sale of commodities. It is now possible to create and sell distinctive nostalgic lifestyles themselves as desirable ways of life. Instead of targeting specific lifestyle groups as potential buyers for specific commodities, it is more profitable to create and stimulate the consumption of commodities associated with distinct lifestyle images. Magazines ranging from *American Health* to *Cosmopolitan* and *Ms.*, including even one called *Lifestyle,* promote particular lifestyles in both their articles and ads. Lifestyle merchandisers, Ralph Lauren and Calvin Klein, do not sell commodities. They produce and circulate the labels that connote a desirable lifestyle, available through the purchase of up-scale commodities bearing Calvin Klein or Ralph Lauren labels. One wears not a dress but a Ralph Lauren, and thereby participates in the nostalgia his ads promote. In buying and wearing a Ralph Lauren or a Calvin Klein, we are actually consuming a simulatory image.

According to Lauren, his merchandising is "not about clothes but about elegance and classicism. The idea [is] to bring back an Old World quality . . . that doesn't exist today." (*New York Times,* April 22, 1986) Actually, that "Old World quality" did not exist even in the past. It is not a historical representation, but the nostalgic simulation, of a past. There was no New England colonial style in colonial New England. So-called "colonial style" was a "tradition" invented in the late nineteenth century, to counter the non-WASPish immigration from Southern and Eastern Europe. The image of Victoriana is quite different from any lived reality in any decade in Britain during the long, long reign of Victoria. What is true of lifestyle consumption, is also true of Reagan's politics of nostalgia, where the radio-announcer/actor-as-president embodied images of the past, rather than any politically conservative values however defined. In all three cases, we have an imagistic mockup, conforming to and stimulating our longing for something which we think we've lost, though in actuality we never possessed it—a simulation.

Late-capitalist consumption is the consumption of product characteristics designed to stimulate sales, though claiming to satisfy new needs. Changing product characteristics redefine needs. Rapidly changing product characteristics destabilize needs. With the destabilization of needs, people are less satisfied than before. How is it even possible now to know what one needs? (Leiss 1976, pp. 86–92)

In late-capitalist consumption, social, cultural values have become the signifier for product characteristics, which in turn are the signifier for exchange value. However, in the case of the consumption of lifestyle, social, cultural values are imagistically simulated and circulated as signifiers. The simulation of social, cultural values is much more powerful than the social, cultural values themselves. Decontextualized, the image of social, cultural values can then be juxtaposed with the image and sign of product characteristics to connote a particular lifestyle. Addressees respond to images emotionally and immediately, connecting social, cultural values with product characteristics. In other words, lifestyle based upon social, cultural simulation is perceived as constructed by product characteristics. The consumption of these product characteristics would then be visually constituted for the consumer and present to others the possession of a lifestyle.

Lifestyle is the social relations of consumption in late capitalism, as distinct from class as the social relations of production. The visual construction and presentation of self in terms of consumption relations has by now overshadowed the class relations of production in the workplace. Lifestyle is the new, late-capitalist social relations of consumption, when consumption is no longer the non-developmental other to production, but is itself dynamically developed by the design and production of changing product characteristics, the juxtaposition of image and sign in lifestyle ad format, and the segmentation of consumer market.

Even so, though lifestyle consciousness overshadows class consciousness, class as the social relations of production is still determinative. What one earns determines the extent and quality of one's ability to consume. Household incomes are unequal and becoming even more so. This contradiction adversely affects the lower classes, women, and minorities. (*Infra,* chapter 4, sec. a) Furthermore, goods and services have become more varied across time as well as more expensive. Patricia Ruggles writes: "Increasing prices . . . are not the only source of changes in family needs. Family structures and resources, and even the goods and services available, all change as well. . . . As consumption patterns change, the definition of what is 'necessary' changes also." (*New York Times,* April 26, 1990) Some goods and services, previously considered to be luxuries, are now necessities. With income distribution becoming more unequal, and lifestyle consumption more varied and more expensive, the body is caught up in a new contradiction between *class* and *lifestyle.*

The variety, quality, and choice available to the consumer depend not only on income but also on education. The hierarchy of income structured by the labor market slants minorities, women, children, the sick, and the disabled disproportionately to the lower income levels. But income affects education and information, so that the higher incomes usually are better informed in regard to consumption choices. Therefore, they can better exercise their choice, and have better housing and medical care, healthier food and eating habits, and higher qualities of living. On the other hand, the poor and needy, who are usually less educated and informed, are more vulnerable to the new juxtaposing ads, which stimulate them to consume goods and services they do not need. They are therefore further constrained in the variety, quality, and choice of their consumption.

According to Bloom and Koreman (1986), the top economic quintile has 4.23 times as much to spend as the lowest quintile. Though expenditure on food increases with income, at each quintile level of income the consumption of food represents a smaller percentage of that quintile's total expenditure. The top quintile spend 2.76 times as much on food as the lowest quintile. But the former's food expenditure represents only 14 percent of its total expenditure, whereas the food expenditure of the lowest quintile represents 21 percent of its total expenditure. Eating better yet spending proportionately less on food, the top quintile have more left for other consumer items. They accordingly spend 3.42 times as much on housing, 2.3 times as much on health and personal care, twice as much on education, and 23.8 times (!) as much on personal insurance, pensions, and social security, as the lowest quintile. In such ways are the quality of lifestyle constituted, for those who can afford it.

Clair (Vickery) Brown (1987) has shown that women entered the workforce in large numbers only after 1950, when food consumption has already improved for the upper and middle incomes. The extra income earned by married women went to improve transportation, recreation, and personal insurance, i.e., goods and services other than basic dietary necessities. Both trends, interacting upon each other, contributed to a new class distinction based upon visible consumption.

> Class differences (manifested in economic distance) became more visible as they became centered on transportation and recreation rather than food and family size. . . . The combination of having basic needs met for most families and of having consumption made more public seems to have increased the desire for inequality across classes since 1973. . . . In our culture, growth has resulted in a greater need for paid work, and affluence has intensified the desire for class differences in consumption. (p. 48)

Be this as it may, the usual analyses of the variety, quality, and choice of consumption assume that product characteristics satisfy needs, and that consumers, in exercising their choice, know what they need. But such is not the case. For example, data clearly show that African Americans constitute 11 percent of the US population, and have lower income and less money to spend on daily necessities. Yet they make up 17 percent of the soft-drink market, and consume 50 percent more Scotch per capita than whites. (Marable 1983, pp. 159, 161) Do African Americans really need more soft drinks and Scotch than other groups of people? At one level, they don't "need" to consume proportionately more of these items. At another level, they "need" these items as displacement for the other needs in food, clothing, and shelter beyond their reach. That's freedom of choice for them!

d. The Semiotics of Late-Capitalist Commodity

Because of (1) the design and production of commodities as changing product characteristics; (2) the relay of juxtaposed images and signs in the new advertising; and (3) the repeated use of social, cultural values to sell product characteristics—the late-capitalist commodity has become even more mysterious than the industrial-capitalist commodity analyzed by Marx. Instead of being a simple correlation of use value and exchange use, the late-capitalist commodity has become a *semiotic hybrid* of social, cultural values, changing product characteristics, and exchange value.

Marx posited that a commodity embodied both exchange value and use value, with the production of the former culminating in the consumption of the latter. He emphasized that exchange value was purely quantitative, whereas use value was qualitative. The former was dynamic and problematical, the latter slow-changing, relatively stable, and unproblematical. The seeming stability of use value, I propose, depends on the social, cultural values generated and sustained by non-exchangist practices in other relatively autonomous terrains. Capitalist production not only puts pressure on use value, but ultimately cannibalizes the social, cultural values generated by non-exchangist practices.

In late-capitalist production, the use value of commodity has become changing product characteristics. Advertising connects changing product characteristics to social, cultural values by means of the relay of juxtaposed images and signs. The late-capitalist commodity has in effect become a *semiotic hybrid* composed of

$$\frac{\text{(destabilized) social, cultural values}}{\text{(rapidly changing) product characteristics}}$$
$$\text{(quantitative) exchange value}$$

located in an expanded, accelerated terrain of production and consumption, which has absorbed all other terrains of non-exchangist, social practices. Within this hegemonic terrain, consumption is no longer the static other to production.

From the standpoint of production, product characteristics have displaced seemingly stable, slow-changing use value as the signifier for exchange value. The design and production of the changing characteristics of automobiles, diet foods, or any other late-capitalist commodity utilize clusters of open-ended, ever-changing systems of differences without stable identities. "The most powerful way to position a product is to define what it is not," said Marcio Moreira of McCann Erickson Worldwide, an advertising agency. (*New York Times*, May 27, 1990)

The design and production of product characteristics have been refined with the help of systems analysis and market research. Changes in product characteristics are undertaken primarily for the sake of the production of exchange value. They sometimes improve the satisfaction of socially, culturally defined needs, though often they destabilize established concepts of needs. An example is the "Microbrew" coffeemaker recently designed and produced by Farberware, Inc., which brews coffee in a microwave oven. The design intersects two sets of available statistics, plus a market research commissioned by the company. Though coffee drinking is on the decline, the consumption of high-priced, home-ground coffee is growing at about 20 percent a year; and 54 percent of coffee maker purchases are made by households of two or fewer persons, usually older people, students, or young couples. On the other hand, approximately 80 percent of American households now own a microwave oven, but most of them say they find its use limited. The market research commissioned by Farberware found that there was indeed interest in the concept of a microwave coffee brewer, but more for a two-cup than a six-cup size. The resulting product is "Microbrew," which can brew one to two cups of coffee in the microwave in less than four minutes. "We are selling perception as much as reality," said the general manager of Farberware. "We want to fill a need in the consumer's mind, and it really doesn't matter if the need is real or imagined." (*New York Times*, May 27, 1989)

By now, the use of social, cultural values as signifiers for product characteristics has become an integral part of the advertising and marketing of late-capitalist commodity. With social, cultural values becoming the signifier of product characteristics, and product characteristics in turn the signifier of exchange value, the late-capitalist commodity is a much more effective means for the production of exchange value, than the industrial-capitalist commodity with its correlation of relatively stable use value and dynamic exchange value.

From the standpoint of consumption, we no longer consume unproblematic use values to satisfy the needs defined by stable social, cultural values. Instead, we consume packages of changing product characteristics which are really the signifier of exchange value. Such is the case, by now, in the consumption of many late-capitalist commodities. Sometimes, we even consume the signifier of the signifier of exchange value, i.e., social, cultural values. This occurs when we consume a product because of the social, cultural values associated with it—for example, the scientific value or the nostalgia associated with certain commodities, the social, stylistic snobbery associated with upscale commodities, or the patriotism associated with "buy American." In consuming late-capitalist commodities, we face a new dilemma of simulation. Are we consuming product characteristics as the signifier of exchange value, or social, cultural meanings as the signifier of the signifier of exchange value?

The late-capitalist commodity is therefore a *semiotic hybrid* in an expanded, accelerated terrain of production and consumption. Marx's analysis of the dual aspects of exchange value and use value embodied in the industrial-capitalist commodity presupposed the dynamic development of production and the relative stability of consumption. But, in late capitalism, discursive, systematic and semiotic practices have destructured this nineteenth-century structure of production, by developing consumption as well as production. By now, the development of production and consumption by a combination and recombination of structural, discursive, systematic and semiotic practices has destroyed any distinction between quality and quantity. Instead, the late-capitalist commodity as a semiotic hybrid intersects open-ended, ever-changing systems of social, cultural meanings, systems of product characteristics and systems of exchange value, with each system constituted as differences without identity. The power of the late-capitalist commodity stems precisely from its being a semiotic hybrid intersecting these systems. I shall discuss the implication of the hegemony of the late-capitalist terrain of production and consumption in Chapter 3.

On this account, I am critical of Wolfgang Haug's concept of commodity aesthetics, because it is still founded on the old Marxist binary oppositions. (Haug 1987) Haug makes a distinction between use value, and the promise of use value, as well as between the objective promise of use value and the subjective promise of use value. The promise of use value, before its actual use, constitutes for Haug the realm of commodity aesthetics. And the aesthetics of monopoly commodity utilize mythical supersigns (e.g. recognition, love, health, happiness, manliness, natural purity, and so on) to organize individual imaginations.

Haug's observations regarding the mythical supersigns are quite pertinent. But the foundation for his concept of commodity aesthetics as the promise of use value still presupposes the oppositions between the satisfying object and the needing subject, between real and false needs, between exchange value and use value, and between production and consumption. The commodity aesthetics of Haug works on the second terms of all these oppositions, i.e., the subjective promise of use value and the needing subject. It leaves untouched all the first terms of the oppositions. Haug has simply superimposed his concept of commodity aesthetics onto the orthodox Marxist concepts of the production of commodity as exchange value. He therefore has not confronted the problem created by the collapse of all oppositions in the hegemonic terrain of production and consumption, and the emergence of the late-capitalist commodity as a *semiotic hybrid* of

$$\frac{\text{(destabilized) social, cultural values}}{\text{(rapidly changing) product characteristics}}$$
$$\text{(quantitative) exchange value}$$

Neither merely subjective, nor merely objective, simulation is built into the design, production, marketing, and consumption of the late-capitalist commodity as a semiotic hybrid. Alluring and sexualized, the multi-level, simulatory hybrid is the object of late-capitalist desire, reworking our very personality make-up by means of the consumption of lifestyle.

Leiss, Kline, and Jhally observe that a high proportion of all commodities today are cloaked in layers of symbols and images. They have in effect become "receptacles for the generalized play of meanings, as 'fields' for human states of feeling which are projected onto the physical and sensual substance of the object." Late-capitalist commodities "are recognized as psychological things, as symbolic of personal attributes and goals, as symbolic of social patterns and strivings." The result is "a situation in which people are surrounded by things that are themselves 'alive.' . . . This resonance between persons and things, circulates freely through all of society's information channels." (1988, pp. 242–43) I propose that, in the new connection between things and humans, it is not so much that the late-capitalist commodities are "alive," as that we ourselves have become commodified. We are accordingly less "alive," since our feelings are instigated by the signs of social, cultural values, and our needs repackaged by changing product characteristics. The result is the new phenomenon of lifestyle consumption.

3 The Hegemony of Exchangist Practices

In the first two chapters, I argued that, unlike earlier epochs of capitalism, consumption and production in late capitalism are developing in tandem. No longer is consumption changing simply because of the development of production. Rather, production and consumption are developing conjointly, accelerating and expanding by means of the combining and recombining of structural, discursive, systematic, and semiotic components. The result is an unprecedented hegemony of exchangist practices, which I discuss in this chapter.

This hegemony means the collapse of the hierarchical relations between the terrain of production/consumption and other hitherto relatively autonomous terrains of non-exchangist, reciprocal social practices. Under the new hegemonic regime, all non-exchangist practices are valorized for the production and accumulation of surplus value. This is the dynamics underlying the de-territorialization and re-territorialization of terrains of non-exchangist practices and values. Therefore, concepts such as "relatively autonomous terrain" or "multi-level structure"—derived from critiques of earlier structurations of capitalism—are no longer useful in analyzing late capitalism.

Instead of locating them within the structural grids appropriate to and derived from earlier epochs of capitalism, we need to analyze the workings of late-capitalist exchangist practices which subvert and break through these grids. A fundamental issue in methodology is involved here, i.e., the categories of analysis that we use should be able to elucidate the phenomena at hand, rather than likening and reducing the new problematic to an earlier, more familiar configuration. Here, I want to acknowledge my indebtedness to other critical thinkers who helped to enlarge our understanding of the dynamics of exchange value.

Feminist materialists have made an important contribution to the critique of exchange value. Kuhn and Wolpe (eds. 1978) emphasized the hitherto unrecognized and therefore untheorized contribution of women's labor to the production of exchange value, in the forms of patriarchal family and the gender division of labor. Young, Wolkowitz, and McCullagh (eds. 1981) continued with their studies of the subordination of women at the international level. *The Review of Radical Political Economy* devoted a special issue on this problem, in Spring 1984. And Hartsock (1983), in a study of class, gender, and power showed how social reproduction and the gender division of labor were imbedded in a set of production and reproduction relations that empowered men. She urged that the Marxist analysis of production relations should be enlarged into a feminist historical materialism.

With an earlier and different set of assumptions and concerns, Polanyi argued, with cogent insight, how the capitalist economy was the first and only one to emerge out of and become separate from society, and would inevitably engulf society itself. For a self-adjusting market economy "could not exist for any length of time without annihilating the human and natural substance of society." (1957, p. 3)

> Ultimately . . . the control of the economic system by the market is of overwhelming consequence to the whole organization of society: it means no less than the running of society as an adjunct to the market. Instead of economy being embedded in social relations, social relations are embedded in the economic system. (p. 57)

Polanyi's thesis, I suggest, anticipated the problematic of late capitalism, which, rather than being contextualized by non-exchangist, reciprocal social practices, has valorized all of the social.

Habermas (1975) used a system crisis concept to analyze "advanced capitalism." He characterized the latest epoch of capitalism as three interconnecting systems—the economic, the political-administrative, and the sociocultural. Each system possesses its own steering mechanism, and is open-ended, providing for input and output. Each is crisis prone.

The economic system requires an input of work and capital. Its output consists of consumable values, which are distributed over time among different social strata. Typically, economic crises are output crises, i.e., problems in the realization of the exchange value necessary for another round of production. The economic system of advanced capitalism cannot shoulder these crises by itself. Thus, the political-administrative system intervenes with its output of sovereignly executed decisions, to moderate the economic crises. Nevertheless, administrative decisions can never reconcile and fulfill the imperatives from the economic system. This leads in turn to a rationality crisis of the political-administrative system. The rationality crisis of the political-administrative system is also a legitimation crisis, from the standpoint of the public, that provides for the sovereignty of the state. From that latter standpoint, the legitimation crisis in turn requires an input, and therefore an expenditure of generalized motivations, from the sociocultural system. The sociocultural system receives its input of goods and services from the economic system, and of legal, administrative acts, and public, social security from the political-administrative system. These inputs do not replace but rather erode the traditions which support the patterns of motivation that are crucial in sustaining the continued existence of the two other systems. The result is a motivation crisis of the sociocultural system.

Concluded Habermas:

a) Because the economic system has forfeited its functional autonomy *vis-à-vis* the state, crisis manifestations in advanced capitalism have also lost their nature-like character. . . .

b) Economic crises are shifted into the political system through the reactive-avoidance activity of the government in such a way that supplies of legitimation can compensate for deficits in rationality and extension of organizational rationality can compensate for those legitimation deficits that do appear. There arises a bundle of crisis tendencies [in the political system, the] limits [of which] are determined by, on the one hand, the fiscally available quantity of value . . . and on the other by supplies of motivation from the socio-cultural system. . . .

c) The less the cultural system is capable of producing adequate motivations for politics . . . the more must scarce meaning be replaced by consumable values. To the same extent, the patterns of distribution that arise from socialized production for non-generalizable interests are endangered. (pp. 92–93)

What is most intriguing, from my standpoint, is Habermas' central thesis of the impact of advanced capitalism's production of consumable values on such non-exchangist values as rationality, legitimation, motivation, and meaning. He saw these non-exchangist values as being located in two non-economic systems, and it was the linkages of these three open-ended systems that provided him with the means to discuss the devaluation of non-exchangist values by exchange value. That devaluation or valorization of non-exchangist practices, I agree, is the outstanding feature of late capitalism.

However, I question Habermas' metaphoric conceptualization of political-administrative and sociocultural practices as "systems," even though admittedly open-ended ones. It is true that systems analysis increasingly intrude, in political-administrative and sociocultural practices; but that does not constitute these practices as two open-ended though connecting systems. In a sense, Habermas was translating the concept of multi-level structure into interconnecting open-ended systems. Since system is used here as a metaphor, I pose the question as to whether the triple, interconnecting use of the same metaphor is adequate in describing the dynamics of late-capitalist exchangist practices.

Instead of discussing structural or systematic grids, I shall analyze in this chapter the hegemony of exchangist practices from the standpoint of poststructuralist semiotics, since semiotics has become so crucial a component of exchangist practices in late capitalism. To some extent, Jeremy Shapiro anticipated my approach in a seminal article published in 1972: "One-Dimensionality: The Universal Semiotic of Technological Experience." Twenty years after the publication of this article, late capitalism, or more specifically the late-capitalist commodity, has developed farther than Shapiro ever dreamed.

In Chapter 2, section d, I showed how the late-capitalist commodity became a three-level semiotic hybrid:

$$\frac{\text{(destabilized) social, cultural values}}{\text{(rapidly changing) product characteristics}}$$
$$\text{(quantitative) exchange value.}$$

The universalization of commodity relations means that commodity in late capitalism is no longer just a combination of use value and exchange value, but a semiotic hybrid. This semiotic hybrid works to break down the boundary separating exchangist and non-exchangist terrains. In other words, use value in terms of rapidly changing product characteristics implies destabilized social, cultural values.

Capitalist production organizes exchangist practice as a terrain in which all the first terms of the sign correlates which structured the capitalist commodity moved to the center, while all the second terms were located along the periphery. Thus, *quantity, exchange value, production,* and *reproduction of capital* occupied the center of the terrain of industrial-capitalist production, while *quality, use value, consumption,* and *reproduction of labor* (i.e., social reproduction) got pushed to its periphery. Each second term acted as the signifier for the development of the first term as the signified. Thus, quality is the signifier for the development of quantity; use value the signifier for the development of exchange value; consumption the signifier for the development of production; and the reproduction of labor (i.e., social reproduction) the signifier for the reproduction of capital. All the first terms in these sign correlates are dynamic and problematical; the second terms, though historically changing, are relatively stable and unproblematical. The development of all these first terms has led to the expansion and acceleration of the terrain of exchangist practices.

But other non-exchangist terrains of reciprocal social practices also existed, such as social reproduction, gender, and sexuality, and psychic make-up (as distinct from "psychology" as a social-science discipline which studies psychic make-ups). These other terrains have been, until recently, relatively autonomous and generated non-exchangist values. I don't mean that the practices in these terrains were free of obligations or power relations, only that they were not directly organized by the production of exchange value. However, in late capitalism, expanded, accelerated production and consumption have valorized all hitherto non-exchangist practices as means for the development of production.

Use value is not a value in and of itself. Its qualitative distinction depends on its occupying a dual semiotic position, straddling the boundary of production/consumption. Within the terrain of production/consumption, use value is the signifier or expression of exchange value as the signified—although in everyday life we are led to believe use value is the signified and exchange value the signifier. Use value is the means for the development of exchange value. But the specific quality of use value, i.e., its utility, depends on the social practices in other, relatively autonomous, non-exchangist terrains. The "usefulness" of a commodity refers to the prevailing social practices regarding what is important, what is preferable, what is necessary. Therefore, the use value or utility of a commodity, in one sense the signifier for exchange value as the signified, is at the same time the signifier for the non-exchangist social, cultural values generated in other relatively autonomous terrains as the signified. In other words, use value refers to, as well as depends on, the social, cultural values in other non-exchangist terrains. It is in this sense that I call use value a *transference*. Because of its double semiotic location, use value is able to bridge exchangist terrain and non-exchangist terrain, being a signifier for both.

With the concept of use value as a transference, I now can propose development and its other, i.e., underdevelopment, as the binary logic which underlies capitalist production. The development of exchange value does not appear out of thin air. In fact, even thin air is subject to the depletion that accompanies the development of production—witness the accelerated depletion of the ozone layer surrounding the earth. Capitalist development is always at the expense of some body, some relationship, some thing—whether it be labor, non-exchangist values, or global resources. *Development requires its opposite, i.e., underdevelopment.*

However, the difficulty in exposing this binarial logic is that, up until now, Marxist as well as non-Marxist theorists have tried to confine the problematic of development in the terrain of production alone. Thus, for Marxists, the opposite of development is dependent, uneven, or unequal development in the peripheries or urban centers. And for non-Marxists, there simply is no opposite, only delayed development in third-world countries. In other words, underdevelopment has been conceived strictly as a negative economic phenomenon, a lack. However, I shall define *underdevelopment* more generically as the other to *capitalist development.* Just as "Orientalism" as the other in Western discourse does not tell us anything about the social, historical reality of Asia, so "underdevelopment" as the other of capitalist development cannot be comprehended from within the economic discourse of capitalist development.

Underdevelopment is not a stable signified, but an open-ended proposition. Being the other of the development of exchange value, underdevelopment cannot be fully comprehended from within the terrain of production and consumption. It is, instead, a series of ever-expanding, deeper exploitation and depletion, extending from the economic (or terrain of production), to the non-economic. Underdevelopment is not just the economic exploitation of labor, of women, of minorities, of the peripheries, but also a series of ever-deeper, penetrating exploitations and depletions, i.e., the valorization, of non-exchangist social, cultural values and global resources. Thus, underdevelopment as exploitation and depletion, for the sake of capitalist development, can only be understood outside of the terrain of production, i.e., from the standpoint of the valorization of former relatively autonomous terrains of social reproduction, gender, sexuality, and psychic make-up, i.e., the accelerated, expanded transformation of bodily needs. It is not merely the delay and the complication of capitalist development as a universal norm, but the destabilization of human bodily needs for the sake of capitalist development.

The concept of use value as a transference helps us to understand the workings of underdevelopment. Yet, how can the development of exchange value be the underdevelopment of its signifier, use value, when we actually witness in late capitalism the development of consumption? The point I am arguing is that as long as there were non-exchangist terrains to generate and sustain social, cultural values, use value seemed relatively stable, although the development of exchange value was actually slowly depleting the social, cultural values in other relatively autonomous terrains. But the late-capitalist development of production and consumption involves the transformation of hitherto relatively autonomous, non-exchangist practices into means or signifiers for newly constructed product characteristics as use value, which are, in turn, means for the social, cultural values that have now become apparent.

The transformation of non-exchangist practices ensues from the development of the second terms in the terrain of production and consumption. The valorization and commodification of non-exchangist practices is an underdevelopment, since qualitative distinctions and the satisfaction of bodily needs are now means for the production and the accumulation of exchange value. Development of the second terms in the terrain of exchangist practices *and* valorization of all the non-exchangist practices in other, former, relatively autonomous terrains are concurrent and interdependent movements. They are two aspects of the fundamental dynamics of development and underdevelopment by the hegemony of exchangist practices in late capitalism. In other words, bodily needs are underdeveloped "for the sake of" developing exchange value.

Everything is being valorized. Nothing is the same as before. Take, just as an example, one changing phenomenon, nostalgia—the longing for a present absence. The destabilization of social and cultural values accompanying the production and consumption of rapidly changing product characteristics has transformed *nostalgia* from longing for a lost yet familiar past, to the postmodernist simulation of a past that never was. *Nostalgia* is filling a vacuum that the destabilization of social, cultural values created. There is a modern history of nostalgia yet to be written. Elsewhere, I argued that, before industrial capitalism, nostalgia was not a temporal concept, but the longing that people experienced for a lost yet familiar space. With the coming of industrial capitalism, nostalgia became the longing for a former, more familiar time, within an episteme of development-in-time. (1982, p. 40) However, in late capitalism, mock-up images of the past proliferate as signifiers for diverse purposes. Ralph Lauren's "colonial New England," "Victorian England," and "Safari Africa" sell lifestyle consumption; Ronald Reagan's "America" sells neo-conservative politics. In a world of the meta-communication and meta-signification of images, we enjoy and consume simulations of the past. That sentiment can enhance exchange value. Late-capitalist nostalgia is an ongoing simulatory, repackageable sentiment. Nostalgia isn't what it used to be. With the collapse of stable, linear space-time framework, it no longer is a representation of a past, but a simulation.

What I am arguing casts a new light on the debate between Baudrillard and Jameson concerning the simulatory signs of postmodernism. Baudrillard has argued that simulation results from the destabilization of all referents in late capitalism. Instead of the real, we are now left with only the hyperreal, i.e., simulation without referents. "The hyperreal transcends representation only because it is entirely in simulation. . . . It is reality itself today that is hyperrealist." From within the hyperreal, we cannot discern the logic nor the contour of this new "neo-capitalist cybernetic order." (1983, pp. 147, 111)

Jameson, on the other hand, insisted that postmodernism is not a relatively autonomous culture, but rather "the cultural dominant of the logic of late capitalism." (1984, p. 85) According to him, Ernest Mandel's late or multinational or consumer capitalism constitutes "the purest form of capital yet to have emerged, a prodigious expansion of capital into hitherto uncommodified areas." (p. 78) Thus, according to Jameson, aesthetic production has become integrated into commodity production generally: "the frantic economic urgency of producing fresh waves of ever more novel-seeming goods, at ever greater rates of turnover, now assigns an increasingly essential structural function and position to aesthetic innovation and experimentation." (p. 56)

I propose that the destabilization of referents results from the development of the second terms in the terrain of production/consumption *and* the valorization of former, relatively autonomous non-exchangist terrains. This is characterized by changing combinations and recombinations of structural, discursive, systematic, and semiotic practices. Baudrillard was wrong; the simulation of postmodernism is not absolute. Moreover, postmodernism requires a critique undertaken from the standpoint of the hegemony of exchangist practices, i.e., the new problematic of bodily needs provoked by the development of use value *and* the valorization of non-exchangist practices.

But two aspects of Jameson's critique of postmodernism, I feel, need elaboration. First, I would characterize postmodernism as exchangist both in content (or signified) and in expression (or signifier). The content of postmodernism is neither realist representation nor modernist expression. Realist representation assumes the stability of the referent, and a mimetic equivalence between the signified and the referent. Modernist expression abandons the mimetic project, in favor of a formalist, aesthetic reordering of the signified. Postmodernism, finally, takes as its project the sign without a stable referent. Furthermore, postmodernism is itself a signifier, an expression, for exchange value. There is no relative autonomy of the aesthetic terrain any more, since "art" is now thoroughly valorized in the marketplace. With the collapse of aesthetics as a relatively autonomous practice, postmodernism is exchangist both in content and as expression. In content, postmodernism plays on the sign lacking a stable referent. As expression, it accepts the end of the bourgeois project of aesthetic integrity. This duality explains the love-hate relations of postmodernism to late capitalism. *If* (to extend the argument of Walter Benjamin) the work of art became mechanically reproducible in the age of photography and film, thereby losing its aura, *then* the work of postmodernism becomes infinitely recontextualizable and exchangeable in the age of cybernetic and semiotic practices. (Benjamin 1969, cf., Hayles 1987)

Secondly, I would like to go beyond Mandel's multifactored, multivariable study of capitalist production since World War II. In *Late Capitalism,* Mandel proposes six basic variables in the late-capitalist mode of production: (1) the organic composition of capital in general, and in the two departments of the production of means of production and of consumer goods in particular; (2) the distribution of constant capital between fixed and circulating capital; (3) the development of the rate of surplus value; (4) the development of the rate of accumulation; (5) the development of the turnover time of capital; and (6) the relation of exchange between the two departments. According to Mandel, "the history of capitalism, and at the same time the history of its inner regularities and unfolding contradictions, can only be explained and understood as a function of the interplay of these six variables." (1975, p. 39)

Mandel spent most of his effort in analyzing the interdependent workings of the six variables. Capitalism, according to him, is the generalization of commodity production and competition. In other words, capitalism is the extension of the capitalist conditions of appropriation, valorization, and accumulation. However, the extension of the conditions of appropriation, valorization, and accumulation, i.e., over-capitalization, decreases the rate of profit. Late capitalism, with its growing monopolistic sector and state intervention, cannot avoid this crisis. Rather, to the extent that commodity production and competition become even more extended, the crisis becomes even more generalized.

> The expansion of credit, the "industrialization" of wholesale and retail trade, the extension of the service sector, and the innovations of the third technological revolution in the transport and tele-communication sector as well as in such activities as inventory control, permitted a considerable acceleration of the rotation of circulating capital, which further contributed to the rise in the rate of profit after the Second World War. Subsequently, however, the increasing expense of fixed capital investment projects, the lengthening of the time necessary to build new factories and productive complexes, the declining rate of self-financing and the growing trend towards credit contraction, restricted the shortening of the turnover-cycle of fixed capital and of circulating capital, and tended to immobilize more and more capital in conditions where it could no longer operate productively, and thus in turn depressed the rate of profit again. (pp. 558–59)

But no matter how complex and sophisticated, Mandel's analysis is fundamentally a critique of the structure of production. On the one hand, he sees late capitalism as "generalized universal industrialization for the first time in history," with the mechanization, standardization, over-specialization, and parcelization of labor "penetrating into all sectors of social life." (p. 387) On the other hand, he continues to analyze the crisis of late capitalism as a crisis solely of the capitalist relations of production. Mandel does not see consumption (cf., pp. 389ff), the state (chapter 15), and ideology (chapter 16) as incorporated into, transformed by, and therefore also transforming the hegemony of exchangist practices in late capitalism. Mandel places consumption, the state, and ideology in ancillary roles, though accentuating the crisis of late-capitalist production and accumulation. Although the implication of his "generalized universal industrialization" is a new capitalist configuration, in it, consumption, the state, and ideology are still superstructural and relatively autonomous, where their interaction with production does not lead to any new, totally different kind of crisis. Late capitalism is for him not different, but "merely a further development of the imperial-ist, monopoly-capitalist epoch." (p. 9)

The regulation school of Michael Aglietta and others, from my stand-point, is an improvement in conceptualization, since it analyzes late capitalism in terms of the development not only of production and consumption, but also of social reproduction. According to Aglietta, in order to accumulate, production must be consumed and capital re-produced. The reproduction of capital requires the reproduction of la-bor. And the reproduction of labor involves not only labor's current consumption, but also its maintenance from one generation to another. There is no general, automatic equilibrium over time. "To speak of reproduction is to show the processes which permit what exists to go on existing. In a system whose internal relationships are in course of trans-formation, not everything does continue to exist, . . . transformation means rupture, qualitative change." (1979, p. 12)

To explain for the accumulation of capital across crises, Aglietta intro-duces the concepts of regime of accumulation and mode of regulation. In the words of Alain Lipietz, a leading proponent of the regulation school:

> A *regime of accumulation* describes the fairly long-term stabilization of the allocation of social production between consumption and accumulation. This implies a certain correspondence between the transformation of the conditions of production and the transfor-mation of the conditions of the reproduction of wage-labor, be-tween certain of the modalities in which capitalism is articulated with other modes of production within "a national economic and social formation," and between the social and economic formation under consideration and its "outside world." . . .
>
> The regime of accumulation must therefore be materialized in the shape of norms, habits, laws and regulating networks which ensure the unity of the process and which guarantee that its agents conform more or less to the schema of reproduction in their day-to-day behavior and struggles. The set of internalized rules and social procedures which incorporate social elements into individual behavior (and one might be able to mobilize Bourdieu's concept of habitus here) is referred to as a *mode of regulation*. (1987, pp. 14–15)

Thus, a regime of accumulation encompasses a larger terrain than the structure of production, or even of production/consumption, since it includes social reproduction. And a mode of regulation, at once social and subjective, is the *habitus* necessary to support a successful regime of accumulation.

According to Aglietta, the structural transformation that capitalist countries experienced from the end of the nineteenth century to the middle of the twentieth century required a new mode of consumption based upon "the domination of commodity relations over non-commodity relations." (1979, p. 81) For a regime of accumulation, new production requires new consumption. The new regime of accumulation requires new social norms instituted as part of what Aglietta calls a new mode of regulation.

The USA leads all other countries in this extension of commodity relations. "Fordism" is the name Aglietta gave to the new set of commodity relations. Fordism is not just the assembly-line production of new commodities, but also the consumption of new commodities—e.g., standardized housing and the automobile, together with all their supporting goods and services. New social norms, such as the minimum wage standard, social security, unemployment insurance, and old-age retirement benefits are legislated, to insure the continuity of both production and consumption. Collective bargaining is the centerpiece of the new commodity relations, implicating capital, labor and the New Deal state. Fordism, according to Aglietta,

> marks a new stage in the regulation of capitalism, the regime of intensive accumulation in which the capitalist class seeks overall management of the production of wage-labor by the close articulation of relations of production with the commodity relations in which the wage-earners purchase their means of consumption. [It] is thus the principle of an articulation between process of production and mode of consumption, which constitutes the mass production that is the specific content of the universalization of wage-labor. (pp. 116–17)

Fordism is that mode of regulation which accounts for the central importance of socialized consumption under the new regime of accumulation. Regulation for this socialization of consumption results from the class struggle between capital and labor, with the state acting as the hegemonic instrument of the dominant class in the struggle. Both the collective bargaining between capital and labor under state sponsorship *and* the social welfare legislation of the New Deal were necessary to regulate the socialization of consumption. Fordism prospered in the two decades immediately after the end of World War II. However, by the sixties, this mode of regulation began to falter, as its regime of accumulation became increasingly more difficult. By then, the fall in real social wage costs came to an end in the USA. More intransigence on the part of capital to preserve its profitability *and* labor's increased complaints of the new workplace discipline rendered collective bargaining ineffective. At the same time, the increases in social welfare support necessary to sustain social consumption became politically more contentious, as the prospect of capital accumulation diminished.

Aglietta sees the crisis of Fordism as leading to neo-Fordism, a new regime of accumulation and a new mode of regulation that attempted to take advantage of the newly available automation. Neo-Fordism did not introduce automation; rather, automation was available and could be used in capital accumulation. "The principle of work organization now in embryo is known as the recomposition of tasks. . . . The problem is to know whether the change in work organization made possible by the introduction of automatic production control can canalize the class struggle into forms compatible with the law of accumulation." (pp. 122–23)

Lipietz sees the changes since the early 1970s as a combination of the crisis of Fordism at the center *and* the emergence of peripheral Fordism in those third-world countries that possess the combination of an autonomous local capital, a sizeable middle class, and significant elements of the skilled working class. This peripheral Fordism (i.e., men working in the automobile industry) often coexists with primitive Taylorization (i.e., women in the electronics and textile industries). The development of peripheral Fordism is heavily internationalized. It does not follow the "bicycle/moped/small car/big car" developmental trajectory of the mass production at the center. Instead, "in Brazil, where workers still go on foot, the motor industry began by making large and medium-sized cars designed in Germany, for a middle class that already existed in both Germany and Brazil." (1987, p. 110)

Unlike Mandel, who approaches the problem of capital accumulation in late capitalism primarily from the standpoint of the structure of production, the regulation school analyzes Fordism and Fordist crisis in terms of the interdependent, interacting relation between production/consumption and social reproduction. However, the difference between the regulation school and my arguments comes out most clearly in regard to the assumption of "the habitus" underlying its concept of mode of regulation—an assumption borrowed from Pierre Bourdieu.

According to Bourdieu,

the habitus, the durably installed generative principle of regulated improvisations, produces practices which tend to reproduce the regularities imminent in the objective conditions of the production of their generative principle, while adjusting to the demands in-scribed as objective potentialities in the situation, as defined by the cognitive and motivating structures making up the habitus. (1977, p. 78)

For Bourdieu, as well as for the regulation school, the habitus is non-exchangist, relatively stable. As "a matrix of perceptions, aperceptions, and actions" it is

the product of the work of inculcation and appropriation necessary in order for those products of collective history, the objective struc-tures (e.g., of language, economy, etc.) to succeed in reproducing themselves more or less completely, in the form of durable dispo-sitions, in the organisms (which one can, if one wishes, call indi-viduals) lastingly subjected to the same conditionings, and hence placed in the same material conditions of existence. (pp. 83, 85)

I question whether the concept of habitus is sufficient for late capital-ism. I would argue that the hegemony of exchangist practices, by means of the combination and recombination of structure, discourse, systems analysis, and semiotics, is *underdeveloping* the habitus. Instead of the habitus, we have in late capitalism the valorization of social reproduc-tion, gender, and sexuality, and even psychic make-up. In other words, the regime of accumulation in late capitalism can no longer rely on a relatively stable, relatively autonomous mode of regulation, but needs to underdevelop and thus destabilize it.

Harvey has used the concepts of the regulation school to advance the thesis of *flexible accumulation,* for the "period of rapid change, flux, and uncertainty," since 1973, although he warned it is "by no means clear" that the new systems of production and marketing—characterized by more flexible labor processes and markets, geographical mobility, and rapid shifts in consumption practices—warrant the title of a new regime of accumulation, or that the revival of entrepreneurialism and neo-conservatism, coupled with the cultural turn to postmodernism, war-rant the title of a new mode of regulation. (1989, p. 124) In Chapter 1 of this work, I relied on Harvey's analysis of "the political-economic trans-formation of late twentieth-century capitalism." (1989, part 2) And I am especially impressed by his argument regarding the new international financial systems, and the postmodernist architecture and design of the city.

However, I would like to take issue with his concept of "time-space compression." It is not that I disagree with it, but, rather, I don't think his analysis goes far enough to bring out the new space-time experiences in late capitalism. Harvey defined that term as

> processes that so revolutionize the objective qualities of space and time that we are forced to alter, sometimes in quite radical ways, how we represent the world to ourselves. I use the word 'compression' because a strong case can be made that the history of capitalism has been characterized by speed-up in the pace of life, while so overcoming spatial barriers that the world sometimes seems to collapse inwards upon us. (p. 240)

I agree that the acceleration and expansion of production and consumption has compressed our experience of time and space. Harvey traces this acceleration and expansion back to industrial capitalism. But I would argue that space-time compression in late capitalism has led to fragmentation and simulation. "Space and time are no longer the framework of our perception." (Lowe 1982, p. 161) Instead, bits and pieces of different simulatory spaces and simulatory times are valorized to produce and hype the consumption of late-capitalist commodity as a semiotic hybrid. Harvey himself had worked on space as built environment. And I have argued that simulation of the past has become a signifier for use value.

The new experience of simulatory space/time makes postmodernism quite different from modernism. Harvey argues for the continuity from modernism to postmodernism. I would say that modernism was a formalist aesthetic, appropriate to the relativity of space-time in the early twentieth century. But postmodernism with its space-time fragmentation and simulation is not only different from modernism, but is no longer a relatively autonomous aesthetic. The hegemony of exchangist practices, embodied in the late-capitalist commodity as a semiotic hybrid, has made postmodernist culture signifiers of destabilized, repackageable use value.

Marxists are accustomed to the proposition that there is a structure of production/consumption, and a culture which reflects or interacts with that structure. This parallels the subject/object dichotomy in mainstream, academic knowledge. But in late capitalism, everything is destabilized; nothing is relatively autonomous. Thus, I do not accept the proposition that the body is constructed by the social relations of production, which then is supplemented by a bourgeois psychology, whether Freudian or behavioral. Nor do I accept the ideology of an autonomous individual self with stable identity. By locating the problematic of the late-capitalist body within the hegemonic terrain of exchangist practices, I intend to abandon the hitherto equally compartmentalized studies of the family, sexuality, and psychology. In their stead, I propose to study late-capitalism's valorization of social reproduction (chapter 4), gender and sexuality (chapter 5), and psychopathology (chapter 6), for the sake of capital accumulation. All practices conjoin to code our bodily needs as signifiers of exchange value; no body remains unaffected.

4 Social Reproduction Practices

Social reproduction is one aspect of the circuit of capitalist production/consumption. It includes not only the everyday maintenance of the existing working population and their families, but also the natal production and the post-natal nurturing and socialization—including child-rearing, informal learning, schooling, technological and professional education, medical, health, and social services—which are all necessary to the reproduction of labor. Otherwise, there can be no reproduction of capital. It is therefore a complex of social relations connecting and intersecting production/consumption and so-called "culture."

Industrial-capitalist production, as many critics have pointed out, was predicated upon the underdevelopment of social reproduction. And Marx criticized capitalist political economy for utilizing wage labor as a commodity, without having to pay for the social reproduction of labor. The onus of social reproduction was thus left to the non-exchangist practices in an increasingly capitalized world. Such an underdevelopment assumed the relative stability of slow-changing human needs and the unpaid labor of women in satisfying these needs.

But this assumption is no longer viable in late capitalism. In the late twentieth century, capital continues to exploit and underdevelop the remaining non-exchangist social-reproduction practices in the urban ghettoes and in the peripheries, without having to pay for them. However, at the center, the expanded, accelerated, and systematized development of both production and consumption requires a more diversified, differentially skilled workforce, as well as bodies recoded in terms of changing, new needs. Thus commodified goods and services for natal production, health care, child- and preschool-care, urban/suburban socialization, and formal education and training, have almost totally replaced the non-exchangist social-reproduction practices formerly provided by household, kin, and local community.

The valorization of social reproduction increases the cost of the reproduction of capital. Part of the increase can be discounted by accelerating the entire process of production/consumption. (Mandel 1975, p. 225) Part of the increase is paid for by the double exploitation of lower paid women and minority workers in the center and the peripheries. Nevertheless, such "reproduction conditions increased both the size and value content of the consumption basket, hence decreased relative surplus value production." (O'Connor 1984, p. 150) Furthermore, neither labor nor capital can afford to finance the higher cost—the former not having sufficient income, the latter not wanting to diminish its profit. Hence, the late-capitalist state has to step in with an array of different programs to support social reproduction goods and services. But the state does not produce exchange value; nor can it fundamentally alter social hierarchy by redistributing wealth and status. In effect, the late-capitalist state plays a role in processing the cost of social reproduction.

Aglietta has pointed out that

> the flows of the income and the institutional mechanisms by which these needs are met vary greatly from one social formation to another. Differences arise according to whether taxes and other charges are more or less socialized, i.e., brought within an institutional mechanism for balancing out the risks and costs of collective expenditures. The differences between the direct wages paid to simple labor-power in different countries are linked in part to divergences in the ways in which these needs are covered. (1979, pp. 179–80)

Therefore, the central problematic here is not the growth of welfare and entitlement since the 1960s, but the inclusion of social reproduction within the expanded, accelerated circuit of production/consumption, i.e., how the hegemony of exchangist practices valorized and commodified social reproduction practices. Yet, that problematic is obfuscated at the most advanced center of late capitalism, i.e., the USA, by blaming the state for the decline of traditional non-exchangist practices. This, of course, is not shortsightedness, but an inherent aspect of the neoconservative politics of nostalgia and displacement.

I shall examine in this chapter certain linkages in the problematic, namely the changing household and the politics of "the family," reracialization, and the bio-technical systematization of the body. These are some of the more visible practices that construct our bodily lives.

None of them can be studied in isolation, nor in terms of models derived from earlier epochs. All of them are now transformed, by means of a recombination of structure, discourse, systems analysis, and semiotic communication/signification, within the context of the hegemony of exchangist practices, and therefore must be located in that context or terrain.

a. Changing Household and the Politics of "The Family"

The Family, as Collier, Rosaldo, and Yanagisako affirmed, "is an ideological unit rather than merely a functional unit." It is a "symbolic opposition to work and business, in other words, to the market relations of capitalism." The Family as ideology "is part of a set of symbolic oppositions through which we interpret our experience in a particular society. . . ." (1982, pp. 34–35) It presupposes an opposition between the public and the private. More recently, Coontz (1992) has shown The Family to be a recent nostalgia rather than a past reality. In effect, she argues there is no linear history of the family, whether developmental or devolutionary. And May (1988) showed the cold-war origins of this new white middle-class family ideal, or what I would term imaginary, since it is very much promoted by the meta-communication of image.

But the family is only one type of household, since not all households are families. The two are not synonymous. According to the United States Census Bureau, a household as the basic unit of living can be either family or non-family. Family household consists of either a married couple or other related persons living together. And a family can be a couple with or without children, a single parent with children, or a non-parental adult with related children. Non-family households consist of unrelated persons, at times even children, who share the same living quarters. Taken in this sense, family is one type of household, and the nuclear family is one of a variety of families. The politics of "The Family," on the other hand, displace changing households and varieties of families with the imaginary of a heterosexually married, two-parent family as the norm, thus marginalizing all other families and households.

I argue in this section that the late-capitalist household located in the hegemonic terrain of exchangist practices is neither a viable retreat, nor an institutionalized private space. With the breakdown between the public/private dichotomy, the household has become instead a center of consumption. The wage income of the average male bread earner alone can no longer finance the consumption of the ever new, specialized goods and services which household members increasingly deem necessary. This is due also, in part, to the changing composition of households, and changing jobs in the labor market, accentuated by the recession of 1973. The correlations of this trend are working wives and mothers, and the various entitlement programs that the welfare state makes available to the middle class. The Reagan-Bush administrations could not reverse the trend, which began in the postwar era, but, rather, sought to displace it with neo-conservative attacks against the State for eroding Family values. The household, in effect, is undergoing structural, discursive, systematic, and semiotic recombination in late capitalism.

The household is becoming more varied, and its size is declining. In 1970, 70.5 percent of all households were married couples, 8.7 percent were female-headed families, 1.9 percent, male-headed families, and 18.8 percent, non-family households. The average size of the household was 3.14 persons; and the average size of the family was 3.58 persons. By 1990, 56 percent of American households were married couples, 11.7 percent were female-headed families, 3.1 percent, male-headed families, and 29.2 percent were non-family households. The average size of the household in 1990 was 2.63 persons; the average size of the family, 3.17 persons. For African-American households, 35.8 percent were married couples in 1990 (it was 53.3 percent in 1970); 31.2 percent were female-headed families (21.8 percent in 1970); 4.3 percent, male-headed families (2.9 percent in 1970); and 28.8 percent, non-family households (22 percent in 1970). (*SAUS, 1992*, pp. 46–47) Quite obviously, the changes in African-American households have been much more dramatic. I will discuss that in section *b*.

The changing composition of households is reflected in marriage and divorce rates across time. (*Ibid.*, pp. 90–91 for figures) From 1970 to 1988, the rate of first marriages has gone down, while the average age and the median age of first marriages have gone up. There are many reasons why different persons get married; among them, romance is probably an important consideration. And the delay in marriage can be attributed to economic hardship, non-marital sexual activities, and perhaps fear of commitment. But the constancy of marriage depends on many factors other than romance, which soon fades. From 1970 to 1988 the rate of divorce has gone up. Nevertheless, remarriage after divorce has also gone up. That certainly indicates a romance for the married state. And the question as to whether there is a decline in family values is debatable, since, no matter what they are, family values are very much touted.

Are marriage and divorce the causes for family household formation
and breakup? To answer in the affirmative is to set the stage for the
"dissolution of family and family values" argument. Can it not be said
that marriage and divorce rates are merely the reflection of changing
household formation? Besides, what leads to marriage and divorce?
There are so many imponderables. Most people got married, I suspect,
for reasons that subsequently needed to be re-examined and revised, if
not rejected. Marriage sometimes turns out well, but quite often, it does
not, as is proven by the plethora of data on abuse and battery in the
American family.

I would argue that the major factor in explaining changing household
composition from the postwar era to the present, is its location at both
ends of the expanded, accelerated circuit of production/consumption.
Wages and incomes from production provide for the maintenance of the
household; and the consumption of household goods and services is an
important avenue for realizing some of the capital necessary for another
round of production. A major thrust to expand the consumption of
household goods and services paralleled expanded wages and incomes in
the postwar era. Here is where the imaginary of The Family, i.e., the
white, middle-class suburban nuclear family ideal, became so powerful.
The imaginary fueled the consumption of new goods and services, redefining what we believe to be our daily necessities.

In the five years after World War II, with the increase in discretion-
ary income allowing for the consumption of goods and services other
than basic necessities, consumer spending increased 60 percent, but the
amount spent on household furnishings and appliances rose 240 percent. Furthermore, governmental policies promoted massive developments of single-family houses in the suburbs. Between 1950 and 1970, the
suburban population doubled from thirty-six million to seventy-four
million. Eighty-three percent of the nation's growth during those years
took place in the suburbs. (May 1988, pp. 165, 170)

The increase in suburban housing resulted in greater reliance on the
automobile—especially the station wagon, which the housewife/mother
used to transport the bread-earning husband and the children, and to
bring home the canned, frozen food from the new supermarket. In turn,
the increased reliance on the automobile resulted in the need for new
roads, highways, and superhighways to drive on. The shopping mall,
interspersed along the highways, soon followed. This was a new lifestyle
for the white middle class, but not for the minorities. As Coontz quite
properly reminds us, a quarter of the US population was living in pov-

erty in the mid-1950s, and a third of US children were living at poverty level at the end of that decade. (1992, pp. 29–30)

Both Strasser (1982) and Cowan (1983) showed that the American housewife in the postwar era had become increasingly dependent upon canned and frozen foods, refrigerators, freezers, dishwashers, washing machines, and dryers. These are supposedly labor-saving devices which afforded the housewife greater leisure. But Schor discovered that the postwar housewife did not gain that promised leisure. Instead, labor-saving appliances often require more rather than less attention. In the meantime, the standard of cleanliness has placed increased demands on the housewife. As a result, there has been no decline in the amount of time that the housewife spends on domestic labor. (1991, chapter 4)

Besides the military-industrial complex, enlarged household consumption is one major means to realize capital accumulation in the expanded, accelerated, and systematized terrain of production/consumption. George Katona, for example, found that nearly the entire increase in the gross national product in the mid-1950s was due to the increased spending on consumer durables and residential construction. (Cited in May 1988, p. 167)

But the wage income of the average male bread-earner alone can no longer finance the consumption and aspiration of the ever new, specialized goods and services which household members increasingly deem necessities. As a result, more and more wives and mothers have joined the ranks of working women to enlarge the female labor force. The trend was further accentuated by the end of postwar prosperity in the late 1960s and the recession of 1973, when households were already hooked on commodified lifestyles. Women in the postwar era began to go out to work in ever greater proportion. Between 1940 and 1950, there was a 29 percent growth in the number of women in the labor force. In the 1960s, the number of women at work grew by 39 percent. And that rate accelerated to 41 percent in the 1970s. (Coontz 1992, p. 163) In 1960, 37.7 percent of all women and 31.9 percent of married women worked; by 1990, 57.5 percent of all women and 58.4 percent of married women worked. In 1960, one-third of the civilian labor force was female. That increased to 38 percent in 1970; 42.5 percent in 1980; and 45 percent in 1990. (*SAUS 1992*, pp. 387, 383)

Wives, mothers, and other women work because they have to, for the sake of household consumption. In 1980, 58 percent of white females and 77.7 percent of African-American females worked for financial rather than non-financial reasons. (*SAUS 1982–83*, p. 384) Minority women, with lower incomes, at more risk of heading poor-income households, are more likely to work than white females. In 1960, 37.8 percent of the female adult working population and 48.2 percent of minority females were in the civilian labor force; in 1970, 43.4 percent of females and 49.6 percent of minority women worked; those figures increased to 51.6 percent of females and 53.8 percent of minority females by 1980. (*SAUS 1982–83*, p. 276)

In married-couple households, the woman is slightly more likely to work if her husband's income is below average, than if it is above average. The additional income of the working wife is sufficient to increase the couple's total household income to the point of exceeding the income of a family where the husband's income is above average, but the wife does not work. It is not so much that higher income households have working wives, as working wives put their households into higher income brackets. (Smith 1979, pp. 10, 12) The working wife's pay is a substantial increase in the household income, even though household expenses are also increasing considerably because she works. Inflation further complicates the problem of cost in the standard of living. On March 31, 1986, *Newsweek* reported that "it now takes two wage earners to sustain the same middle-class lifestyle that one income could provide 20 years ago."

The rate of working women who are married and have children under the age of six has increased from 18.8 percent in 1960, to 30.3 percent in 1970, to 45.1 percent in 1980, and 59.9 percent by 1990. (*SAUS 1992*, p. 377) More mothers are working, and, consequently, they have less time for child-rearing. Thus, more children have working mothers, though this is more likely in African-American than white married-couple families, and more likely in white than African-American single-parent families. In 1980, 52 percent of white children and 64 percent of African-American children in married-couple households had working mothers; 66 percent of white children and 57 percent of African-American children in single-parent households had working mothers. (Grossman 1982)

On the other hand, some working women are delaying marriages and having fewer children. After the initial postwar boom, the median age at first marriage for females has been increasing, from 20.2 in 1955 to 21.6 in 1979, although the median age for males increased only in the 1970s. (*SAUS 1982–83*, p. 82) Working women have fewer children than non-working women. (Moore and Hofferth 1979, p. 128)

With women working, and with the spread of different methods of contraception, families with children have decreased from 57 percent of all families or 49 percent of all households in 1960, to 52 percent of all families or 38 percent of all households in 1981. In other words, only somewhat more than half of all families or a little more than one-third of all households now have children, though African-American families with children increased from 56 percent of all African-American families in 1960 to 63 percent in 1975, and then dropped to 61 percent by 1981. ("U.S. Children and Their Families," p. 11; *SAUS 1982–83*, p. 43)

For different reasons, both working and non-working mothers are using various kinds of preschool childcare. As the family gets smaller, working mothers rely less on household help, and have to make different childcare arrangements. In 1958, more than half of the preschool children under the age of six whose mothers worked full time had at-home childcare, and another quarter received care in the homes of others. By 1977, slightly more than one quarter of children with working mothers were cared for at home; almost half in another home; and another 15 percent received care in group care centers. ("U.S. Children and Their Families," p. 14) For full-time working mothers, the pattern has been shifting away from childcare provided at home by others, to daycare in another's home or group care center.

The increasing use of childcare is not due solely to mothers working. The general trend is for both working and non-working mothers to use group care, at least among those who can afford it. Group care provides commodified socializing and educational advantages to preschool children, which many parents now consider a necessity. In 1967, 31.6 percent of three- to five-year-olds were enrolled in nurseries and kindergartens; by 1981, the number had jumped to 57 percent. The increase in nursery school enrollment has been particularly strong, jumping from 5.8 percent in 1967 to 21.4 percent in 1981. Working mothers are somewhat more likely than non-working mothers, white mothers somewhat more likely than African-American mothers, and married mothers slightly more likely than single mothers to enroll their children in preschool group cares. (*SAUS 1982–83*, p. 142)

Suransky (1982), Postman (1982), and Winn (1983) have focused on the so-called erosion and disappearance of childhood. From their point of view, children now are no longer as innocent, i.e., "child"-like, as before. This, I suggest, is not so much a problem of lost innocence, as a condition related to the valorization and commodification of social reproduction. Children are being raised with the help of television. They have become precocious consumers of the goods and services which replaced many of those personal, non-exchangist relations which formerly went into social reproduction. Children are now much more attuned to the needs of consuming commodities and services than to the needs of intersubjective social relations, more object- than subject-related. In other words, socialization has become education in consumer goods and lifestyle. In turn, parents approach children as commodities, in what Ehrenreich and Nasaw (1983) called "the emotional economy of the American family." Thus, kids are both "dependent consumers and likable commodities" in late-capitalist USA. On a local TV show I caught recently, an interviewee remarked offhandedly yet presciently, with no irony intended, "children are our most precious commodities."

In the segmented and resegmented labor market, women consistently earn less than two-thirds of comparable male wages. Furthermore, increasing numbers of working women are not supplementing the income of the male household head, but supporting themselves in single-parent households. These women have less money and also less time to raise children. In 1960, 6 percent of white families and 21 percent of African-American families with children under eighteen were headed by females; by 1982, the figures were 15 percent for white families and 46.6 percent for African-American families. ("U.S. Children and Their Families," p. 6) In 1982, 15.3 percent of white children under eighteen were living with mothers only, 1.9 percent with fathers only, and another 2 percent with neither parent, for a total of 19.2 percent of all white children not being raised in a married-couple household. In that same year, 47.2 percent of all African-American children lived with mothers only, 2 percent with fathers only, and another 8.4 percent with neither parent, for a total of 57.6 percent of all African-American children not being raised in a married-couple household. The percentage for Hispanic children fell between those for whites and African Americans. ("Marital Status and Living Arrangements: March 1982," p. 5) The reality is that inequality of income exists between male-headed and female-headed households, as well as between white and African-American households, with African-American female-headed households accounting for almost half of all African-American children, at the bottom.

But male incomes have also suffered since the end of the prosperity in the late 1960s, and the recession of 1973. As Robert Solow summarized:

The most important fact of American economic life is that the real income of the average family, which had been rising at about 3 percent a year in the 1950s and 1960s, fast enough to double every twenty-five years, slowed to a crawl (or worse) about 1973. For the past twenty years, growth has been negligible.

And inequalities have increased, with the bottom worsening, the middle barely getting by, and the few at the top enriched. (*New York Review of Books*, March 25, 1993, p. 12) The result is that a fifth of the nation's children are poor, as are almost a fourth of its preschoolers and almost half of its African-American children. In 1970, 10 percent of the nation's children lived in one-parent households; the figure has more than doubled since. In 1960, one in twenty-five children was born to an unmarried mother; now it is one in four. (*New York Times*, December 27, 1992) These figures are the product, not of declining family values, but of changing households in the accelerated, expanded circuit of late-capitalist production/consumption.

In spite of the trend toward two or more incomes per household, it may very well be that these incomes cannot support the commodified goods and services needed by the late-capitalist household. Yet the continuing valorization and commodification of household needs is necessary for capital accumulation. Who is going to pay for health care, unemployment, and retirement? Here, inevitably, the State has to step in. But Americans have had a love-hate relationship with the State. On the one hand, the so-called middle-class Americans, that is the majority, feel entitled to government services and tax write-offs—for example, deduction on home mortgage interests, and social security benefits. On the other hand, they view the State as an encroachment on their personal liberties, and are susceptible to conservative attacks on the chicaneries of the welfare state.

In the 1960s, provoked by public concern for poverty, the federal government under Johnson embarked on a series of welfare legislation. This legislation included Aid to Families with Dependent Children; food stamps and expanded school lunch programs; the Juvenile Delinquency and Youth Offenses Control Act of 1961; the 1962 social services amendments to the Social Security Act, which fundamentally increased and expanded support for service delivery by the various states; the Economic Opportunity Act of 1964, which provided Job Corps for urban dropouts, Neighborhood Youth Corps for part-time workers, work study programs for poor students going to college, and the Community Action Program and Volunteers in Services to America (VISTA) to eradicate poverty; and the enactment of hospital insurance for the old (including Medicaid) in 1965. Then, in 1972, the extension of Supplementary Security Income to the aged, blind and disabled. All of these by now familiar programs constituted public welfare to subsidize late-capitalist social reproduction.

Through successive acts and amendments, the emphasis of public welfare policy has changed from concern for the poor to universal entitlement. The primary thrust of the 1962 social services amendments was rehabilitation of the poor through social casework services. But, as Gilbert has pointed out, "from 1962 to 1980 there were a consistent loosening of social service eligibility standards and a concomitant broadening in the client base of the welfare state." (1983, p. 50) With increases in the range of federal social services, culminating in the Title XX amendments of 1974, the "provisions are directed more at enhancing human development and the general quality of life than at reducing poverty." (pp. 50–65) Instead of initiating a war on poverty, public welfare became universal entitlement. As Coontz points out, the dramatic growth in government social expenditures since the 1960s has been in social insurance programs, such as worker's compensation, disability, and Medicare. And these programs benefit primarily the white middle class. Even at the height of the Great Society anti-poverty initiative, between 1965 and 1971, 75 percent of America's social welfare dollars were spent on the non-poor. (1992, pp. 79–80) Contrary to popular opinion and neo-conservative rhetoric, public welfare as a whole benefits those in the middle-income brackets much more than those at the lower-income levels.

It is this change from social services for the poor to universal entitlement, in the name of human development and the quality of life, that primarily accounts for the increase of human resources outlays as a percentage of the total federal budget—from 28.4 percent in 1960, to 38.5 percent in 1970, to 53 percent in 1980. Though the figure declined to 49.5 percent of the total federal budget in 1990, the absolute figures for outlays in human resources almost doubled between 1980 and 1990. (SAUS 1992, p. 317)

The impact of public welfare on the poor is at best only ameliorative. Plotnick and Danziger found that, in 1972, only 42 percent of the total federal, state, and local expenditures of $185 billion on social welfare programs went to people whose earned income fell below the official poverty line, while 58 percent went to those with income levels above the official poverty line. However, the 42 percent of social welfare expenditures going to the poor did cut the percentage of officially poor people from 20 percent to 12 percent of the population. With the addition of in-kind transfer programs, the percentage of officially poor people fell to 6 percent. Thus, the war on poverty did lessen absolute poverty. Neverthe-less, Plotnick and Skidmore discovered that relative poverty, reflecting degrees of income inequality, hardly changed at all throughout the 1960s and 1970s, despite all the social welfare programs. (quoted in Page 1983, pp. 88–89) The problem, as Piven and Cloward point out, is that, by now, "almost half of the aggregate income of the bottom fifth of the popula-tion is derived from social welfare benefit. The poorest people in the country are now as much dependent on the government for their subsis-tence as they are on the labor market." (1982, p. 15) Therefore, the poor are more dependent on government support and more vulnerable to any changes than the rest of the population.

The public welfare policy of the late-capitalist state reconfirms the social reproduction of existing class, race, and gender hierarchies as determined by the expanded, accelerated, and systematized production and consumption. The middle classes have come to expect support from public welfare, whereas the lower classes can hardly live without it. Be-cause of that, the Reagan-Bush administrations found great difficulty in cutting universal programs that benefit middle-income households, al-though they succeeded in slashing benefits for the poor.

I propose that late-capitalist production and consumption have al-tered household composition, including the married-couple family. In this, the state has played only a subordinate, ameliorative role. It is the hegemony of exchangist practices that is subverting the binary opposi-tions between wage labor and domestic labor, the workplace (public) and the home (private), and culturally constructed male and female gendered roles. Thus, our inherited oppositional homologies of *man : woman = production* (wage labor) *: social reproduction* (domestic labor) *= public : private* no longer prevail.

On the other hand, The Family is a highly important and useful imaginary. More than a sign, it is an image that can arouse culturally constructed nostalgia and longings. It does not matter that The Family, with its working father, housekeeping mother, and their one or two children, does not represent most of American households. Nor does it matter that most of us have had anxious, conflicted family lives. The imaginary is a repository of coded and by now unreal longings which can be mobilized for diverse purposes. As we all know, The Family is used by many for diverse ethical, social, religious, and political purposes. Furthermore, it is also used by corporate advertisers as a signifier for the commodification of household goods and services. In other words, the imaginary is a means to ease and justify the commodification of the household. Thus, The Family as an imaginary is out there, readily available to play an important semiotic role, precisely because it is not actual.

In actuality, production and consumption practices in late capitalism are *meta-coding* the binary oppositions which underlaid the culture we inherited from industrial capitalism—i.e., over-coding the public/private, work/home, masculine/feminine dichotomies. At the imaginary level, The Family is *over-charged* with those coded longings that have no place in investing themselves in the hegemonic terrain of exchangist practices. But The Family by itself is not sufficient. To be effective, it needs an imaginary enemy or opposite, namely, the State. The dichotomy between The Family and the State, a free-floating opposition, camouflages the collapse of the binaries that founded our cultural heritage. Thus, quite miraculously, The Family can join forces with the free-market ideal of capitalism against the State, totally ignoring late-capitalist exploitation and underdevelopment of households for the sake of capital accumulation. This is one of the most impressive accomplishments of the right in the last two decades. The imaginary of The Family has nothing to do with the history of the family. It is more than nostalgia, and it is more than ideology. The Family is an integral part of the political culture of late capitalism.

b. Re-Racialization

In this section, I shall restrict myself to the issue of race as it pertains to African Americans. I take the term "race" not in any biological or genetic sense, but as a discursive construction with real effects. I will not discuss here the problematics of ethnic minorities, e.g., Hispanics, Native Americans, Asian Americans—not because they are unimportant, nor undeserved of their own specific analyses, but because I cannot hope to encompass all the important issues in one single volume. (Otherwise, I will never be able to finish this one.) Let me simply state that ethnicity, also a discursive construction, is different from race, and that the problematic of the former is totally different from that of the latter. I do not accept the argument that ethnicity and race are analogous. Nor do I agree that African Americans can partake of the old American myth of social mobility like ethnic minorities, since social formation in the USA up until now has always been founded on the marginalization, i.e., the othering, of African Americans. In other words, it is racialized and racist, through and through. In fact, quite a number of successful minorities buy into the racist marginalization of African Americans, as a part of their own ascription to the white/black dichotomy.

The social reproduction of African Americans is conditioned by class and race, with low income levels and ghetto-ization for most. These conditions create higher infant mortality rates, higher unemployment for youths, lower wages, higher stress, and higher instances of heart attacks for African Americans, when compared with the whites. Conditions in the last two decades have become worse for these African Americans, as opposed to the minority of middle-class, well-educated African Americans who struggled successfully to improve their lot. But all of these are obfuscated by the imaginary of The Black Family as the negative other to the imaginary of The Family, i.e., The White Family. The Black Family is everything that The White Family is not. The Black Family lacks discipline and is afflicted by an excess of sexuality. The imaginary of The Family functions to obfuscate the changing reality of American households. The negative imaginary of The Black Family reduces the problematic of African-American social reproduction to manageable, racist dimension. The fault lies in "the decline of The Black Family." It is their own fault! Thus the re-racialization of the last two decades works at two levels, each reinforcing the other. On the one hand, the social reproduction of African Americans is worsening. On the other, we don't see this as a racial and racist problem.

We all know the disparity between social reproduction in the USA as a whole and the social reproduction of African Americans. In 1989, the infant mortality rate for African Americans was more than twice as high as for whites, and life expectation at birth at least six years less. (*SAUS 1992*, pp. 76, 80) Let us recapitulate just a few figures from Coontz (1992) to fill in the conditions between birth and death. Economic gains for all segments of African Americans, except for the few college graduates, have either stagnated or reversed since the mid-1970s. The number of African Americans with incomes 50 percent below the official poverty line has increased by 68 percent since 1978, and the number of those living in poor urban areas has increased by 20 percent. Forty-five percent of African-American children live in poverty for several years of their childhood. And even college-educated African-American males make only 75 percent as much as white males, and are four times as likely to be unemployed. Finally, "an Asian or Hispanic who finished only the third grade or who earns less than $2,500 a year has a higher chance of living in an integrated neighborhood than does a black person who has a Ph.D. or earns more than $50,000." (p. 234) This is not to say that there is no discrimination against Asian and Hispanic Americans in many parts of the country.

These very disturbing and undeniable figures need to be explained or at least explained away. Some on the right propose the genetic inferiority of African Americans as an explanation. There may be quite a number of people who are receptive to that argument, although saying it in public leaves one open to accusations of racism. And nobody wants to be tagged a racist nowadays, not even David Duke. Nevertheless, various displaced code words and images are often used to activate the unspoken racism that is prevailing in the country.

A much more effective explanation than genetic inferiority, and much more respectable for both the mainstream press and the academic world, is the thesis of the decline of the African-American family. Statistics are easily available to show the decline in the nuclear couple family, the rise in female-headed households, the rising number of unemployed and criminalized youths among African Americans. All the figures contribute to the argument that not only are African Americans the other, but their families are the negation of The Family.

There are several gross, unwarranted assumptions in this argument. One is that The Family is self-sufficient and is therefore responsible for social reproduction. The other is that this norm is a value to which all other types of households must conform. The third is that African-American families and households are, or at least should be, the same as those of the whites, regardless of socioeconomic and cultural differences. And the final assumption is that there is such a thing as The Family which can be traced across time to show whether it is rising or declining. I reject all of the above as unwarranted assumptions. Moreover, I reject the whole argument concerning the decline and fall of the African-American family, though not because I believe that African American family households are not suffering, nor because I believe that there is such a thing as The African American Family. I reject it because the argument judges African-American households in terms of a white imaginary, thus obfuscating the damages inflicted on African-American social reproduction by changing production and consumption practices.

In addition to the biological reduction and declining African-American family, the Reagan-Bush administrations have argued that affirmative action is reverse discrimination against the majority. The argument upholds the assumption that we can all compete in a level field. What is most intriguing about the argument is that it encourages denial. It denies that there is any significant racial discrimination in this country. It denies the socioeconomic, cultural differences which disadvantage certain people in the marketplace. And it denies that past discrimination has any impact on us at the present. The argument in effect lends support to the ideal of a free market. But the free market ideal denies the reality of a political economy; just as the imaginary of The Family denies the reality of changing households in the changing political economy. The thesis of reverse discrimination, together with the imaginary of The Family and the free market ideal, in effect, circulate as constricted ideological values. These values encourage denial. And by providing compartmentalized explanations for specific issues, they ultimately obfuscate the hegemony of exchangist practices in late-capitalist USA.

It is against this background of deteriorating conditions for African Americans and increasing criticism of the government's welfare policies and affirmative action, that William Julius Wilson, a mainstream sociologist and a social democrat, introduced his thesis, *The Declining Significance of Race* (1978). Wilson sees race as a distinct category from class, and argues that by now "as the influence of race on minority class-stratification decreases . . . class takes on greater importance in determining the life chances of minority individuals." (2d ed., 1980, p. x) He justifies his thesis on two grounds. There is a changing African-American social structure, with a small middle class, a much larger lower class, and even a new, growing underclass. Until the recession of 1973, the conditions of the African-American middle class had been improving, especially among the well-educated young. On the other hand, the conditions of the lower- and under-classes have worsened. That, to Wilson, is an indication of the rising importance of class differences in the problems confronted by African Americans. And this is true not only for blacks but also non-blacks. Furthermore, Wilson argues, in *The Truly Disadvantaged* (1987), that public welfare policies and affirmative action based upon consideration of race do not and cannot deal with the fundamentally socioeconomic problems of the urban ghetto population. Wilson urges policies based upon class, instead of race-specific policies or behavioral modification.

From the standpoint of public policy, there is merit to Wilson's argument. Wilson is neither denying the existence of racism, nor merely celebrating the rise of an African-American middle class, as some of his critics claimed. He is trying to shift the public policy debate from race to class, since, from his standpoint, the problems currently facing African-American lower- and under-classes in the ghettoes are socioeconomic, and can never be resolved by race-specific policies. I agree that there is probably somewhat more support for class-specific, rather than race-specific policies in the USA at large, although in hard times the middle classes would not be likely to look out for the lower classes.

But the merit in Wilson's argument is based upon a false premise. Unlike others, I would criticize Wilson at the conceptual, i.e., methodological, level. He conceives of class and race as two discrete sociological categories. Classes, according to Wilson, are differences in "relationships . . . within the market where different commodities are bought and sold and where people with various resources (goods, services, or skills) meet and interact for purposes of exchange." (1980, p. 156) In other words, class, according to Wilson, is a social relations of exchange, in the Weberian sense. It has nothing to do with race. Race, on the other hand, is a separate category, and Wilson urges that it be considered "as a special problem within the general context of political economy." (p. 162) If I interpret Wilson correctly, class stratification based upon the social relations of exchange is non-racial; race runs deeper than class, but needs to be considered as a special case within the context of the US political economy since World War II. It is this categorical separation between class and race that enables Wilson to compare the relative importance of the two, and to say that race is now not as significant.

Unlike the sociological approach of Wilson, Omi and Winant conceive of race as a socio-historical formation, emphasizing its political, contestable character. "Racial categories and the meaning of race are given concrete expression by the specific social relations and historical context in which they are embedded." (1986, p. 60) They therefore vary over time and space. "The meaning of race is defined and contested throughout society, in both collective action and personal practice. In the process, racial categories themselves are formed, transformed, destroyed and re-formed." (p. 61) Race is not a biological essence, a stable thing in itself. It is "an unstable and 'decentered' complex of social meanings constantly being transformed by political struggle." (p. 68) It is present everywhere in the Social, whether covertly or overtly.

In accordance with their concept of racial formation, Omi and Winant see the "racial upsurge" of the 1950s and 1960s as a dramatic transformation of the American political and cultural landscape. During those two decades, new ideas of racial identity, new modes of political organization, and new definitions of the role of government in promoting "equality" were explored and contested. (p. 89) These new ideas were first promoted by the civil rights movement, and then by the new social movements, the latter spearheaded by the black movement. In turn, the right counter-attacked in the 1970s and 1980s. Omi and Winant see three main currents in the reaction against the racial upsurge—the far right, the new right, and neoconservatism. The far right are admitted white racial supremacists. The new right react against the recent changes by rallying around the traditional ideas of nation, community, and family. And the neoconservatives rely on the values of individualism, the free market, and freedom from government intervention. With the exception of the ideals fostered by those on the far right, the prevailing racial reaction "claims to favor racial equality. Its vision is that of a 'color-blind' society where racial considerations are never entertained. . . ." (p. 113) Instead, the problem for them is the new racial injustice of reverse discrimination.

To some extent, Omi and Winant's racial formation is confirmed by Weir, Orloff, and Skocpol (eds. 1988), and by Roediger (1991), though they also go beyond Omi and Winant's social-constructivist approach. Weir, Orloff, and Skocpol, in the introduction to their collaborative anthology, argue for an "institutional-political process" in the formation of the welfare state in the USA. And this state formation needs to be understood in relationship to capitalist economic development, urbanization, and transformations of liberal values—but not in an outright economistic sense. What is relevant to my argument here is that Weir, Orloff, and Skocpol, when discussing the peculiarities of the American welfare state, point to white Southern agrarian interests working through an undemocratic one-party seniority system in the Congress to affect public policies from the New Deal to the Great Society. Thus, Franklin D. Roosevelt got his social security programs for Northern urban workers by preserving white Southern agrarian interests. (1988, pp. 16–27) In other words, race has always been a hidden but important factor, in this case at the very foundation of our social security programs. And this race is not mere racism, but economic interest based upon existing racial stratification and racism.

Again, Roediger argues that, in the nineteenth century, "whiteness was a way in which white workers responded to a fear of dependency on wage labor and to the necessities of capitalist work discipline." Instead of joining forces with slave labor, wage labor considered itself free labor and distanced itself from the former. "[M]ade anxious by fear of dependency," the white working class "began during its formation to construct an image of the Black population as 'other'—as embodying the preindustrial, erotic, careless style of life the white workers hated and longed for." (1991, pp. 13–14)

Omi and Winant are correct in emphasizing the pervasiveness of racial formation in the USA. However, there is also the need to state the obverse aspect of the pervasive racial formation, namely, the context of late-capitalist production, consumption, and social reproduction. This context, I have argued throughout this volume, cannot be analyzed in terms of an orthodox Marxist structural order, but as a hegemonic terrain of exchangist practices, with the recombination of structural, discursive, systematic, and semiotic components. And the very structural, discursive, systematic, and semiotic components are premised on the pervasiveness of racism. In other words, race operates within a hegemonic terrain, and that terrain takes advantage of existing racism. In reality, the two are intertwined.

Let us forget about the search for origin, since that search is a retrospective ordering which distorts and reduces the synchronic problematic. If we forgo the search for biological origin of race or only conscious intentional discrimination, then we can see race is *always* present in the USA, whether in outright discrimination and segregation, or implicitly in the very construction of the outlooks and values of the majority. The latter depends on the othering and marginalization of African Americans, since there is *already* at work in the construction a dichotomic "logic" of white versus black, center versus periphery. Race is neither a monolith, nor an isolatable variable. Therefore, let us abandon the search for an isolatable racism which, in effect, frees all other variables from any responsibility. What is usually termed "the institutionalization of racism" is not something given or static, but the very structuration, discursivity, systems analysis, and semiotics which construct production, consumption, and social reproduction practices by means of this "logic." Regardless of the rise of a small, well-educated African-American middle class, race is now much more insidious and pervasive, much more difficult to combat.

Late-capitalist production practices take advantage of layers of racism, and reconfirm them—unless affirmative action practices intervene, though it is debatable how effective affirmative action can be. At the level of discrimination, whether conscious or unintended, African American workers with the same qualifications are less likely to be employed and more likely to be laid off. Beyond discrimination, African-American workers are the most poorly paid, with the highest proportion of them in the lowest paid categories of work. In addition, they suffer the highest unemployment rate. No one disputes these facts. The disputes center around different explanations, such as lack of education, poor work discipline, and the culture of poverty. These characterizations precisely reconfirm African Americans as different, i.e., as a "race." But these characterizations are not explanations so much as evidence of the structural, discursive, systematic, semiotic constructions which separate African Americans as a "race." Take, for example, another usual explanation: that jobs are available in the suburbs, but the urban poor often lack access to them. But isn't this suburbanization a development which presupposes its other, i.e., the underdevelopment of the urban center? Is this complex postwar suburban development and urban underdevelopment solely due to the "economics" of investment capital seeking a higher rate of return, or is there not deep racism at work too? Finally, is not the reserve army of unemployed African-American workers useful in disciplining the workforce?

The point is that the deeply ingrained dualism between the so-called subjective (or psychological) and the so-called objective (or socioeconomic), i.e., between mind and body, prevents us from recognizing the pervasiveness of racism. On the one hand, we search for intentional and legally defined discrimination; on the other, we excuse the unintended as objective and therefore not discriminatory. But the structural, discursive, systematic, and semiotic construction of production practices that are racist is neither merely objective nor merely subjective. The old dualism of subject/object, mind/matter prevents us from recognizing the underlying dichotomous logic of white/black, center/periphery that is always, already at work. But, for African Americans, racism goes beyond the subjective/objective distinction—they experience it going and coming. Nevertheless, they are often accused of being paranoid! Of course, one can learn to overlook and repress it!

The new lifestyle consumption reconfigures racism in several ways. In general, those with less income and education are more vulnerable to the

packaging, marketing, and advertising, i.e., the semiotics, of new commodities. Since higher percentages of African Americans are in the lower
income groups, they are more likely to be victimized, by succumbing to
repackaged, advertised needs. More specifically, lifestyle segmentation,
based on systems analysis, enables corporations to target select groups
for the marketing of specific commodities, e.g., advertisements for cigarettes and liquor that target the ghetto population. Finally, the issue is
not the declining significance of race and the emergent importance of
class, but, rather, the overshadowing of class, i.e., the social relations of
production, by lifestyle, or the new social relations of consumption.
Lifestyle consumption makes us accept those with similar lifestyle characteristics through the consumption of similar commodities, and alien-
ates us from class solidarity or cross-race politics. It is easier now to
accept an African American with a similar upscale lifestyle, and to abhor
those with downscale or dissonant lifestyles.

Racism is not a single, discrete, isolatable item, nor is it the result of a
conspiracy. It is always, already present everywhere in the Social. Capital
does not operate as a pure logic. It always utilizes existing values in the
social terrain. Thus, racism is a complex of signs to be utilized for late-
capitalist production, consumption, and social reproduction practices. I
fear that, with the commodification of the social reproduction of most,
i.e., middle-class and white, households, the exploitation of gender becomes less productive of surplus value, and hence, race has to shoulder a
greater share through the underdevelopment of African-American social
reproduction. In the center of late capital is the ghetto. The development
of the former requires the underdevelopment of the latter. But this logic
is not purely based upon class. It is class filtered through race.

c. The Body and Bio-Technical Systems

Another aspect in changing social reproduction is the new practices of
bio-technical systems in reconnecting, supplementing, decomposing, recombining, decentering, and, in effect, deconstructing the lived body.
This is not just a matter of changing technology or context for the self-
same body. The embodied self is, in late capitalism, undergoing fundamental transformation.

Foucault, in his study of the bourgeois regime of discourse/power,
associated the disciplining of the body with the visual surveillance of the
clinic and the panopticon. This is a gaze which "would be both global

and individualizing while at the same time carefully separating the individuals under observation." (1981, p. 146) In other words, disciplinary discourses constructed bio-power with the aid of a gaze which visually individualized the target of disciplinary discourses. It is the combination of discursive construction (an episteme) and visual individuation (a sensorial hierarchy) which sustained the bourgeois reality of an autonomous bodily self (the content of an ideology).

But that body is currently being transformed by a myriad of bio-technical systems which dissect, deconstruct, recombine, and displace it. As Haraway pointed out, " 'advanced capitalism' and post-modernism release heterogeneity without a norm, we are flattened, without subjectivity. . . . It is time to write *The Death of the Clinic.* The clinic's methods required bodies and works; we have texts and surfaces." (1985, p. 69n) The result she terms the cyborg, or a cybernetic organism. Not all of us are cyborgs yet. Nevertheless, we are certainly more akin to cyborgs than to the individual bodily subject. And with old concepts and boundaries falling apart, new questions and controversies concerning the bodily subject's birth, life, and death are hotly debated. This is the underlying dynamic connecting the seemingly disparate politics of abortion and the AIDS epidemic. In this section, I shall discuss some of the practices of bio-technical systems which are transforming the reproduction of the body.

The expansion of health care in the postwar era was justified by a new discourse of medicine. Until the end of the war, the practice of medicine was based on a biomedical model. (Mishler et al. 1981, pp. 3–19) But around 1950, according to Arney and Bergen, "the language of modern medicine began to identify the structures of life with the normative order of an ecological system that embraced everything that could be spoken about." (1984, p. 162) Partly, advances in medical technology, such as electrocardiographs, linear accelerators, radiation therapy machines, scanners, computerized diagnoses, and others, made the shift possible; partly, it is based on the new logic of systems analysis. As is usual with changing discourses, the new discourse of medicine became an autonomous factor itself, affecting medical production/consumption, technology, and communication.

The new medical discourse, through the shift from a mechanistic to a holistic model, emphasizes relationships, information flows, systems, and ecology. The medical gaze gave way "to an encompassing incorporation, a gaze that attributes meaning to a phenomenon—disease, health, birth, death—in terms of its relations to things in its ecology rather than in terms of slight differences from things most like it." (pp. 62–63) A new relation emerges between the physician and the patient which requires the former to listen to the speech of the latter. It is no longer the silent, visual, objective gaze that Foucault was uncovering for the early nineteenth century. Disease is no longer a specific abnormality or deviation, but a disturbed relationship within a totality of hierarchical systems. The focus of disease has shifted from the acute to the chronic. (Later in this section, I shall discuss the shift from monocausal etiology to etiologic heterogeneity in diagnosing chronic diseases.)

The new discourse offers patients

> not just the possibility of life, but life itself. Medicine became the mediator of the true life, the fulfilled life, the managerially optimized life. As medicine's attention shifted away from disease and toward the person, its goal shifted away from health toward life. It began to map life which came to be identified with the trajectories people follow from conception to death, and to develop a calculus of optimal trajectories together with analyses of deviations from those trajectories. (p. 99)

By raising the expectations of the patient and the public, the new medical discourse is able to generate and mobilize new power. Being more comprehensive, it allows physicians, hospitals, and health maintenance corporations, the pharmaceutical and medical-technology industries, and the regulatory state, to expand the production and consumption of health care goods and services for diverse purposes. "Whereas the taxonomic approach of medicine constantly narrowed medicine's field of vision, the ecological model and systems-theoretic logic are expanding it. All other parameters of medical practice are changing in response." (p. 166)

But, within the expanded discursive coverage, contemporary health care often does not and cannot deliver on the new promises. Strauss, Fagerhaugh, Suczek, and Wiener, in their 1985 survey of the social organization of medical work, observed that medical specialization and technological innovation required expansion of physical facilities, reallocation of workers, integration of new skilled personnel into a continuously changing division of labor, and establishment of complex relationships among a multiplicity of hospital services and departments. The increased technological specialization and complex bureaucratic health structure have led to two important developments. "First, the fragmentation of chronic care, with increasing possibilities that continuity of care will go awry, accompanied by accusatory cries of dehumanization; second, the incorporation of new workers and roles to remedy the effects of fragmented care and dehumanization." (pp. 4–5) They conclude that, given the organizational complexity of the hospital, remedying the situation is shatteringly difficult.

More specifically, from conception to death, biotechnical systems of all sorts are changing received meanings of birth, life, and death.

Artificial insemination, *in vitro* fertilization, and embryo transfer techniques are altering conception and birth. It is now possible to conceive without sexual intercourse, to fertilize outside of the human body, and to give birth to someone else's baby. Not only do these new techniques give hope to couples unable to conceive; sperm banks are in business, selling genetically screened sperms. For example, the Repository for Germinal Choice in Escondido, California, promises in its brochure to "endow future children with the most valuable genes obtainable." These are

> the genes of men whose genetic inheritance appears exceptionally favorable. Valued are physical and mental health, longevity, a sociable personality and the precious and uniquely human quality: the capacity for abstract thought and intellectual creativity.

Surrogacy is another new prospect, with lawyers writing contracts to enable infertile couples to have their baby conceived in the body of another woman.

Blank argues that these new technologies are redefining the "motherhood" which combined the production of the ovum, childbearing, and childrearing. Now it is possible and sometimes necessary to separate the genetic mother, who supplies the egg or the embryo, from the carrying mother, in whose womb the embryo develops till birth, and finally from the nurturing mother, who cares for the baby after birth. In a somewhat similar manner, the "father" can be separated into a genetic father who provides the sperm, and a nurturing father who cares for the child after birth. In effect, the very concept of "parenthood" is being transformed. (1990, pp. 8–11) And we read in the daily papers how new legal and emotional issues are being raised about competing, conflicting rights and responsibilities.

Heart, liver, and kidney transplants give patients a new lease on life.

Some sixteen thousand human organ transplants were performed in 1992. Currently, more than thirty-two thousand people are awaiting various types of organ transplants. But the demands outstrip supplies, and potential transplant patients are placed on waiting lists. Yet neither the patient nor the donor's organ can wait for too long without deterioration. It has to be an organ of the right tissue, blood type, and size for a particular patient, at the right place and right time. About one-half of those patients on waiting lists do get a transplant. But one-fifth to one-third of those on the waiting list die, because of the lack of appropriate organs. (*Business Week,* June 28, 1993) The ethical issue is, who gets a scarce transplant, since another will not—should it be the sickest one, even if he or she is already very old, or the younger one who can use the organ to lead a longer life? (*New York Times,* October 18, 1992) In the meantime, demand creates new market. Thorne and Langner reported that, "however repugnant the idea, the body now has economic value that cannot be wished away or ignored." (*New York Times,* September 8, 1986) Although federal laws prohibit the sale of human organs, the *New York Times,* on September 25, 1985, reported a growing underground market for human organs and cadavers.

In addition, for critically ill patients, there are now available coronary care units, medical intensive care units, surgical intensive care units, respiratory intensive care units, neurological intensive units, and burn centers. The different high-tech equipments in these units have resulted in patients who are neither fully alive nor fully dead, but in a permanent coma. New ethical as well as technical issues of whether to start or when to stop different modes of treatment now confront the doctor, the comatose patient's relatives and lawyers, and the state. (Weir 1989, pp. 34–42, 8)

We have, in effect, moved from a bodily concept of death to a whole-brain concept, or even a neocortically oriented concept of death. As Tristram Englehardt Jr., a leading medical ethicist, points out, when

one's interest is not in the preservation of mere biological life, but in the continuance of a mental life, the focus is on the brain as the sponsor of sentience and consciousness. It is the brain that sustains mental life. The body, in contrast, comes to be seen as a complex, integrated mechanism that sustains the life of the brain, which sponsors the life of a person. One can replace various parts of the body with transplanted organs or prostheses and the person remains the same person. (1986, p. 206)

Nevertheless, the issues of individual birth, life, and death are merely the tip of a much larger, invisible deconstruction and reconfiguration which other, new, biotechnical systems are undertaking on the body. While we are contesting these issues, advances in molecular biology have recently led to the federal government-funded Human Genome Initiative. Headed by James Watson, the discoverer of DNA, at a cost of 3 billion dollars over fifteen years, the project surpasses and is likely to overcome our belief in the integrity of embodied life.

The Human Genome Project seeks to discover the order of some three billion nuclei acid base pairs that make up fifty thousand to ten thousand human genes, and locate them on a "typical" human chromosome set. It is, in effect, a mapping of the molecular genetics of human beings. As the memory of Nazi eugenics fades, the new knowledge of genetics will have many applications, some already useful, others yet to be discovered. New researches are being undertaken concerning the relation between diseases and genes. (I shall deal with the implications of this shortly.) DNA-based genetic testing has already been introduced into health care. It is now possible to predict the likelihood of certain diseases not only for living human beings, but also for fetuses yet to be born. With further simplification of the technology, tests can screen any group of people for possible risks of disease, alcoholism, and even claimed potential criminality. The commercial uses of the technology for pharmaceuticals, insurance risks, and corporate employment are obvious.

Casalino (1991, p. 112) raises important social, legal, and ethical concerns: "Who will screen whom for what purposes? [For example, w]ill individuals be denied employment or insurance because they have been shown to have a genetic susceptibility to, say, breast cancer?" "Will a new human eugenics appear? . . . with individual mating, reproductive, and abortion choices influenced by the definition of what are normal and desirable traits[?]" And, "will the Genome Project further the growing tendency to focus on genetic rather than social causes of social problems and on individual rather than public health?"

Genetic research is altering our understanding of the etiology of diseases. (Holtzman 1989, chap. II) In the early twentieth century, the leading causes of death were pneumonia, tuberculosis, and diarrhea. Biomedical research diagnosed these maladies as being caused by microorganisms; and the cure from the disease involved the elimination of the bacterium believed to have caused the pathology. In other words, there seemed to be a monocausal etiology between the microorganism and the disease. Only later did laboratory tests reveal that not everyone who harbors a pathogenic microorganism automatically develops the disease. In actuality, the etiology of a disease is much more complicated than the simple monocausal relation between it and a microorganism. The decline of pneumonia, tuberculosis, and diarrhea actually came with improvements in public health, such as water purification, sewage treatment, the pasteurization of milk and less crowded housing. Vaccines and antibiotics against the pathogenic bacteria only came later.

In the late twentieth century, with the elimination of these infectious diseases, and with a larger proportion of the populace living from infancy to old age, the leading causes of death are heart disease, cancer, stroke, accidents, and chronic lung disease. These diseases cannot be attributed to specific discovered microorganism. Different people with the same pathogenic condition may develop a disease from different causative factors. The same factor can be incriminated in the etiology of more than one disease. And even though an agent is found to play a role in the causation of a disease, many individuals exposed to a high dosage of that agent will never suffer the disease.

Hence, instead of monocausal etiology, we need to think in terms of etiologic heterogeneity. Some etiologic factors, according to Holtzman, are *discrete,* in the sense that there is already an established causal relation between the factor and the occurrence of the disease in at least some individuals. Discrete factors can be further divided into environmental ones (such as chemicals, physical agents, microorganisms, deficiencies of specific nutrients, weapons) and genetic ones. Recombinant DNA technology permits the search for the genetic basis of disease to proceed directly at the genetic level. But "the possibility of variable expressivity, allelic diversity, and genetic heterogeneity for genetic diseases may make it difficult for investigators to localize or identify disease related genes." (p. 87)

In addition to discrete factors, there are various *modulating* factors, such as age, sex, family, ethnic and racial group, social class, climate, occupation, sanitation, housing, clothing, nutrition, stressors, complex physiological functions, resilience, immunity, social networks, personal habits of smoking and drinking, and pharmacological and recreational drugs. Modulating factors are associational rather than causal. And the boundary between discrete and modulating factors is not static. New discrete factors may be discovered within, and detached from, existing modulating ones. Though our knowledge of the etiology of many diseases will increase, "we will never have complete understanding." (p. 27) There are no " 'magic bullets' (immunization and antibiotics)" for chronic diseases. (p. 36)

Genes, by themselves, do not cause anything. (Hubbard and Wald 1993; Lewontin, Rose, and Kamin 1984) Our information of genes provides a predisposition within a larger context of etiologic heterogeneity. Yet many people, including some scientists, ignore levels of logic and connection to speak of causative genes, homosexual genes, behavioral genes, and good and bad genes.

Nevertheless, even without lapsing into biogenetic babble, advances of genetic knowledge have surpassed the body's integrity and individuality. Genetic science is a semiotic system which "construct[s] and maintain[s] boundaries for what may count as self and others in the crucial realms of the normal and the pathological." The resulting biomedical-biotechnical body is no longer a visible, stable person with the integrity of a self, but a problematic unit conceived "not in terms of laws of growth and essential properties, but rather in terms of strategies of design, boundary constraints, rates of flow, system logics, and costs of lowering constraints." The control strategies concentrate "on boundary conditions and interfaces, on rates of flow across boundaries, not on the integrity of natural objects." Human beings are in effect "localized in a system architecture whose basic modes of operation are probabilistic." (Haraway 1989, pp. 4, 15)

The struggle over the knowledge and the boundary of a biotechnical system is in fact very political. A good case in point is the definition and the research of acquired immune deficiency syndrome, or AIDS, a term adopted by the Centers for Disease Control in 1982. AIDS is a syndrome, not a disease. The syndrome consists of the depletion of, or the inability to replenish, certain white blood cells, thus making that person much less able to fight or contain some infectious diseases. Ordinarily, our body is able to tolerate a number of microorganisms; but with acquired immune deficiency syndrome, i.e., the depletion of certain white blood cells, the body becomes much more vulnerable to them.

Nevertheless, we don't know what exactly AIDS is, or what leads to an immune deficiency syndrome. At a 1984 conference, held by the Secretary of Health and Human Services in an administration under attack for not doing enough to combat AIDS, Robert Gallo came forth to claim that he and his colleagues at the National Cancer Institute had "discovered" the human immunodeficiency virus, or HIV, which could explain for

AIDS. Gallo's HIV is not a virus, but a "retrovirus," which supposedly has the capacity to reverse the ordinary flow of genetic information from DNA to RNA to proteins. The theory is that "retroviruses" can integrate themselves into the host's DNA, thus causing cells to multiply rapidly.

The "human immunodeficiency virus" is a concept, and a contested one. A number of scientists question, on different grounds, Gallo's theory that retroviruses cause AIDS. Furthermore, an AIDS test is not a test for the presence of HIV, but for the antibodies of that virus. And a positive testing does not indicate any specific symptom. Lately, there are counter-claims that some individuals who tested negative for HIV have contracted AIDS. The curious thing is that Gallo and his colleagues had claimed since the late 1970s that their researches on retroviruses would soon lead to a cure for cancer. Of course, that "magic-bullet" discovery has yet to happen. Instead, they now are staking their claim on AIDS. (Goldman and Chappelle 1992) As Treichler points out, the HIV concept is very much a cultural construction of reality. "By repeatedly citing each other's work," Gallo and his colleagues "quickly established a dense citation network, thus gaining early (if ultimately only partial) control over nomenclature, publication, invitation to conferences, and history." (1992, p. 76) We still don't know what's what.

5   Sexuality and Gender Construction

How do exchangist practices construct gender and sexuality in late-capitalist USA? In other words, how have changes in late-capitalist production, consumption, and social-reproduction practices transformed gender and sexuality? In framing the questions in this way, I am already arguing that neither gender nor sexuality is natural, since there is no body-in-itself; both are "socially" constructed. And that construction in capitalist formations is fundamentally determined by production/consumption and social-reproduction practices. Nor do I assume an unconscious sexual identity prior to, and therefore determining, personality formation. I leave the burden of providing the metaphysics of that paradigm to those who need it to explain their theories of personality formations. (Cf., my critique of psychopathology in chapter 6) Section *a*, here, discusses the analytical framework of this chapter; section *b* argues that late-capitalist sexuality is very much a commodified sexual lifestyle; and section *c* is concerned with aspects of late-capitalist gender construction.

a. Gender and Sexuality

To begin with, I shall make a distinction among "sex," "gender," and "sexuality." Admittedly, the three terms are so connected that often we find it difficult to separate them. But I need to distinguish them in order to discuss the changing relations between gender and sexuality in late-capitalist USA. By sex, I mean the perceived physical, anatomical differences between people in having certain organs and traits which we in our culture believe to distinguish man from woman. The term also becomes a verb, as in "having sex," though that transitive act does not necessarily require a "one man/one woman" intercourse. By gender, I mean how we in our culture categorize the differences between man and woman in our social formation. And by sexuality, I mean the modern discourse/power concerning sex which Foucault studied. Obviously, in any social formation, people "have sex" in many different ways. But anatomical differences and sexual activities cannot by themselves account for either sexuality or gender construction. Since the body is a social construction, a social complex, gender and sexuality are necessarily also socially constructed, not "naturally" given.

Different academic disciplines have now come to accept the notion that gender is a social/cultural construction. In support of the notion of its constructiveness, I shall review briefly some of the arguments from the standpoints of anthropology, ethnography, socio-ethnomethodology, and feminist/philosophical critique.

In anthropology, Ortner and Whitehead stated in their anthology that "what gender is, what men and women are, what sorts of relations do or should obtain between them—all of these notions do not simply reflect or elaborate upon biological 'givens', but are largely products of social and cultural processes." They emphasize that "the social-cultural formations most directly bound up with conceptions of gender (and gender-related matters) are prestige structure." (1981, pp. 1, 25) A few years later, Yanagisako and Collier went beyond the cultural construction of gender "to question the universality and analytic utility of our assumptions about sex [i.e., gender] differences." (1987, p. 49) They argued that we must locate gender in the social whole, since gender differences occur and operate differently in different cultures. Most recently, di Leonardo notes the embedded nature of gender, and the need to use different methods, including poststructuralism and Marxism, "to investigate actively the multiple layers of context—or, in another formulation, social location—through which we perceive particular cultural realities." (1991, p. 31)

In actuality, it is only in the modern West that gender is believed to be a universal category founded on the naturalness of anatomical sexual differences. Thus "nature," i.e., anatomical sexual differences, has become for us in the modern West the foundation of gender. But biology is not "nature." It is a nineteenth- and twentieth-century scientific discourse about nature. Whether there is such a thing as Nature in itself is a moot point, since Kant has instructed us that we cannot know a thing-in-itself. Keller (1985, part 3), for instance, has recently argued that the content of science provides us with our knowledge of nature, but science itself is culture-bound, and not value-free. Our knowledge of nature is the product of a specific cultural, scientific construction, which situates nature as the other to culture. The knowledge that biology provides us with, in other words, is the product of scientific construction, not nature-in-itself.

Beyond the constructiveness of gender is the issue as to whether gender is necessarily a male/female bipolarity. This certainly has been the case in the modern Western construction, with its binary oppositions between masculinity/femininity, reason/emotion, active/passive, public/private. But is that necessarily the case with other constructions? Ethnography has provided us with cursory information about the so-called third gender in certain social/cultural formations. (e.g., Herdt ed. 1994) Kessler and McKenna discuss how earlier epochs and other societies had different gender attributions, and that some societies had the practice of a third gender, neither man nor woman. For example, the phenomenon of the berdache seems to have occurred not just in native North American societies, but also in others in Alaska, Siberia, Central and South Asia, Oceana, Australia, the Sudan, and the Amazon region. But the ethnography we have is so colored by the cultural categorization of Western informers that it is hard to separate the information from their Western lenses. (1985, pp. 24–32)

From the standpoint of socio-ethnomethodology, Kessler and McKenna argue convincingly that cultural presuppositions underlie the supposedly value-free scientific study of gender. According to them, none of the current criteria used in the biological determination of gender—such as chromosomes, gonads, internal reproductive organs, pre-natal hormones, external reproductive organs, and pubertal hormones—can by themselves prove to be predictive of gender.

> Although scientists have devised lists of biological criteria which differentiate women from men (chromosomes, gonads, etc.), they always begin by being able to tell females from males in the first place, without any information about these criteria. Although it seems as if the biological facts have an existence independent of gender labels (i.e., there "are" XY chromosomes, etc., and all these together are labeled "male sex"), the process is actually the reverse. Concepts of gender lead to the discovery of "differentiating facts." . . . The biologists' activities are grounded in the everyday gender attribution process. (p. 75)

The movement is from cultural presuppositions to scientific discovery, as each criterion unquestioningly accepts contemporary cultural attributions of gender difference, in the effort to structure scientific data.

Kessler and McKenna conclude, therefore, that "gender is a social construction, that a world of two 'sexes' is a result of the socially shared, taken-for-granted methods which members use to construct reality." (p. vii) Incidentally, Laqueur (1990) has shown that a two-sex model to view human anatomy was a relatively new one in the West, introduced only since the seventeenth century.

Finally, Butler (1990) criticizes those feminists who argue for the naturalness and substantiveness of gender. According to her, gender is a complex of regulations, a cultural production. But from within this culturally produced, regulatory universe, gender is then claimed to be based on nature and/or bodily substance. Gender is, thus,

> the repeated stylization of the body, a set of repeated acts within a highly rigid regulatory frame that congeal over time to produce the appearance of substance, of a natural sort of being. A political genealogy of gender ontologies, if it is successful, will deconstruct the substantive appearance of gender into its constitutive acts and locate and account for those acts within the compulsory frames set by the various forces that police the social appearance of gender. (p. 33)

Binarial gender attributes and heterosexuality are closely intertwined to police and regulate our desire. The naturalization of these attributes, i.e., the claim that gender and heterosexuality are "biological," merely reinforces the regulatory regime. It is a discursive regime that hides itself behind the mask of "nature."

Actually, two fundamental transformations in the disciplinary regime of the body occurred in industrial capitalism. First, as we have just seen, gender, with its newly found claim of being based on nature, and with the new biological science claimed as the discourse of nature, became for the first time ever a fundamental category of social organization. This distinction between man and woman to some extent conformed to the new bourgeois experience of a public/private opposition. Secondly, sexuality also became a new discursive regime, with its emphasis on heterosexual norm and homosexual vice. Both codings seemed to have never occurred before, never elsewhere, though later they influenced other social formations that came under the hegemony of the capitalist/imperialist West. Other social formations had other categories of social hierarchy that were not necessarily along the Victorian man/woman, public/private divide. And sexuality was never an autonomous, discursive regime.

As is well known, it was Foucault who traced modern sexuality to the eighteenth century, when sex emerged from gender subsumption to be separately constructed as discourses of sexuality. Foucault's thesis is that "bourgeois, capitalist, or industrial society, call it what you will—did not confront sex with a fundamental refusal of recognition. On the contrary, it put into operation an entire machinery for producing discourses concerning it." (1978b, p. 69) The discursive construction of sexuality multiplied and intensified pleasure.

> At issue is . . . a process that spreads it over the surface of things and bodies, arouses it, draws it out and bids it speak, implants it in reality and enjoins it to tell the truth: an entire glittering sexual array, reflected in a myriad of discourses, the obstination powers, and the interplay of knowledge and pleasure. (p. 72)

The sexual network focused strategically on four privileged objects of knowledge, namely a "hysterization" of women's bodies, a "pedagogization" of children's sex, a "socialization" of procreative behavior, and a "psychiatrization" of perverse pleasure. (pp. 104–5)

This deployment of sexuality, Foucault argued, formed the basis for the prospect of bourgeois identity, albeit a sexualized identity. There was no sexual identity, as such, before. (This has been corroborated by others, e.g., McIntosh 1968; Weeks 1981; D'Emilio 1983) Take the case of homosexuality. Formerly, gender construction, by subsuming sex, did not construct the homosexual as an individual, nor homosexual identity as a personal prospect. Homosexual identity emerged in the late nineteenth century as a counter-discourse of the repressed, incited bodies of an other. Nevertheless, homosexual identity, as a counter identity within the deployment of sexuality, remained problematical. Though accepting the incitement aspect of sexuality, homosexual identity questioned the repressive aspect. Though accepting the bourgeois ideology of individualism, homosexual identity challenged the sexually repressive construction of bourgeois identity. More recently, some like Katz (1990) have pointed out that the discourse of homosexual abnormality was complemented by the discourse of heterosexual norm. In other words, there was no discourse of heterosexuality before the late nineteenth century!

It was the combination of incitement and repression that founded the bourgeois concept of individual identity. The new sexuality, Foucault argued, was first formed and applied with the greatest intensity within the economically privileged and politically ascendant bourgeoisie.

The primary concern was not repression of the sex of the classes to be exploited, but rather the body, vigor, longevity, progeniture, and descent of the classes that "ruled."

Sex is not that part of the body which the bourgeoisie was forced to disqualify or nullify in order to put those whom it dominated to work. It is that aspect of itself which troubled and preoccupied it more than any other, begged and obtained its attention, and which it cultivated with a mixture of fear, curiosity, delight, and excitement. (1978b, pp. 123–24)

Butler, in her critique of heterosexual gender regulation, points to homosexuality as a series of acts which subvert the regulated order. Going beyond Foucault's notion of the body "as a ready surface awaiting signification," she views it "as a set of boundaries, individual and social, politically signified and maintained." From this standpoint, sexuality "will be shown to be a performatively enacted signification, one that . . . can occasion the parodic proliferation and subversive play of gendered meanings." (1990, p. 33)

My argument is that gender and sexuality in contemporary USA are constructed by the structuration and systematization, the discursivity and counter-discursivity, and the semiotics of late-capitalist production/consumption and social reproduction practices. Foucault's thesis focuses on the deployment of bourgeois sexuality in the nineteenth century as a discursive reality distinct from gender. This deployment, according to him, was linked with capitalist economy through numerous relays. I propose that the separation of gender and sexuality for the bourgeoisie was reinforced by that class's strategic location in the structural opposition between production and social reproduction. In industrial capitalism, production was to social reproduction as bourgeois male was to bourgeois female. Correlating to this structural separation of its gender roles, there emerged for the bourgeoisie the new discursive reality of sexuality, separating sex from gender. In other words, the structural opposition between production and social reproduction meant for the bourgeoisie more distinct gender roles, and the emergence of sexuality as a separate category. On the other hand, this structural opposition between production and social reproduction did not apply to working-class gender roles. Nor did sex emerge as a separate discursive category for the working class.

If that is the case, what then happened to gender and sexuality in late capitalism, given the valorization and commodification of social reproduction, in other words, once the structural opposition between production and social reproduction has collapsed under the hegemony of exchangist practices? I suggest that the development of both consumption and production, in late capitalism, transformed sexuality from a disciplinary to a consumptuary phenomenon. And the valorization of social reproduction is challenging long-held gender roles. Without stable boundaries and identities, gender and sexuality are at once effects and countereffects, or oppositional practices, in that gender and sexuality have become performance acts, precisely because they are effects within the hegemonic terrain of late-capitalist exchangist practices.

b. Sexual Lifestyle and Late-Capitalist Consumption

Bourgeois sexuality presupposed the public/private, outer/inner oppositions. It rested on the structural separation between production and the relatively as-yet-uncommodified social reproduction in industrial capitalism. With the acceleration and expansion of production/consumption and the commodification of social reproduction in late-capitalism, we now have a very different sexuality. It cannot be too much emphasized that, with technological advances, sexual pleasure for the first time ever is wholly disconnected from natal reproduction for the population as a whole. This is the obverse side of natal reproduction without sex. (Blank 1990, pp. 6–8) Separated from social reproduction, sexuality thus becomes a sign to energize, in effect to sexualize, late-capitalist consumption. The result is a sexual lifestyle, as distinct from the bourgeois assumption of an interiorized sexual identity. No longer respecting the outer/inner, the public/private oppositions, the new sexual lifestyle is subverting the opposition between heterosexual norm and its other, i.e., the so-called homosexual vice. We are verging toward polysexuality, i.e., sexual *differences without* stable sexual *identities.*

Immediately after World War II, politicians appealed to sexual discipline and repression, to restore prewar social mores. Public outcry resumed against the menace of the "sex offender," a broad catch-all term which included everything other than the heterosexual norm, from rapists to consenting homosexuals. Then in the 1950s, with public anxiety focused on the "homosexual menace" as well as the "sex offender," many state legislatures passed "sexual psychopath" laws which increased the policing power of mental health professionals over the sexually a-normal. (Rubin 1984, p. 269)

Nevertheless, a new scientific discourse of sexuality emerged within the conservative culture of the postwar era. The new discourse speedily developed a dynamic of its own, at variance from the established discourses of sexual repression. The original impetus for the new discourse can be traced to the publication of Alfred Kinsey's *Sexual Behavior in the Human Male* in 1948. The book came out under the imprint of an obscure academic press in Philadelphia specializing in medical texts. Yet it immediately provoked widespread discussion and made Kinsey a media celebrity, testifying to public interest and receptivity. In 1953, Kinsey's *Sexual Behavior in the Human Female* followed.

The two Kinsey reports provided a quantitative tabulation of sexual behavior among a sample group of human males and females. Some have criticized his sampling as being exclusively white, and containing too many midwesterners, prison inmates, homosexuals and those too willing to volunteer information about their private sexual behavior. But throughout, Kinsey, a trained taxonomist whose previous research topic was the gall wasp, assiduously insisted on the empiricism and objectivity of his reports. For him, sex is "a normal biologic function, acceptable in whatever form it is manifested." (quoted in Robinson 1976, pp. 48ff)

Kinsey's work was a scientific discourse, in contrast to the social, moral, religious discourses of repressive sexual regulation. He eschewed all considerations of the social or ethical implications of human sexual behavior. The sexual behavior he surveyed included masturbation, nocturnal emission, heterosexual petting, homosexual relations, bestial intercourse, as well as heterosexual intercourse. Kinsey was not concerned with love or romance, but concentrated instead on orgasm as the culmination of sexual activity. One type of sexual activity was, from his point of view, as good as any other, as long as it enabled a person to reach orgasm, an outlet, a discharge. Furthermore, he insisted that orgasm as a physiological response was common to both male and female. Among the revealing figures that his study provided, the ones which attracted the widest attention concerned the high incidence of extramarital and homosexual acts among males, and the lower count of orgasm for females.

Instead of the regulation of sexuality on behalf of family, church, law, and mental health, the Kinsey reports approached human sexual behavior on its own terms as a subject of scientific study. Simply reporting the various forms of sexual behavior, they implied that masturbation and homosexuality were as "natural" as orthodox heterosexuality. Reporting that 37 percent of males had at least one homosexual orgasm lowered the taboo barrier against homosexuals. And by counting the incidence of orgasm for females as a well as males, researchers implied the equal importance of orgasm for both genders. The reports were a turning point in opening up the public discussion of sexuality. (Ehrenreich, Hess, and Jacobs 1986, pp. 44–45) Additional studies followed, including William Masters and Virginia Johnson's *Human Sexual Response* (1966) and *Human Sexual Inadequacy* (1970), as well as popular bestsellers, e.g., Helen Gurley Brown's *Sex and the Single Girl* (1962), *The Sensuous Woman* (1969) by "J," Morton Hunt's *Sexual Behavior in the 1970s* (1974), and *The Hite Report* (1976).

Masters and Johnson went beyond the interviewing and reporting techniques of Kinsey through the control and modification of human coitus and masturbation in laboratory conditions. Up until then, most psychiatrists and psychoanalysts followed Freud's hypothesis that female sexuality progressed from "immature" clitoral orgasm to "mature" vaginal orgasm. Masters and Johnson's report on the observed intensity of clitoral sexuality and its central role in female orgasm finally destroyed the exclusive emphasis on vaginal orgasm. Their report asserted "the female capacity for orgasm and the centrality of the clitoris to female sexuality, whether in partnership with another or auto-erotically." (Ehrenreich, Hess, and Jacobs 1986, p. 63) Masters and Johnson could afford to be more daring than Kinsey, since the late 1960s saw a very different discursive contest concerning sexuality than what Kinsey had to face two decades earlier. In the late 1940s, Kinsey's first report had to deflect the brunt of the repressive discourse of sexual regulation. Twenty years later, Masters and Johnson's report came at a conjuncture of a series of semiotic practices regarding sexuality.

In fact, shortly after Kinsey's pioneering work, a new publicity emerged to promote sexuality as a pleasure in itself, wholly unconnected to social reproduction or familistic ideology. This sexual pleasure differed considerably from the use of sexual innuendos and images which aimed at other, non-sexual purposes. In 1953, the year of the publication of Kinsey's second report, Hugh Hefner started his *Playboy* magazine, dedicated to the sexual fantasies of heterosexual men. The magazine consisted of three components: the centerfold and other titillating photos and cartoons of women's bodies; articles dedicated to the appetite and leisure of the male reader; and ads selling various consumer goods to the male reader. Together, the package presented an alternative, sexually oriented way of life for the "liberated" single male. The popularity of the magazine soon attracted advertising revenue from established corporations. The success of *Playboy* led to the publication of many other similar, even more sexually explicit, magazines.

Then in 1962, Helen Gurley Brown came out with her best-selling *Sex and the Single Girl*, which publicized the sexuality of a new group—single, working women. Her book's success testified to the marketability of the single, working woman as a sexualized image, the office worker as a pleasure, not a drudge. Two years later, Brown was hired as the chief editor of *Cosmopolitan* to revamp the then-sedate woman's magazine into one dedicated to the packaging of a sexually oriented, single female.

Rosalind Coward, in an analysis of *Cosmopolitan*, found its articles mostly concerned with career improvement, successful glamorous women, the improvement of sexual and emotional relationships with particular emphasis on the possibilities of female pleasure, and the need for women to have sexual and economic self-independence. The magazine, she points out, is a marketplace of multiple discourses on sexuality—including fashion, medicine, health/fashion, social trends, psychology, and a popular form of sexology. The female heterosexuality presented in the magazine is "liberated" in the sense that it does not refer to family role or childcare problems. The magazine, Coward concluded,

> does not posit a norm of sexual behavior. Instead it places itself precisely in the area of competing definitions, that is the area of the definition of sexuality itself. Its common project is the female body and this appears not as an already defined object but as something subject to competing definitions, often the cornerstone for conflicting ideologies. (1978, p. 16)

The discourse and semiotics of sexual pleasure overstepped the former boundaries set by the discourses of sexual repression. In the 1950s, medical discourse controlled sex manuals, and doctors prescribed sexual norm, for "the married couple." Their advice emphasized heterosexual, marital intercourse as the proper approach. It assumed an active male and a passive female, though the best of the manuals also recommended orgasm for the woman. (Ehrenreich, Hess, and Jacobs, 1986, pp. 47–52) However, by the late 1960s and early 1970s, sexual pleasure as an end in itself has led to a plethora of sex literature in the marketplace. In an analysis of some of this literature, Meryl Altman concludes that, though breaking no new grounds in ideas or morality, it did popularize the findings of Kinsey, and Masters and Johnson. "It is a medium through which the dominant culture, under the guise of breaking taboos, reinforces those taboos, unceasingly telling itself and its initiates what it, and they, already knew." (1984, p. 128)

Kinsey's implied thesis that orgasm was important for both genders, and Masters and Johnson's emphasis on the importance of clitoral stimulation for the woman preceded and might have influenced the radical feminist discourse of sexuality in the late 1960s. Anne Koedt, in "The Myth of the Vaginal Orgasm" (1970), argued that the importance of the clitoris in woman's sexuality meant she did not have to depend upon heterosexual intercourse, since sex with other women would do just as well. Alix Shulman, in "Organs and Orgasms" (1971), supported a female sexuality centered on the clitoris, which "may be stimulated to climax by a hand, by a tongue, or, particularly if the woman is free to move or to control the man's movements, by intercourse." (p. 296) And Barbara Seaman, in *Free and Female* (1972), assured her readers that: "[t]he liberated orgasm is any orgasm *you* like, under any circumstances *you* find comfortable." (p. 73)

The new discourse and semiotics of sexual pleasure took off in late capitalism because, with such commodities as the oral contraceptive pill (introduced in 1960), and then the IUD, we can, for the first time ever, have sex without worrying about natal reproduction. The obverse side of this is natal reproduction without sex, i.e., *in vitro* fertilization, artificial insemination, and ovum transfers. Freed from social reproduction, the new sexuality came to be exploited for the sake of late-capitalist consumption. This is what distinguishes the new sexuality of late capitalism from the bourgeois sexual regulations of industrial capitalism studied by Foucault. It publicizes the promise of sexual pleasure, contradicting the repressive, disciplinary sexuality. The new sexuality is not only discursive and semiotic, but also consumptuary. Quite aptly, the successful sex manual, Alex Comfort's *The Joy of Sex* (1972), was subtitled "A Cordon Bleu Guide to Love-making," and its contents were organized into "Starters," "Main Courses," and "Sauces & Pickles."

New commodities are packaged and produced specifically for the new sexuality. Pat Califia has said, "S/M is not about pain, but about power." (quoted in Ehrenreich, Hess, and Jacobs 1986, p. 130) But sadomasochism as a ritual of dominance and submission, a theater of fantasy, requires such paraphernalia as handcuffs, straps, whips, leathers, etc. Thus, Ehrenreich, Hess, and Jacobs report that S/M theater, previously the practice of a few, is now available to even the midwestern housewife through mail-order catalogues.

From a strictly capitalist viewpoint, it is the ideal sexual practice. . . . S/M owes its entrance into the sexual mainstream to its
paraphernalia: The symbols and gear precede the actual practice
into the homes and imaginations of millions. (p. 124)

Besides the direct consumption of sexual implements, late-capitalist
production/consumption is able to tap the reservoir of sexual fantasy
which the new semiotics of sexuality stimulate. A Lou Harris study reports that sixty-five thousand sexual references a year are broadcast
during the prime afternoon and evening hours on television alone.
"That's an average of 27 an hour . . . including 9 kisses, 5 hugs, 10 sexual
innuendos and between 1 and 2 references each to sexual intercourse and
to 'deviant or discouraged sexual practices.' " Thus a typical American
viewer sees nearly fourteen thousand instances of sexual material during
the popular time slots each year. (*New York Times,* January 27, 1988)

I propose that *the technologies of the look* and *the relay of juxtaposed
images and signs* (cf., *supra,* chapter 2, sec. *b*) are at the center of this
semiotics of sexuality. The two techniques, together with the design and
production of commodities as packages of changing product characteristics, contribute to the construction of sexual lifestyle as a signifier for late-
capitalist production and accumulation of exchange value.

The look in the modern West is sexual. It is an aspect of the primacy of
sight in the modern Western hierarchy of sensing. (Lowe 1982) This
primacy of sight is culturally and historically specific, not universal. Nor
does sex have to be visual in orientation, since seeing is the most distanc-
ing of the five human senses. Specific to the modern West is the look
constituted as the male gaze—visually subjugating and territorializing the
female body. Underneath this look are all the binary oppositions in
bourgeois culture which construct the power of male over female.

Twentieth-century visuality is very much a masculinist one. Photography, cinematography, and television are the technologies of the look,
working to enhance the visualization of sexuality. But technologies are
not neutral. Their applications depend on the assumptions and purposes
of the addressers. Photography, cinematography, and television do not
simply extend the male gaze. With their different techniques of shots,
montage, and narrativity, they repackage and transform the hegemony of
the male gaze in late capitalism.

The article by Coward that I mentioned earlier, which analyzed *Cosmopolitan* magazine, also points to the power of the photo image in
fragmenting, sexualizing, and remaking the female body.

What can be detected in the excess of such advertisements as in many contemporary women's magazines is the multiplication of areas of the body accessible to marketability. This is not a simple process; the imagery of the advertisements makes it clear it is not just marketability that is at stake, it is also the consistent "sexualization" of areas previously not defined as sexual. It is the sexualization of eyes, lips, ears, wrists, legs, feet, hair, mouths, teeth, smells, skin, etc. It is not a matter of exploiting a pre-existent, naturally sensitive body, but the actual construction of parts of the body as sensitive and sexual, as capable of stimulation and excitation, and therefore demanding care and attention if women are to be sexual and sexually desirable to men. The images also reveal the sexualization of situations previously tabooed; work and the street. (1978, p. 16)

This possibility was created by the decontextualizing surrealism of the photo image (Sontag 1978), the dynamic system of looks in cinematography (de Lauretis 1984), and the invasion of images into the home by television. Sex has become a disembodied visual signifier, ever ready for resignification.

Postwar advertising utilizes the technologies of the look in relaying juxtaposed images and signs. Advertising, using images of the new sexuality, captures, mobilizes, and directs the fantasy of the addressee. Sexual image in advertising is the vehicle for a sign content, i.e., the advertising message. The message relays the sexual fantasy onto the promises of the product characteristics. Thus, sexual image in advertising has gone far beyond representation of sexualized bodies, of women's bodies, to the representation of disintegrated body parts, in which each discrete part possesses heightened sexual energy.

Sexual energy is power. The images of disembodied, sexualized body parts, activities and territories have themselves become sign vehicles (signifiers) for other sign contents (signifieds). Take, for example, the ad where Brooke Shields's buttock, sheathed in a pair of tight-fitting jeans, partakes of the promise of penetration by the "male" gaze from behind. A transfer of sexual fantasy, and therefore of energy, occurs in the ad, from Brooke Shields's body part to the tight-fitting jeans. The image of the body part, Shields's buttock, becomes a sign vehicle for the promises invested in the jeans, a package of product characteristics. We not only carry out that fantasy when we purchase a pair of tight-fitting jeans; by wearing and displaying ourselves in jeans, we become conductors in this juxtaposed relay. As consumers we ourselves extend and sustain the relay of juxtaposed images and signs into everyday life.

The characteristics designed into the commodity as a package destabilize and reconstitute the use value of commodity in late capitalism. In this case, the "use value" of a pair of jeans depends on advertising's transfer of the sexual image of Brooke Shields's body part onto the promises of a pair of tight-fitting jeans. The "use value" here is the promise advertising makes to the buyer's sexual fantasy. Sexual image communicates a promise, which is then connected to the characteristics designed into the commodity. It has acquired a value for the buyer, the manufacturer, and the advertiser.

Sexual image is a currency, a powerful sign vehicle or signifier to energize the characteristics of any commodity. Conversely, characteristics are designed and packaged into commodities, with the advertising of sexual image in mind. By now, sexual image—extended and enhanced through the technologies of the look and the relay of juxtaposed images and signs—is ubiquitous in the late-capitalist world. Individual commodities as packaged characteristics partake of, are packaged and marketed as, sexual images. This new simulatory reality accompanies the production and circulation of sexualized commodities as a whole. Instead of a discursive sexuality focused on the promise of bodily pleasure, the new sexuality is now invested semiotically with a constellation of glossy commodities.

The promises of the sexual image can never be fulfilled in themselves; however, a cursory form of fulfillment may be achieved through the consumption of the advertised characteristics of commodities. By wearing a pair of tight-fitting jeans, the consumer participates in a voyeuristic self-enactment of the intended penetration by the "male" gaze in the sexual image. This reveals how powerful that sexual image is as a sign vehicle. The promise always precedes the act. Fulfillment comes not in the promised pleasure of orgasm, but rather through the relay of continuous consumption and display of the sexualized characteristics of commodities—a flaccid dispersion, already an unfulfilled expectation, resulting in frustration and the eternal need for more. The relay is sustained, by ourselves as well as others, through the consumption and display of sexualized commodities.

In Chapter 2, I proposed that lifestyle is the new social relations of consumption—a prospect made possible by the design and production of commodities as packaged product characteristics, advertising's use of the relay of juxtaposed images and signs, and the transformation of the late-capitalist commodity into a semiotic hybrid of social, cultural values, product characteristics, and exchange value. I now suggest that, with the technologies of the look and the relay of juxtaposed images and signs to extend and intensify the gaze, the late-capitalist lifestyle is very much a sexual lifestyle. Lifestyle as a way of life is a visual display, which the consumption of certain types of commodities promotes. Sexual lifestyle is a way of life based upon the consumption of sexualized commodities. We currently present ourselves, and see ourselves and others, as sexual persons who exude the allure and power of the sexualized commodities we consume.

Gay lifestyle is an example of sexual lifestyle—not the only one, but one among many. In the 1960s, with the civil rights movement and the discourses and publicity of the new sexuality, a younger generation of homosexuals and lesbians came out of the closet to claim for themselves a distinct, homoerotic sexual identity. By the 1970s, gay culture had emerged as an alternative lifestyle. On the basis of lifestyle consumption, an urban male homosexual minority with sufficient income transforms itself into the gay lifestyle (although this was less true for lesbians). Gays display themselves as consumers of clothing, holidays, theater and cinema, restaurant meals, cosmetics, and household goods. The gay press became increasingly concerned with the issue of lifestyle by the late 1970s. As Dennis Altman has suggested, the interesting point is that, increasingly, gay lifestyle has become avant-garde fashion in popular culture, as "the adoption of styles and fashions associated with an increasingly visible and assertive gay minority" has become an obvious trend. (1982, p. xii)

Altman sees gay lifestyle as a "product of modern urban liberal capitalism." (p. 51) Rather, I suggest that the change from homosexual identity to gay lifestyle involves a change in personality orientation which late-capitalist production and the consumption of lifestyle has made possible. An oppressed heterodox group, which the discourse of repressive sexuality marginalized as its other, now redefines itself within the context of late-capitalist production/consumption as an alternative lifestyle. Homosexual identity in the 1960s was a counter-discursive ideological practice opposing the heterosexual norm. But the complex of structural, discursive, and semiotic practices soon transformed the social construction of the heterodox self from homosexual *identity* to gay *lifestyle*.

Homosexuality was formerly the other to heterosexuality, in the disciplinary discourses of sexuality. Birken (1988, pp. 92–93) and Katz (1990) both argued that, historically, heterosexuality is, in fact, a discursive construction, concurrent with the construction of homosexuality in the late nineteenth century. The opposition of heterosexuality and homosexuality did not challenge, but rather supported the gender construction of masculinity/femininity in the relatively autonomous terrain of social reproduction in industrial capitalism. However, I propose that the production and consumption of sexual lifestyle in the hegemonic terrain of exchangist practices in late capitalism have destabilized the sexual other.

No longer limited to heterosexuality and its other, the production and consumption of sexual lifestyle in late-capitalist USA has led to the differentiation of the sexual others into increasingly specialized categories—gays and lesbians, "butches" and "fems," sadomasochists, transvestites, fetishists, bisexuals, and those who engage in casual sex, cross-generational sex, and bestiality. As Rubin notes,

> the "modernization of sex" has generated a system of continual sexual ethnogenesis. Other populations of erotic dissidents—commonly known as the "perversions" or the "paraphilias"—also began to coalesce. . . . The perversions are not proliferating as much as they are attempting to acquire social space, small businesses, political resources, and a measure of relief from the penalties for sexual heresy. (1984, p. 287)

In fact, more recently, Isadora Alman, the advice columnist in the *San Francisco Bay Guardian,* made the following reply to a 23-year-old woman who felt confused about her sexuality:

> Leading a gay "lifestyle" (friends, clubs, politics) is not necessarily adjunct to being gay, or vice versa. . . . A person customarily identifies as homo-, hetero- or bi-*sexual* by virtue of the sex of the people with whom they have or want to have sex. A man-crazy woman is certainly not homosexual. If you also want to have sex with a woman or women, you might still define as heterosexual (with side forays) or as bisexual, or as politically gay but basically behaviorally straight. What you want to call yourself is really entirely up to you. What others call you will, of course, be influenced by what is seen of your behavior. (October 27, 1993)

Instead of relying on repressive sexuality to *discipline* the body, we now consume sexual lifestyles as an avenue to *differentiate* the body. Lifestyle consumption has in effect led to polysexuality, challenging and subverting the heterosexuality at the heart of the repressive regulation of sexuality. In other words, we are witnessing the destabilization of the opposition between heterosexual norm and its other, "the homosexual vice."

It is in the context of the production and consumption of sexual lifestyles that I locate the sexual critiques of Judith Butler and Teresa de Lauretis. Butler (1990) states that the notion of natural, stable gender identity is an effect, rather than a cause, of masculine hegemony and heterosexist power. She accordingly argues for performative acts that place in question, and subvert, any and all categories which sustain the heterosexual norm. De Lauretis's conference on "queer theory" in 1990 argues that lesbian and gay sexualities can no longer

> be seen simply as marginal with regard to a dominant, stable form of sexuality (heterosexuality) against which [they] would be defined either by opposition or by homology. . . . Instead, male and female homosexualities . . . may be conceptualized as social and cultural forms in their own right, albeit emergent ones. . . . Thus, rather than marking the limits of the social space by designating a place at the edge of culture, gay sexuality in its specific female and male cultural forms acts as an agency of social process whose mode of functioning is both interactive and yet resistant. . . . (1991, p. iii)

The point we need to remember is that all of us, not just gays, lesbians, bisexuals and the sexual others, participate in sexual lifestyles. To this extent, we are all determined by the production and consumption of sexual lifestyles. The critique of heterosexism is a politics emergent from this context. Nevertheless, we need to ask: will capital subordinate its need for heterosexism, in order to profit from polysexuality?

Jean Baudrillard raised such a prospect:

> [W]hat if Foucault spoke to us so well of sexuality . . . only because its form, this great "production" of our culture, was . . . in the process of disappearing? . . . when sex itself becomes involuted and disappears as a strong referent in the hyperreality of "liberated" sexuality. . . . // Because he remains within the classic formula of sex, Foucault cannot trace this new spiral of sexual simulation in which sex finds a second existence and takes on the fascination of a lost frame of reference. (1987, pp. 13–16)

Commodified sex, overcommunicated, oversignified, and oversold, may not be as gripping as it used to be.

c. Gender Construction in Late Capitalism

Gender is socially constructed, rather than biologically destined. But the term "social construction" is a catch-all tag for all sorts of methodological approaches. It opens up a whole new terrain of untested, related issues. We need to admit the different approaches and debate the issues involved. To say that gender is socially constructed is to admit that it is historical and changing, and therefore open to contestation.

I propose that the social construction of gender in late-capitalist USA should be analyzed as a set of related, sedimented, though often conflicting practices—practices of production, consumption, and social reproduction which consist of structural, discursive, counter-discursive and semiotic components. Thus, there is a complex of discourses, rather than a single discourse, of gender. However, before I go further, I need to make clear the implications of my approach to gender construction.

To begin with, I reject any biological determinism or fundamentalism. I do not even accept the assumption of some social constructivists that gender begins with anatomical sex differences as a bipolarity, and that its social construction is scripted on an already bi-polar biological substratum. Rather, I suggest we need to turn our perspectival priority the other way around. In no social formation, at any place, in any time, except in the bourgeois capitalist order, is gender considered to be biologically determined. Other social formations did not even know biology as a scientific discourse of nature; they had other, totally different, all-encompassing, holistic concepts of nature. And if we insist that gender constructions are scripted on biological differences, that is our interpretation of their social formation, not their lived social reality. I further suggest that, in the bourgeois capitalist formation, gender is not actually biologically determined. Foucault (1970) had pointed out that biology is a nineteenth-century discourse of nature. And Kessler and McKenna (1985) have shown how science is culturally founded, before it provides us with the so-called data from which to generalize. The new discourse of biology "naturalized," i.e., disguised and obfuscated, the capitalist construction of gender, providing it with a scientific gloss. And it still remains a part of the dominant ideology at present.

Furthermore, gender is not a universally fundamental category of social hierarchy or stratification. It is true that, in capitalist social formation, gender is a fundamental category of social order, and its male/female polarity parallels and reinforces such other bourgeois polarities as public/private, reason/emotion, outside/inside, active/passive, etc. Thus, we are supposedly either men or women, partaking of either of these bipolar characteristics, although there are the "abnormal" and "deviant" who do not fit the polarities. But no other social formation orders its population in terms of the category of gender, nor along such starkly bipolar cultural dichotomies. At least among those social formations that I know something about, gender is not even a fundamental category of social order. For example, Barlow (1991) argues that, in late imperial China, women were discursively constructed as virtuous mothers and good wives, but never as "women"; men, too, were constructed not as "men," but as fathers, sons, husbands, rulers, and subordinates. Woman and man were never constructed in terms of a universal gender category, outside of social hierarchy.

Finally, it is only within a social formation ordered by bipolar gender category, i.e., only within a bourgeois capitalist order, that sexuality emerged as a separate, though related, discursive reality—the grounds on which our beliefs in individual identities are justified. Other social formations (again, as far as I know) do not discursively order sex in terms of a heterosexual/homosexual polarity. Therefore, what we often assume to be the norms in regard to gender and sexuality are really quite exceptional—specific and peculiar to only the capitalist social formations. And they are now undergoing changes. Instead of universalizing our own norms and projecting them onto others, we should accept the peculiarities of the bourgeois capitalist order of things.

In the previous section, I presented the argument that bipolar sexuality is under assault by the commodification of sexuality and the sexualization of consumption in late capitalism. In this section, I argue that gender construction has recently become much more conflictual. I shall analyze gender construction in late-capitalist USA in terms of changing structural, semiotic, and discursive components.

In industrial capitalism, social reproduction remained outside of the terrain of production. Bourgeois gender construction was gridded by the demarcation between production and social reproduction, work and home. That structural demarcation supported the dichotomous gender construction of male and female in terms of the various binarial oppositions. The everyday language and practices of the urban middle classes presupposed and reinforced these oppositions. This newly reinforced binarial gender was further supported by the new discourses of heterosexuality and its homosexual other. In other words, bourgeois gender construction and sexuality were gridded by the industrial-capitalist structuration of production and social reproduction, as well as by the rationalization, i.e., the binarization, of middle-class culture.

This naturalization persisted into the post-World War II era. David Schneider, in his 1960s ethnography of "the American family," discovered that what made a person male or female in American culture then was "the kind of sexual organs he has." Beyond the minimal required body parts, certain other characteristics were believed to indicate gender identity.

> Men have facial hair and are said to have hair on their chest, but women do not. Temperamental differences are held to correlate with the differences in sexual organs. Men have an active, women a passive quality, it is said. Men have greater physical strength and stamina than women. Men are said to have mechanical aptitudes that women lack. Women have nurturant qualities which men lack. Men tend toward an aggressive disposition said to be absent in women. (1980, p. 41)

Because of these different qualities, Schneider reported, it was the prevailing belief that men and women were fit

> for different kinds of activities and occupations. Men's active, aggressive qualities, their strength and stamina, are said to make them particularly good hunters and soldiers and to fit them for positions of authority, especially where women and children are concerned. Women are presumed to be nurturant and passive in ways that make them particularly good at teaching school, nursing, food preparation, and homemaking. Men's mechanical aptitudes are said to make them good at working with machines—at designing, building, and repairing them—in ways which women cannot match. (*Ibid.*)

(By 1980, in the second edition to his work, Schneider admitted that things have changed.)

From this standpoint, the most interesting structural changes in late-capitalist USA are the entry of women into the labor force for production, the commodification of social reproduction, the disjunction between sexual intercourse and natal reproduction, and the sexualization of consumption. These new developments are subverting the structural foundation upon which bipolar bourgeois gender construction rested.

After the end of World War II, there were concerted efforts to get working wives and mothers back into the home. Lower-income women always had to work, assuming they could find work. Nevertheless, for a variety of reasons—rising expectations in living standards, personal self-esteem, and feminist ideology—women of all income levels entered the labor force in ever larger numbers. The turning point came in the 1970s, with rising consumer expectations, and declining wages, when the number of working women over the age of sixteen increased from 29.7 million to 42.1 million in the decade. In 1970, 40.8 percent of women sixteen years and older were working, comprising 37.7 percent of the civilian labor force. By the end of the decade, in 1980, 47.7 percent of women were working, increasing their share of the labor force to 42.4 percent. In 1990, 53.5 million women, or 54.3 percent of all women, were working, comprising 45.4 percent of the civilian labor force. (*SAUS, 1992*, p. 383)

Women are more likely to obtain employment in those occupations providing for supportive services, e.g., nursing rather than doctoring, secretarial work rather than executive management, public school teaching rather than college teaching. These are jobs which take advantage of women's culturally constructed "nurturing" traits, leading men to expect these traits of women and women expecting themselves to provide them. Pringle (1989) confirms our everyday experience by showing how dichotomous gender and sexuality roles reinforce the "femininity" of the secretary at the bottom of the bureaucratic workplace. There is power at play here. Besides, these are also jobs which pay poorly. On the one hand, women's gender construction is utilized in these jobs. On the other, the lower wages in these jobs reflect and reinforce the cultural subordination of women. In 1980, almost half of all employed women worked in occupations that were at least 80 percent female, and more than two-thirds of all men were employed in occupations that were at least 80 percent male. (Reskin and Hartmann 1986, p. 7, cited by Williams 1989, p. 2)

Nevertheless, efforts in enforcing equal employment policies have gradually enabled some women to obtain jobs customarily considered the preserve of men, i.e., jobs that require traits which are culturally considered to be "masculine"—doctors, executive managers, unionized craft workers. Also, these jobs always pay better. The better pay is often justified as requiring more training and better skills, though sometimes it is justified the other way around, i.e., the men who work at these jobs need higher pay to support family households. Nevertheless, the women who take these jobs soon acquire the traits required of them. Freeman (1990) shows how successful middle-level female managers often take on traits formerly considered to be "masculine," e.g., becoming more ambitious, more task-oriented. However, even when women become college and university professors, both their male colleagues and their male and female students often still expect them to provide more nurturing support than male professors.

On the one hand, the structure of production utilizes and reinforces existing dichotomous gender construction. On the other, the large-scale entry of women into the labor force is putting some pressure on gender construction. In other words, the structure of production no longer simply confirms gender construction, as before.

A different though related set of statistical changes reveals the impact of working women on the home. In 1960, 18.8 percent of married women with children under the age of six worked; in 1970, 30.3 percent of them were working; that increased to 45.1 percent in 1980, and to 59.9 percent by 1991. (*SAUS 1992*, p. 377) In effect, most married women with children under the age of six now work. With women in production, the home has become a center of consumption. And much of the formerly unpaid social-reproduction work is now valorized and commodified. In effect, late capitalism has absorbed social reproduction into an enlarged circuit of production/consumption. At the production end, women provide cheaper wage labor, putting pressure on higher male wages. At the consumption end, the commodification of social reproduction increases the variety of goods and services that were formerly considered peripheral, and are now perceived as necessities. The privacy of the home is invaded by production and consumption practices. From the standpoint of gender construction, this structural transformation means the end of the bourgeois family ideal of a working father and a domestic mother. Mothers now often shoulder both tasks, i.e., wage-earning and homemaking. Admittedly, some fathers take on some customarily "domestic," i.e., "female" gender tasks.

All of the structural changes affecting gender construction are also concurrently semiotic changes—semiotic in the sense of the communication and also signification of gender traits. Socially constructed gender traits, formerly accepted as being simply a man or being a womanly woman, are now leading to clashes and dissonances both at home and in the workplace. What was formerly accepted as "natural," is now being questioned, defended, and modified, both in the workplace and at home.

In addition, the widespread use of the Pill to prevent contraception since the 1960s has brought a disjunction between heterosexuality and natal reproduction. This unprecedented disjunction has affected both social reproduction and consumption. It means that social reproduction can no longer claim sole jurisdiction over sexuality, and that sex can be consumed for its own enjoyment without natality. (Blank, 1990, 6–9) But the disjunction has also made sexuality a floating signifier, pervading the entire social terrain. In effect, it has made possible late-capitalist sexual lifestyles.

We therefore need to be cognizant of the impact of this disjunction on gender construction. Formerly, dichotomous gender construction, with the support of production and social reproduction, was able to command and normalize sexuality. In other words, heterosexual normalization supported dichotomous gender construction. But, now, with free-floating sexuality pervading the social terrain, bipolar, dichotomous gender construction is being challenged by gay, lesbian, bisexual, and polysexual lifestyles, and unisexual fashions. Sexuality has turned the table on gender construction, by exceeding the normalization and control of the latter.

Gender and sexuality are more demanding and more confusing for most of us than ever before. Conflicting demands tear us between disciplinary and consumptuary sexualities, between old and new gender roles, between the diverse demands of sexuality and gender. Ruth Moulton reports massive anxiety among men and women in regard to gender and sexual roles in recent years. The anxiety manifests itself in sexual attitudes and behavior, in marriages and divorces, in dual-career marriages, in the issue of careers versus children confronting women, as well as between women and men at work. (1980, pp. 272–81)

Pressures on dichotomous gender norms have led to increasing ideological conflicts among feminists, neoconservatives, religious leaders, and sociobiologists. Each proposes a different discourse of gender based on a different set of assumptions.

The 1950s reinforced traditional gender attribution. But in the 1960s, middle-class women, trained to fill dichotomous gender roles, found themselves in new positions of production and social reproduction, and yet they were still expected to maintain their internalized gender attributes. The second feminist movement responded to the resulting contradiction between traditional gender construction *and* the changing position of women in production/consumption and social reproduction. Equal-rights feminism and radical feminism were two such responses.

Equal-rights feminism derives from a liberal tradition stretching all the way back to Mary Wollstonecraft, and is concerned with the problem of gender discrimination in the public sphere. It promotes such reforms as affirmative action, special protection for women in the workplace, reproduction rights, and welfare. More recently, equal-rights feminists are arguing for equal pay for comparable work. However, the discourse of equal rights does not directly confront the problems between traditional gender roles *and* new positions in production and social reproduction, which many women face. Equal-rights feminism, in upholding the ideal of equality, does not challenge gender construction outside the public sphere. In that sense, it is a customary liberal response to a new problem.

Radical feminists, on the other hand, have undertaken a direct critique of the contradiction between existing gender attribution and new positions in production and social reproduction, primarily in terms of women's bodily needs. Unlike the liberal problematic of gender equality, the problematic of women's bodily needs cuts the ground from under existing gender attribution. Radical feminism directly confronts the issue of male power over women, which stems from existing gender attribution.

As an example of radical-feminist critique, *Our Bodies, Ourselves,* (1973) a best-selling manual originating from a Boston radical feminist health collective, justified the discourse of women's bodily needs on the ground that it wrests control over women's bodies from the control of male medical discourse. As was explained in the preface:

> For us, body education is core education. Our bodies are the physical bases from which we move into the world. . . . Learning to understand, accept, and be responsible for our physical selves, we are freed of some of these preoccupations and can start to use our untapped energies. Our image of ourselves is on a firmer base, we can be better friends and better lovers, better *people,* more self-confident, more autonomous, stronger, and more whole. (p. 3)

Epistemically speaking, radical feminists based their answers to women's bodily needs, not on equal, universal rights, but on difference, as they came to realize the inadequacy of the equal-rights approach, and as they developed their own arguments in terms of the specific, different bodily needs of women. Thus, Seaman concluded: "However, women *are* different from men. Our sexuality is both less and more: less in that it is easily suppressed and more in that the limits of our potential almost defy measurement. . . . Also, we are different reproductively." (1972, p. 18)

Churches, neoconservatives, and familistic ideologues are fighting back with traditional arguments to shore up dichotomous gender attribution. Instead of recognizing that changes in gender construction are due to the hegemony of late-capitalist exchangist practices, they prefer to scapegoat "big government," feminists, liberals, and radicals for subverting dichotomous gender attribution. They insist that gender is natural and universal, and therefore ought not to be tampered with. They appeal to the emotional ties people have invested in religious beliefs, and to a nostalgic, idealized past, in order to shore up their argument. Some are even promoting the wild men, or wild women, within ourselves!

Neoconservative and traditionalist efforts receive further support from the new "scientific" discourse of sociobiology. Since the Second World War, biology underwent transformation from a functionalist science of organisms to a systematic science of inter-species behavior and adaptation. Edward O. Wilson, one of sociobiology's leading promoters, claimed that the discipline is "the systematic study of the biological basis of all forms of social behavior, including sexual and parental behavior, in all kinds of organisms, including humans." (1978, p. 2) Actually, in the name of sociobiological evolution, some of the most trite dichotomous gender attributions are resurrected. For example, David Barash wrote in one of the leading college textbooks on sociobiology, *Sociobiology and Behavior* (with a foreword by Edward O. Wilson):

> Women have the primary child-care roles in all human societies. Men are significantly less concerned with infants and children. . . . males of our species, like other mammals, must have less confidence in their paternity than females. . . . It is therefore adaptive for females to invest heavily in the well-being of the children. . . . The woman can be counted on to take care of the kids. . . . By competing with other males, [the male] can retain access to his female and also possibly attract additional mates. . . . Of course . . . modern twentieth-century life would have greatly diffused these more primitive, biologically generated tendencies, but they may well persist nonetheless, taking different forms in different cultures. (1982, pp. 323–24)

The contending discourses of feminists, neo-conservatives, traditionalists, and sociobiologists approach the problem of gender construction at different levels of specificity. Equal-rights feminists approach present-day problems for women from within the liberal tradition. The approach does not question the breakdown of the opposition between public and private, and work and home, in late capitalism. The subject matter of radical feminist discourse is woman and her bodily needs; its argument is based upon the newly perceived differences between man and woman, which the destructuralization of the opposition between production and social reproduction has exposed. Neoconservative, religious, and familistic discourses, on the other hand, claim that gender is natural, rather than cultural and historical, and insist that traditional gender relations are universal and normative. They refuse to accept the new problems women face in late capitalism, skirting contemporary problems by appeals to nature, science, and the Bible.

Lastly, I see transsexualism as symptomatic of the tension of gender construction and sexuality in late capitalism. Transsexuals are persons who have undergone psychological, hormonal, and surgical procedures of gender transformation. Harry Benjamin, a pioneer in gender transformation, distinguishes transsexuals from homosexuals and transvestites, arguing that each category is fundamentally different. Homosexuality involves sexuality with a partner of the same gender. For homosexuals, gender is not a problem. Transvestism, i.e., cross-gender dressing, is an act which requires no partner, with the majority of transvestites being heterosexuals, not homosexuals. But "transsexualism is a sex and gender problem, the transsexual being primarily concerned with his (or her) self only, a sex partner being of secondary although occasionally vital importance." (1966, p. 26) The transsexual is not a transvestite. He or she does not derive sexual pleasure in cross-gender dressing. Rather, the transsexual regards the self as really a person of the opposite gender, wrongly placed in his or her present body. Psychotherapy does not satisfy the transsexual. He or she requires hormonal and surgical transformation of gender. The transsexual regards the issue as a problem of gender identity, not one of sexual object choice.

Kessler and McKenna point out that, unlike homosexuals, transsexuals accept the dichotomous constructions of gender and of sexuality. Their complaint is that their own bodies have the wrong genitals, and therefore they have wrongly gendered bodies. Kessler and McKenna found

that the transsexual, through his/her concerns with "passing," and the medical and legal professions, through their treatment of transsexualism, reveal the production of the natural attitude toward gender. The transsexual produces a sense of the facticity of gender in social interaction in the same way everyone produces it. The natural attitude allows no exception, so the transsexual, an apparent exception, is seen as not an exception after all, but rather an example of the "objective" truth of the facts. (1985, p. 114)

Transsexuals believe they belong to one of the two dichotomous genders, though other people, as well as their own body, might indicate they belong to the opposite gender.

Jan Morris, a writer who had a transsexual gender operation, reflected recently "that one's sense of gender may be partly acquired . . . or at least powerfully influenced by the state of society." Her point is, historically speaking, quite insightful. She wondered:

Would my conflict have been so bitter if I had been born now, when gender line is so much less rigid? If society had allowed me to live in the gender I preferred, would I have bothered to change sex? Is mine only a transient phenomenon, between the dogmatism of the last century, when men were men and women were ladies, and the eclecticism of the next, when citizens will be free to live in the gender role they prefer? (1974, p. 172)

From my standpoint, transsexualism is a late-capitalist solution to a capitalist problem. Earlier epochs and other societies have had different gender attributions. (Epstein and Straub eds. 1991; Garber 1991; Herdt ed. 1994) We have ethnographic information concerning the berdache in some North American societies, the Xanith in Oman, and woman-to-woman marriage in some African societies. (Shapiro 1991, pp. 262–68) But transsexualism is quite different from these.

Only in capitalist society has sexuality been separately constructed, apart from and in addition to gender construction. Nevertheless, in the modern West, both sexuality and gender are constructed on the basis of the same, existing sociocultural dichotomies, to doubly bound gender and sex. This *double-binding* of gender and sexuality is specific to the modern West, since other, earlier sociocultural formations never had discourses of sexuality, nor sexual identities. The regime of capitalist production requires the double disciplining of the body by both gender and sexuality, in order to demarcate social reproduction from the production of exchange value. In turn, bourgeois personal identity became both a sexual and a gender issue. Transsexualism is not primarily a sexual identity problem. It is a gender identity problem, which the pressures of bipolar sexual identity in late capitalism accentuate. The specific situation results from the combined, heightened demands of both dichotomous gender attribution and bipolar sexuality. Nevertheless, late capitalism has come up with technical solutions to the problem, made possible by advances in psychotherapy, endocrinology, and transplant surgery.

Raymond (1979) condemned transsexuals for accepting and confirming the existing dichotomous construction of gender, when they change their gender. But by the 1990s, Kate Bornstein, "a transsexual lesbian whose female lover is becoming a man," considers herself a "gender outlaw," the very title of her recent autobiography. Bornstein sees transsexuals as being on the borders of the male/female bipolarity. And her project is to criticize the rigid polarity of bipolar gender construction.

I found out that gender can have fluidity, which is quite different from ambiguity. If ambiguity is a refusal to fall within a prescribed gender code, then fluidity is the refusal to remain one gender or another. Gender fluidity is the ability to freely and knowingly become one or many of a limitless number of genders, for any length of time, at any rate of change. Gender fluidity recognizes no borders or rules of gender. (1994, pp. 3, 51–52)

6   Redisciplining the Subject

Psychology is a meta-discursive discipline in capitalist social formations, in the sense that it is a crucial, necessary supplement to the capitalist construction of the human person. Its primary function is to supplement other disciplines of enlightenment by individualizing the person and constructing bourgeois subjectivity. However, with the hegemony of exchangist practices in late capitalism, and the collapse of the distinction between public and private, between inside and outside, I argue that the construction of a subjective self, apart from society, becomes even more problematical. Here, the burden is not upon me to justify the concept of individual identity or the integrity of the discipline of psychology. Instead, let me present a puzzle to all those interested in supporting the legitimacy of psychology as an autonomous branch of knowledge—a puzzle which needs to be unpacked before proceeding to any total acceptance of it.

All other human disciplines are reflexive enough to make a distinction between the discipline, and the subject matter it studies. Thus, sociology is the study of "society," in the sense that "society" is the subject matter for the discipline of sociology, although lately Laclau and Mouffe question the viability of the concept of "society," substituting for it the much more open-ended concept of "the Social." Similarly, economics is the study of economy; and so on. Even historians are belatedly distinguishing the "history" constructed by their discipline from the past they seek to represent. But what is psychology? It is at once the discipline and the subject matter.

For example, most histories of psychology are histories of the discipline. Is it possible to have a history of psychology, in the sense of the psychology of other peoples in other spaces and times? In fact, can that category, let alone the discipline, be fruitfully applied to others? But this is not merely a question of the hermeneutics of psychology as a discipline for the social formations of other spaces and other times. The inability or refusal to make a distinction between a discipline and its subject matter is most revealing. In collapsing the two, it becomes well nigh impossible to make a distinction between the second-degree concepts of the discipline and the first-degree concepts in the discursive construction of reality, thus universalizing its claims and enhancing its ability to supplement the capitalist construction of the person.

The argument of this chapter is that, if the person in late capitalism is socially constructed by the changing practices of production, consumption, social-reproduction, gender, and sexuality, then we need to explain that person in these terms, rather than reducing the person with a discrete psychologistic paradigm. Section *a* shows how the discourse of psychiatry, facing different theories, has abandoned any attempt to deal with the person, resorting instead to a multiaxial, systemic, diagnostic classification of symptoms of illness. Section *b* discusses changing mental health practices beyond the discipline of psychiatry, which nevertheless utilize the discourse of psychiatry. And Section *c* concerns the inability of psychopathology to deal with illnesses which go beyond the paradigm. There is not a relatively autonomous realm which can be comprehended by the discipline of psychology. It is a most important disciplinary practice.

a. The Discourse of Psychiatry

Psychiatry is a Foucaultian discourse—a "discipline" in both senses of the word. *The Diagnostic and Statistical Manual of Mental Disorders* (hereafter *DSM*) is the discourse of the American Psychiatric Association (APA). Besides being a manual for the discipline or profession, it has over the decades come to provide a common standard of terminology and classification for hospital administrators, the legal profession, social-welfare agencies and the public at large. Thus, the influence of *DSM* goes considerably beyond the profession of psychiatry. This section analyzes the postwar changes in the discourse of psychiatry.

A reading of the three editions of *DSM* (1952, 1968, 1980) reveals that the discourse has become less coherent, more eclectic and systematic, with the approach shifting from etiology to symptomatology. To a considerable extent, biomedical diagnosis of mental disorders provided the basis for the coherence of *DSM*-I (1952 ed.), an approach which tends to reduce the psycho-social dimensions of mental disorders. By removing the biomedical model from subsequent editions of the *DSM*, the APA ended any possibility of internal coherence of the discipline, making it at once more eclectic and more influential.

Concurrently, the discourse also became more systems oriented. We can trace the importance of systems analysis back to *DSM*-I. A justification for the first edition was the felt need, at that time, for a standardized terminology to bridge differences generated by experiences in diagnosing prewar, wartime and postwar patients. In the foreword of *DSM*-II (1968 ed.), the emphasis was on the usefulness of its standardized nomenclature to mental hospitals, psychiatric clinics, office practice, general hospitals, and community mental health centers, as well as in consultations to courts and industrial health services. (p. viii) However, it was *DSM*-III (1980 ed.) that consolidated the reliance on systems analysis by requiring a multiaxial, systemic, diagnostic approach. (I shall elaborate on this later.) The 1980 edition thus definitively removed the discourse of psychiatry from the biomedical etiological model. In effect, the discourse deals only with the classification and amelioration of symptoms of illness, not the patient himself or herself.

DSM-I, using a biomedical approach to the psychical, divided all mental disorders into two major groups. The first group consisted of "those in which there is a disturbance of mental function resulting from, or precipitated by, a primary impairment of the function of the brain, generally due to diffuse impairment of brain tissue." The second group included all "those which are the result of a more general difficulty in adaptation of the individual, and in which any associated brain function disturbance is secondary to the psychiatric disorder." (p. 9) Psychotic disorders (such as affective disorders, schizophrenic reactions, and paranoid reactions), psychoneurotic disorders, and personality disorders accordingly all belonged to the second group. In between these two major groupings was a minor group of "mental deficiency" attributed to "primarily a defect of intelligence existing since birth, without demonstrated organic brain disease or known prenatal cause. This group will include only those cases formerly known as familial or 'idiopathic' mental deficiencies." (p. 23)

DSM-I's division of mental illnesses into two major groupings was based upon a binary opposition between a positivity and its negative other, not on two distinctly positive sets of criteria. The first group of mental disorders were "caused by or associated with impairment of brain tissue function." (p. 2) Those in the second group were a polyglot of "disorders of psychogenetic origin or without clearly defined physical cause or structural change in the brain." (p. 5) In other words, illnesses in the first group were all reducible to the biomedical model, whereas illnesses of the second group were due to causes *other* than the impairment of brain tissue function. The impairment of brain tissue function remained the sole positivity, the only scientifically measurable and verifiable, criterion. Furthermore, *DSM*-I announced that some disorders in the second group probably would prove later to be caused or associated with impairment of brain tissue, and, if that were to be the case, they would be moved into the first group.

DSM-I's diagnostic approach to mental disease followed that of the medical etiology of somatic illness. But the dominant model of disease, as George Engel pointed out, was

> biomedical, with molecular biology its basic scientific discipline. It assumes disease to be fully accounted for by deviations from the norm of measurable biological (somatic) variables. It leaves no room within its framework for the social, psychological, and behavioral dimensions of illness. The biomedical model not only requires that disease be dealt with as an entity independent of social behavior, it also demands that behavioral aberrations be explained on the basis of disordered somatic (biochemical or neurophysiological) processes. Thus the biomedical model embraces both reductionism, the philosophic view that complex phenomena are ultimately derived from a single primary principle, and mind-body dualism, the doctrine that separates the mental from the somatic. (reprinted in Mezzich and Berganza, eds., 1984, p. 39)

The first group of mental disorders in *DSM*-I were somatic-based, i.e., read from observable symptoms to somatic disorders, with the latter supposedly causing the former. Although mental disorders in the second group were not somatic-based, their symptoms were still etiologically diagnosed on the assumption that observable symptoms could be reduced to a few discrete, measurable causative agents—analogous to the somatic-based mental disorders of the first group. This, I suggest, is a case of reduction, where an etiological model of somatic diagnosis is used to explain symptoms which are acknowledged as not necessarily somatic or solely somatic in origin.

DSM-I considered the human person to be a "psychobiologic unit" (pp. 1, 105). But within that unit the biologic etiologically retained the priority over the psychical. *DSM*-I emphasized that the psychobiologic unit possessed a "personality structure." (p. 34) Though acknowledging that "apparent or obvious external stress precipitat[es] the condition," it insisted that "unconscious internal conflicts are not to be considered as external stress." (p. 47) In other words, a personality structure was a more or less self-contained psychobiologic unit. It then reacted to stresses coming from the outside. Etiologically, the psychobiologic unit was more fundamental than the external, social environment which surrounded it. The psychical was subordinate to the somatic, as well as being discrete from the Social.

Because it had embraced such dualisms as somatic and psychical, personality and society, as well as an implicit somatic bias against the non-somatic, *DSM*-I necessarily had to add a set of "qualifying phrases" to its binary classification—"with psychotic reaction," "with neurotic reaction" and "with behavioral reaction." These qualifying phrases bridged the gap between an often hypothetical somatic etiology and observable clinical symptoms of mental disorders. The qualifying phrase "with psychotic reaction" obviously would be redundant, when used in diagnosing psychotic disorders; "with neurotic reaction," when used diagnosing psychoneurotic disorders; and "with behavioral reaction," when used in diagnosing personality disorders. But qualifying phrases were necessary in other cases, because the existing etiological diagnosis, based upon biomedical models, could not explain for so many symptoms resulting from the reality of embodied-being-in-the-world.

Later, *DSM*-III (1980 ed.) would explain that, in *DSM*-I, "the use of the term 'reaction' throughout the classification reflected the influence of Adolph Meyer's psychobiological view that mental disorders represented reactions of the personality to psychological, social, and biological factors." (p. 1) But I see the problem as far more than simply an issue of "reaction," because that term implies and calls up an entire set of other related concepts. If mental disorders represented the "reactions" of the personality to psychological, social and biological factors, then (1) is "personality" a substratum prior to "mental disorder"? (2) is "personality" apart from, and then a reaction to, "psychological, social, and biological factors"? and (3) what is the relation among "mental disorders" and "representation" and "reaction"—in other words, which does what to whom? It is not Meyer, but the underlying unquestioned dualistic, biomedical, etiological, reductionistic assumptions that provoke such unanswerable questions.

The second edition, *DSM*-II, introduced a new diagnostic nomenclature which, rather than classifying mental disorders into two major groups supplemented by three qualifying phrases, as did *DSM*-I, dispersed the two groups under ten categories: mental retardation; organic brain syndrome psychoses; psychoses not attributed to physical conditions listed previously (including schizophrenia); neuroses; personality disorders and certain nonpsychotic mental disorders; psychophysiologic disorders; special symptoms; transient situational disturbances; behavior disorders of childhood and adolescence; and conditions without manifest psychiatric disorders and nonspecific conditions. The terminology for the categories came from different diagnostic approaches. Thus, mental retardation and organic brain syndrome psychoses were biomedical; neuroses were psychodynamic; and behavior disorders of childhood and adolescence were developmental. In other words, the diagnostic nomenclature of *DSM*-II abandoned the binary oppositional logic of the standard nomenclature of *DSM*-I.

DSM-II replaced *DSM*-I's three qualifying phrases with a five-digit classification system. The first three digits designated major disease categories, the fourth specified additional detail within each category, and the fifth coded "certain qualifying phrases that may be used to specify additional characteristics of mental disorders." (p. 3)

The second edition claimed it "tried to avoid terms which carry with them *implications* regarding either the nature of a disorder or its causes and has been explicit about causal assumptions when they are integral to a diagnostic concept." And "in the case of diagnostic categories about which there is current controversy concerning the disorder's nature or cause," it "has attempted to select terms which it thought would least bind the judgment of the user." (p. viii)

Along with its stated attempt to abandon a causal, etiological approach, *DSM*-II also de-linked symptoms of mental disorders from specific concepts of personality make-up, whether biomedical and psychodynamic. It no longer employed the concepts "psychobiologic unit" and "personality structure." Mental disorders were no longer due to the reaction formation of a psychobiologic unit or personality structure, but became simply clusters of symptoms dispersed in the new field of diagnostic nomenclature. And "individuals may have more than one mental disorder." (p. 2) With the above changes in assumptions, *DSM*-II encouraged a multiple diagnostic approach.

Nevertheless, *DSM*-II still retained a proclivity for biomedical etiology. Thus, "mental retardation" occupied first place in *DSM*-II's new diagnostic nomenclature, "to emphasize that it is to be diagnosed whenever it is present, even if it is due to some other disorder." (p. 121) And *DSM*-II advised that

> any mental disorders, and particularly mental retardation and the various organic brain syndromes, are reflections of underlying physical conditions. Whenever these physical conditions are known they should be indicated with a separate diagnosis in addition to the one that specifies the mental disorder found. (p. 4)

Furthermore, many terms in the diagnostic nomenclature, representing the practices of various schools, similarly retained an underlying dualistic, mind/body assumption.

The 1980 edition of *DSM* (*DSM*-III) extended and consolidated changes *DSM*-II had initiated. The three most important were (1) classification of mental disorders by symptomatology; (2) the further de-linking of mental disorder and the individual person; and (3) introduction of a system of multiaxial diagnostic evaluation. Together, the changes made the third edition much less etiological and coherent, much more eclectic and systematic.

(1) Mental disorder in *DSM*-III no longer consists of "a discrete entity with sharp boundaries (discontinuity) between it and other mental disorders, as well as between it and No Mental Disorder." Instead, it became "a clinically significant behavioral or psychological syndrome or pattern that occurs in an individual and that is typically associated with either a painful syndrome (distress) or impairment in one or more important areas of functioning (disability)." The intended inference is obviously "that there is a behavioral, psychological, or biological dysfunction, and that the disturbance is not only in the relationship between the individual and society." (p. 6)

DSM-III's approach was clinical and descriptive. "For some mental disorders," it stated, "the etiology or pathological processes are known." However, for most,

> the etiology is unknown. . . . The approach taken [here] is atheoretical with regard to etiology or pathological process except for those disorders for which this is well established and therefore included in the definition of the disorder. (pp. 6–7)

DSM-III admitted that different theoretical orientations allow for the fact that "clinicians can agree on the identification of mental disorders on the basis of their clinical manifestations without agreeing on how the disturbances come about." The approach is, therefore, "'descriptive' in that the definitions of the disorders generally consist of descriptions of the clinical features of the disorders. These features are described at the lowest order of inference necessary to describe the characteristic features of the disorder." (p. 7)

DSM-I's standard nomenclature had classified all mental disorders under two major binarial groupings, plus three qualifying phrases. *DSM*-II's diagnostic nomenclature had dispersed mental disorders into ten categories. *DSM*-III increased its diagnostic categories to eighteen, and rearranged them in the following order: disorders usually first evident in infancy, childhood, or adolescence; organic mental disorders; substance use disorders; schizophrenic disorders; paranoid disorders; psychotic disorders not elsewhere classified; affective disorders; anxiety disorders; somato-form disorders; dissociative disorders; psychosexual disorders; factitious disorders; disorders of impulse control not elsewhere classified; adjustment disorders; psychological factors affecting physical condition; personality disorders; a separate "V" code for conditions not attributable to a mental disorder that are a focus of attention or treatment; and additional codes. In *DSM*-III, a mental disorder is no longer "a discrete entity with sharp boundaries (discontinuity)." It has become only "a clinically significant behavioral or psychological syndrome or pattern." (p. 6) The course of a mental disorder varies among individuals. Thus an individual may suffer from several syndromes or patterns of dysfunctions.

(2) Its new approach, according to *DSM*-III, seeks to counter the common misconception "that a classification of mental disorders classifies the individual, when actually what are being classified are disorders that individuals have." Therefore, *DSM*-III avoids the use of such phrases as "a schizophrenic" or "an alcoholic," in favor of the term "an individual with Schizophrenia" or "an individual with Alcohol Dependencies." The new approach also counters the conception

> that all individuals described as having the same mental disorder are alike in all important ways. Although all the individuals described as having the same mental disorders show at least the defining features of the disorder, they may well differ in other important ways that may affect clinical management and outcome. (p. 6)

DSM-III provides a less individualistic, more behavioral and adaptive concept of the person. It defines identity as "the sense of self, providing a unity of personality over time. Prominent disturbances in identity or the sense of self are seen in Schizophrenia, Borderline Personality Disorder, and Identity Disorder." (p. 361) Personality now consists of

deeply ingrained patterns of behavior, which include the way one relates to, perceives, and thinks about the environment and oneself. Personality *traits* are prominent aspects of personality, and do not imply pathology. Personality *disorder* implies inflexible and mal-adaptive patterns of sufficient severity to cause either significant impairment in adaptive functioning or subjective distress. (p. 366)

Nevertheless, for *DSM*-III, a person is still an "individual," in opposition to "society."

DSM-III distinguished between "behavioral, psychological, or biological dysfunction" and "conflict between individual and society." The former is mental disorder, the latter "social deviance." (p. 6) The underlying assumption thus remains intact: the individual exists prior to social reality, and it is the individual's unconnected emotionality that constitutes the treatable problem. Nevertheless, *DSM*-III abandoned any attempt at individual diagnosis, as the following discussion shows.

(3) To compensate for its descriptive symptomatology, *DSM*-III introduced a multi-axial evaluation, which required (whereas *DSM*-II just encouraged) that "every case be assessed on each of several 'axes,' each of which refers to a different class of information." (p. 23) There are five axes.

Axis II covers personality disorders and specific developmental disorders. On the other hand, Axis I covers clinical syndromes. These two axes are intended to comprehend the entire classification of mental disorders. The separation between Axes I and II, according to *DSM*-III, is to ensure "that consideration is given to the possible presence of disorders that are frequently overlooked when attention is directed to the usually more florid Axis I disorder." (p. 23) *DSM*-III advises that "on both Axes I and II, multiple diagnoses should be made when necessary to describe the current condition." Axis III includes physical disorders and conditions. "The separation of this axis from the mental disorders axes, is based on the tradition of separating those disorders whose manifestations are primarily behavioral or psychological (i.e., mental disorders) from those whose manifestations are not." (p. 8) The purpose of Axis III is to permit "the clinician to indicate any physical disorder or condition that is potentially relevant to the understanding or management of the individual." (p. 26).

The first three of the five axes constituted the official diagnostic assessment. The remaining two—Axis IV: severity of psychosocial stressors, and Axis V: highest level of adaptive functioning past year—were "available for use in special clinical and research settings and provide information supplementing the official *DSM*-III diagnoses (Axes I, II, and III), that may be useful for planning treatment and predicting outcome." (p. 23)

The multiaxial evaluation of clinical symptoms, and the refusal to link symptoms to any concept of personality structure or psychobiologic unit, actually transform *DSM*-III's diagnostic categories from a descriptive symptomatology to a closed system of labeling. The result is a one-level, free-floating ordering of syndromes or patterns, which is useful for sorting out illnesses, and naming and classifying them in terms of observable symptoms.

As it became more eclectic, systematic, and less coherent, the discourse of psychiatry became ever more controversial. In 1989, the American Psychiatric Association came out with a new four-volume revision of *DSM*-III *Treatment of Psychiatric Disorder*. The new manual offered extensive reviews of all the major therapies and medications commonly employed to treat any illness. However, this time, the work cannot even claim to be official. Because of various objections and disagreements, it is published as a report of the APA's Task Force on Treatments and Psychiatric Disorders. (*New York Times*, December 14, 1989)

b. Changing Mental Health Practices

The breakdown of the discursive coherence of psychiatry can be understood as adjustments, at once reflexive and initiative, within the larger context of the changing production and consumption of mental-health practices, both private and public. In this section, we discuss the numerous factors at work to reconstitute that context.

Most directly, the discursive shift from the biomedical etiology of *DSM*-I to the systematic symptomatology of *DSM*-III enabled the psychiatric profession to provide and control a common set of terminologies for comprehending and commanding the expanding, increasingly diverse psychotherapeutic practices. This came at a time when the ratio of psychiatrists among those providing mental health services declined. Between 1975 and 1990, the aggregate number of psychotherapists (including psychiatrists), clinical social workers, marriage and family counselors expanded by 275 percent—from 72,000 to 198,000. Yet the number of psychiatrists increased only from 26,000 to 36,000. (*New York Times,* May 17, 1990) Thus, in 1975, over one-third of the mental health service providers were psychiatrists; whereas by 1990, that percentage dwindled to 18 percent. Nevertheless, the systematization of its discourse in *DSM-III* enabled the profession to consolidate and enlarge its influence. (Kirk and Kutchins 1992, pp. 5–6, 8)

The committee that drafted *DSM*-I worked closely with the Biometrics Branch of the National Institute of Mental Health. The chief of the branch served as statistics consultant to the APA committee, and prepared the majority of the sections on "Statistical Reporting" and "Statistical Classification of Mental Disorder" of *DSM*-I. (p. x) By the 1960s, the practice of systems analysis had prevailed in government, as well as large corporations and institutions. The microcomputer revolution of the 1970s further expanded the practice. Thus, the multiaxial system of *DSM*-III was able to connect the discourse of psychiatry more closely to the systems practices of health maintenance organizations, insurance companies, the government, courts, and ultimately large corporations.

Systems analysis facilitated the psycho-pharmacological treatment of mental disorders. Using the multiaxial systems, a psychiatrist can sort out symptoms and connect them to the corresponding pharmacological treatments. Such treatment, Rosenbaum and Sonne complained in 1986, "seldom (or never) deals with the causes of illness. It is exclusively directed toward alleviating symptoms." (p. 3) Indeed the drugging of patients has reached virtually epidemic proportions in many areas of patient management. Paul Lerman, for instance, found that the excessive use of antipsychotic drugs originated with the onset of the deinstitutionalization of mental patients in the 1960s. Unusually large amounts of drugs were prescribed in nursing homes, special children's treatment facilities, board-and-care homes, group homes, and halfway houses, as well as in special hospital units and correctional facilities. (1982, pp. 59, 103)

According to Richard Warner, the new drug lithium carbonate, which was approved by the Food and Drug Administration (FDA) in the early 1970s, altered the diagnosis of schizophrenia and its relation to manic depression. Until the mid-1970s, schizophrenia was very widely diagnosed in the USA. American psychiatrists tended to label as schizophrenics those who would have been labeled manic-depressives in Europe. Even patients with no clear psychotic features were labeled as latent and pseudoneurotic schizophrenics. In the 1960s, a research project found psychiatrists in New York, when compared to their counterparts in London, to be twice as likely to diagnose schizophrenia, four times less likely to diagnose psychotic depression, and ten times less likely to label a psychotic patient as suffering from mania. (1985, pp. 17–18)

However, psychiatric diagnosis in the USA changed radically in the 1970s. Practitioners began to emphasize manic depression rather than schizophrenia. Warner attributes the change to the introduction of lithium carbonate, a drug found highly effective in controlling manic-depressive illness, as well as being considerably more pleasant and probably less potentially harmful than the most common alternative drugs then available. Lithium carbonate, however, is generally not beneficial for schizophrenic patients. Though the drug was known earlier, it was not available in the US market until 1970, when the FDA finally gave permission for its use in the treatment of mania. Whatever the reason for the delay, the availability of the drug was followed within a few years by a major revision of the APA's classification system for mental disorders. (pp. 18–19)

Unlike the two previous editions, *DSM*-III limited the diagnosis of schizophrenia to those illnesses exhibiting its specific features for at least six months. In addition, it

> excludes illnesses without overt psychotic features. . . . Illnesses with onset after mid-adult life are also excluded. . . . Furthermore, individuals who develop a depressive or manic syndrome for an extended period . . . are not classified as having Schizophrenia but rather as having either an Affective or Schizoaffective Disorder." (p. 181)

In other words, the introduction of a new drug effective for manic depression correlated with a broader diagnosis of manic depression and a narrower diagnosis of schizophrenia in psychiatric practice. The actual change in practice preceded the official discursive change, from a broad diagnosis of schizophrenia in *DSM*-II to a much more restrictive diagnosis in *DSM*-III. That is, the narrower diagnosis of schizophrenia preceded *DSM*-III, just as the broader diagnosis preceded *DSM*-II.

Beyond systems analysis and the production and consumption of new psycho-pharmaceutical drugs, other nonpsychiatric factors, such as the movement to deinstitutionalize mental patients, the proliferation of various psychotherapeutic practices, and the availability of new governmental funding, were all exceedingly important in contextualizing the changes in the discourse of psychiatry.

Lerman's study of the different trends in the complex phenomenon of deinstitutionalization found that, since the mid-fifties, there have been fewer clients using traditional mental institutional facilities. But that did not result in a decline in the total number of mental patients, or even a lessening of their pathologies, since the decline in the number of mental patients in traditional institutions was accompanied by "rising rates of admission, shorter lengths of stay, and heavy reliance on general hospitals or community centers associated with local hospitals." (1982, p. 77) Group homes, alcohol and drug centers, halfway houses, homes for the emotionally disturbed, and board-and-care homes, all of which were formerly unavailable, now supplemented these countervailing trends.

Richard Mollica's survey of changing mental health practices in south-central Connecticut from 1950 to 1975 confirms Lerman's findings. According to Mollica, mental hospitals there accounted for two-thirds of all patient-care episodes in 1950, and for all practical purposes were the only source of psychiatric care for lower-class patients, since support for outpatient treatments did not exist at the time. In 1975, an entirely different pattern of care had prevailed. By then, state mental hospitals accounted for only 23 percent of all patient-care episodes. In contrast, public outpatient care (provided mainly by the regional community mental health center) had expanded from 8 percent of all patient care episodes in 1950 to 33 percent. (1987, p. 370)

In 1950, according to Mollica, psychiatrists in south-central Connecticut were virtually the only providers of active treatment for mental illnesses; twenty-five years later, many types of psychiatric professionals and paraprofessionals engaged in outpatient settings. By then, psychiatrists, psychologists, social workers, and clergy counselors were all delivering privately supported outpatient psychotherapy. In contrast, non-professional mental health workers were providing psychiatric care at community mental health centers along with other professionals, and were the primary and regular providers of treatment on all state mental hospital inpatient units. Psychiatrists were primarily used as consultants at the state mental hospitals. (p. 372)

The declining number of mental patients in the traditional institutions and the development of different types of outpatient care meant that psychiatrists were losing control of patients to psychotherapists and paraprofessionals in a much more diversified market, which involved both more producers and more consumers of mental health services. Seen in this light, it now becomes clear that changes in *DSM*-III were efforts to recognize and accommodate newer treatment approaches.

Thus, the introduction to *DSM*-III emphasized how the multiaxial system of diagnosis could be used in psychodynamically oriented treatment, functional analysis of the behavior disturbance, family therapy, and somatic therapy. (pp. 11–12)

Deinstitutionalization, another important factor, is not a single phenomenon. Castel, Castel, and Lovell's study of mental medicine and the state in postwar USA points out that deinstitutionalization describes (and in part conceals) three related processes, which have profoundly altered mental health institutions, professions, and practices. Yet these processes did not do away with either the fact of institutionalization, the recognition of professional competence, or the predominance of technique. (1982, p. 298)

First, institutionalization is far from obsolete as a solution to the problems of mental health and other forms of deviance. Hospital admission procedures and functions have been redefined and have become more restrictive, and new alternative institutions have been created, thereby rationalizing and to some degree reinforcing custodial programs. Second, the medical model did not prepare psychiatry to handle outpatients, whose problems were social and political as well as psychological, in community mental health centers. Nor was psychiatry prepared to handle new issues like drugs, counter-culture, feminism, and gay liberation. And third, with new clients in new institutions, the number of different kinds of available therapy increased, as did the number of cases in which specialists of all styles felt competent to intervene. The result was the extension of the jurisdiction of mental medicine to cover a large number and a greater variety of social groups, and the continued viability of the modes of treatment, ranging from the most archaic to the most modern, all of them functioning together as parts of a comprehensive system. (p. 306)

This new model Castel, Castel and Lovell called "enhanced normality." (p. 307) Its aim is no longer to heal the sick or even merely to maintain the health of the "healthy." Rather, "enhanced normality" seeks to correct deviations from the norm and to maximize individual efficiency. Underlying this normalization are the assumptions that human beings are open to technological manipulation, and that the social environment is amenable to scientific control.

Psychiatry has always been a normative discipline. At its height, it was a disciplinary practice based upon the biomedical model of etiology. Changes in mental health practices since the 1960s were due to the

greater variety in the production and consumption of the psychotherapeutic regulations of dis-eased bodies. The changes did not follow a
detailed plan. The production and consumption of antipsychotic drugs,
the deinstitutionalization of mental patients, the proliferation of psychotherapeutic treatments and of new facilities all came about because of the
efforts of private enterprises and the state working in tandem. All these
treatments do not necessarily lead to much improvement. But then, that
was never the purpose. The fundamental dynamic here is a marketplace
lubricated by greater governmental financing. There is always money to
be made in the maze of psychosis and social failure.

According to Lerman, the accelerated reduction of inpatients in the
1960s was associated with the availability of significant new fiscal resources from an expanding welfare state. In order to take advantage of
these new federal funds, a state was required to provide new matching
funds for the specific grant-in-aid programs. The government's willing-
ness to fund new welfare programs depended on public entrepreneur-
ship capability and skills, as well as philosophical agreement with the
objectives of a long-range plan. (1982, p. 103)

Castel, Castel, and Lovell confirmed that the practices of mental medicine in the United States were the outcome of the workings of various
forces, none of which can operate independently of the others. Competition, conflict, exchange, and reinterpretation produce a dynamic
equilibrium. The state manages, rationalizes, standardizes. It provides a
central source of information, coordinates diverse initiatives, and plans
long-term projects. However, even when the central government does
intervene directly, it is rarely to set up wholly new government-run
institutions. (1982, pp. 317, 318)

Andrew Scull (1977), on the other hand, would argue that this shift in
social control styles and practices reflects the structural pressures to
curtail sharply the costly system of segregative control once welfare pay-
ments, providing a subsistence existence for elements of the surplus
population, make available a viable alternative to management in an
institution. Such structural pressures are greatly intensified by the fiscal
crisis encountered in varying degrees at different levels of the state apparatus; a crisis engendered by advanced capitalism's need to socialize more
and more of the costs of production. (p. 152)

As is the pattern in late-capitalist USA, government financing enlarges
the market, but does not fundamentally alter its working. The social
impacts of the valorization of psychopathology have varied according to

age, ethnicity, and income. Between 1950 and 1970, institutional resi-
dence rates for white males and females under 65 either went down, or
were stable. The rates for African-American males and females all went
up. And rates for both African-American and white males and females
over 65 all rose. (Lerman 1982, p. 61–2) Mollica confirmed that, in south-
central Connecticut, state mental hospitals reduced its resident population by two-thirds from 1950 to 1975, in spite of the fact that in the
same period their admission rates quadrupled. What has resulted is a
"revolving door" syndrome. In addition, large numbers of elderly patients were discharged into nursing homes. But the lower classes are
always much more dependent on state-provided services than on private
mental hospitals.

Mollica concludes that deinstitutionalization, as well as the shift of
higher classes of patients to private inpatient facilities, has contributed to
a pooling of the most socially disabled patients in the public inpatient
units. This "creaming" effect has essentially overloaded the state facilities
with the most socially disabled patients who have no hope of receiving
effective treatment. Lower-class patients receive most of their outpatient
services at the community mental health centers. Furthermore, even at
these centers, the poor are disadvantaged because they are channeled to
the categorical treatment units, rather than the psychotherapy units. The
former provide their patients with organic therapies and brief counsel-
ing contacts; they rely heavily on nonprofessional staff. In contrast, the
psychotherapy unit is staffed by professionals who meet with their patients on a weekly basis, and provide individual, group, and family psychotherapy. (1987, p. 375)

c. The Bounds of Psychopathology

The various discursive practices of psychopathology all assume a bio-
psychic self, with discrete social environmental factors as impinging on
such a self. Thus, by emphasizing therapeutization of the self, they dis-
regard that there is no self without the Social, no "society" without lived
bodies, and that it is not possible to deal with one without the other. I
argue that psychopathology, by reinforcing the ideology of the individual subject, plays a vital role in displacing sociopathology. This displacement subjectivizes the sociopathology inherent in late capitalism; and
what cannot be psychopathologized becomes sociologically the deviant.

I am arguing for the need of sociopathology, in order to reassess and relocate seemingly psychic disorders in a broader, more critical perspective. Crucial personal disorders cannot be adequately dealt with as mere psychopathology. Let me cite two cases in point: anorexia nervosa and schizophrenia.

Anorexia nervosa is a pathological desire for thinness which afflicts upper- and middle-class, and is now spreading among lower-class, young women. Brumberg, in *Fasting Girls* (1988), persuasively argues that, although they can be traced back to the Middle Ages, fasting and food refusal are transformed by cultural and social systems, to give new meanings in different historical epochs. "Thus the modern clinical term 'anorexia nervosa' should be used to designate only a disease of modernity." (p. 3) Unlike religious fasting, anorexia nervosa as a term first appeared in the late nineteenth century to refer to an upper-class problem, when refusing food operated as a decorous emotional tactic within a family where food was plentiful and connected to love. But post-World War II world, preoccupied with dieting and the image of a slim female body, transformed the dynamics of anorexia nervosa, as well as making it an epidemic for middle-class young women. "By the 1970s and 1980s the cultural imperative for control of appetite became extraordinarily troublesome precisely because the stimulus to eat (and not to eat) was everywhere." (p. 266)

Central to anorexia nervosa is a problem in the patient's perception of her own body image. The patient believes that her body does not conform to an ideal image of bony thinness. The belief reveals either an inability to assess one's own size accurately, or, even when assessed accurately, an extreme disparagement of one's own size. (Garfinkel and Garner 1982, p. 125) This belief leads to a pathological disciplining of one's own body, in the vain hope of conforming to an ideal body image. Garner and associates, in surveying *Playboy* magazine and the Miss America beauty pageant, found that the ideal of female beauty has become ever thinner over the years. This, in spite of the fact that other researchers discovered that, over the same period, the average woman under the age of thirty actually gained, and not lost, weight. (pp. 109–110) While most agree that anorexia nervosa is over-represented in the upper classes, Garfinkel and associates found that the pathological thinness has spread among all classes. (p. 102) The pathology is obviously worsening. A study of one specific locale showed that the incidence of anorexia nervosa, occurring most prominently in the fifteen to twenty-four age group, almost doubled between the 1960s and the early 1970s.

The pressure of the new body image on women is tremendous. Wayne and Susan Wooley wrote that, unlike young women of fifty years ago, young women of the present generation have probably "gone through" more than one body. (*MS.,* November 1986)

> Before the advent of widespread dieting, the experience of the body was relatively continuous for most women, marked only by the gradual change of normal growth, by a period of rapid qualitative as well as quantitative change at puberty, and by pregnancy. . . . The majority of young adolescents [today] go on weight-loss diets, and, of course, the majority of weight-loss diets are followed by regain of the lost weight, often with an "overshoot." Thus by mid-adolescence young women have cognitive and sensory memories of many forms of the body-self. (p. 90)

Even more recent studies reveal that, by adolescence, girls begin to suffer a higher rate of depression than boys, due to their preoccupation with appearance. Said one researcher: "Body image is a huge part of how girls think of themselves." (*New York Times,* May 10, 1990)

Caprice Benedetti, a 5-foot-10-inch fashion model weighing only 125 pounds, confesses that "this whole business is deception. It's false advertising. It's total fantasy. How can a pear-shaped body put on a pair of leather pants and a tight shirt and look 5-10, 120 pounds and not pear-shaped. It's a shame. We give women false expectations and we make them feel worse about themselves. I know I'm putting something on that most people can't wear." (*New York Times,* January 5, 1993)

In the previous chapter, I suggested that the technologies of the look and the relay of juxtaposed images and signs are at the center of a semiotics of commodified sexual lifestyle. In late-capitalist USA, body image overdetermines the social, and therefore the self-reconstruction of women. Women are much more vulnerable to body image than men. I argue that the latest version of anorexia nervosa is much less a psychopathology, than a late-capitalist sociopathology.

An even more intractable problem is schizophrenia. Most agree that it is characterized by abnormalities of speech and action, emotional flattening, delusions, and auditory hallucinations. And it is more likely to afflict the young. But we don't really know the etiology or the proper treatment of schizophrenia. There are no objective characteristics for its diagnosis. Medications are able to reduce, selectively, some of the symptoms usually associated with schizophrenia. But we cannot define schizophrenia in terms of the types of treatment. In fact, some patients diagnosed as schizophrenics do not respond to pharmacological treatment. Two major problems are that these symptoms can vary markedly over time, and that there can be a large area of overlapping with other psychiatric groups. (Schied 1990, p. 24)

As noted in the last section, *DSM*-III made the diagnosis of schizophrenia much more restrictive than *DSM*-II. Pawelski, Harrow and Grossman (1987) sampled 214 young, nonchronic patients who were hospitalized during the early phases of various psychotic disorders. Under the criteria of *DSM*-III, only thirty-nine of them were diagnosed as schizophrenics, while 175 were diagnosed as non-schizophrenics. However, if *DSM*-II criteria were used, the same group would yield 109 schizophrenics and 105 non-schizophrenics. This is not surprising, since the diagnostic criteria for *DSM*-III were much more restrictive than for *DSM*-II. But what *is* surprising is that, in comparing post-hospital recoveries among the patients, Pawelski, Harrow and Grossman found,

> the outcome differences between *DSM*-III and *DSM*-II schizophrenics were not large and the *DSM*-III were not superior to *DSM*-II in terms of separating schizophrenics and nonschizophrenics on the measures of overall outcome during the early posthospital phase. (p. 91)

At present, researchers assume that a combination of biological predisposition and environmental circumstances lead to the manifestation of the illness.

> According to this model, a predisposition to schizophrenia is inherited or acquired developmentally and forms the basis for indices of vulnerability to the disorder. This vulnerability is modified by all life events that increase or decrease the likelihood that schizophrenia will emerge in early adulthood. (Straub and Hahlweg 1990, p. 1)

The model consists of three major categories: enduring vulnerability characteristics; external environmental stressors; and development of psychotic symptoms. Enduring vulnerability characteristics, such as disturbance of information processing, psychophysiological response anomalies and social competence deficits, are assumed to be there before, during, and after a schizophrenic episode. External environmental stimuli comprise social stressors (discrete life events) and nonsupportive social networks, (especially in a family with high levels of expressed emotions). (pp. 1–3)

Psychopathology is recognizing the importance of social, environmental factors. For example, Zubin (1986), in proposing a multicausal approach to the etiology of schizophrenia, includes a spectrum of models ranging from the genetic, via the internal environmental (e.g., infectious disease and viral), the neurophysiological and the neuroanatomical, the developmental, and the learning, to the ecological (i.e., the social). In addition, Zubin points to such factors as low socioeconomic status, physical and social deficiencies in the milieu, minority or marginal status, ghetto niche, and educational and vocational limitations, as all leading to higher risks of developing schizophrenic episodes.

However, psychopathology presupposes the pre-eminence of a dynamic psychic self. It cannot provide for any ordering of the different aspects of the social, ecological as a meaningful framework. How can such factors as "low socio-economic status," "physical and social deficiencies in the milieu," "minority or marginal status," "ghetto niche" and "educational and vocational limitations" constitute a social, ecological framework within which the human person is located? Is the person still fundamentally a psychobiological entity? We are in effect confronted with an intractable dualism between the psychological and the social, the individual and society, the inside and the outside, with the psychic inside being privileged.

Psychopathology introduced the concept of *stress* to mediate the persisting dualism. *DSM*-I made a distinction between "external precipitating stress" and "unconscious internal conflict," cautioning psychiatrists not to confuse the two. The manual advised that whenever a stress could not be determined, the clinician should record it as undetermined. The clinician should not presume "that a particular environmental stress is severe because one or even several individuals react[ed] poorly to it, since these individuals may have had poor resistance to that particular stress." (pp. 47–48) In other words, unconscious internal conflict was assumed to be the dynamic, external stress was only a precipitant.

DSM-III lists severity of psychosocial stressors as the fourth in its multiaxial diagnostic evaluation. Yet only the first three axes constitute the official psychiatric diagnostic assessment. Axis IV together with Axis V are available for use only in special clinical and research setting, and provide information to supplement the official diagnoses of Axes I, II, and III in planning treatment and predicting outcome. And mental disorder is defined in *DSM*-III as a clinically significant behavioral or psychologic syndrome or pattern that occurs in an individual. . . . In addition, there is an inference that there is a behavioral, psychologic, or biologic dysfunction, and that the disturbance is not only in the relationship between the individual and society. When the disturbance is limited to a conflict between an individual and society, this may represent social deviance . . . but is not by itself a mental disorder." (p. 363)

The current vulnerability/stress model in the study of schizophrenia (e.g., Wong, et al., 1986, p. 79) assumes that certain individuals have an underlying and enduring psychobiological vulnerability to schizophrenic disorder. Psychotic symptoms and their accompanying behavioral disabilities then emerge or become exacerbated when stressors impinge upon these individuals. However, as Day (1986) points out, psychopathologists who study stress cannot agree on what constitutes a stressful life event. (see also Popplestone and McPherson 1988, pp. 318–20)

From the standpoint of sociopathology, psychopathology's concept of stress to mediate the psychic and the social not only perpetuates the dualism between the two, but operates as a buffer to preserve the assumption of a psychodynamic self from having to deal with the problematic reality of sociopathology.

I propose that it is the hegemony of exchangist practices in late capitalism that has fundamentally reconstructed bodily needs and their satisfaction. Old social, cultural values are circulated and consumed as nostalgic images to sell newly packaged product characteristics. New social, cultural values are produced as signifiers of exchange value. But exchange value, a mere quantity, cannot provide any meaningful human ends beyond mere accumulation. Bodily needs are now constructed and satisfied for the sake of the production of exchange value. The combination and recombination of structural, discursive, systematic, and semiotic components in late-capitalist practices of production, consumption, social reproduction, gender, and sexuality create a reality for the embodied self which is deeply ambivalent, conflictual, and self-defeating. The result is the fundamental sociopathology of late capitalism. Late-capitalist exchangist practices are inherently sociopathological; not to be pathological in the current situation is unimaginable. The contradictions are no longer class-specific, but undercut class, ethnic, gender, and sexual distinctions as this exchangist reality spread, although different classes, ethnicities, genders and sexualities are determined by these practices differently.

Psychopathology is a displacement, a reduction of sociopathology. Instead of locating schizophrenia in a social context, it provides a narrower, bio/physio/psychological model. The reduction may not be successful, in that most people do not fully recover from schizophrenia. But it has led to the proliferation of various psychotherapeutic practices in the late-capitalist marketplace, which are subsidized with government funding. Though it may be a failure from the standpoint of the dis-eased body, psychopathology is a success as late-capitalist commodification.

As displacement, psychopathology is not socially neutral. Mental illnesses are hierarchically distributed in terms of classes, ethnicities, genders, and marginal groups. Lower-class persons have more symptoms of mental illness than upper-class persons (Dohrenwend and Dohrenwend 1969); women have more neurotic symptoms than men (Gove and Tudor 1973); and people who are single, divorced, or separated from their spouses have more mental symptoms than married people (Gove, 1972). (All cited in Horwitz 1982, p. 62)

Furthermore, psychotherapy is more likely to be sought out by those who can afford it. Horwitz (1982) showed how different groups recognize and accept the psychopathologizing of mental illnesses, and found that "an individual's location in social space predicts the probability that he or she will recognize and label mental illness." (p. 83) Those from higher social classes, who possess more education and cosmopolitan culture, are more likely to recognize and label mental illness, as are all women. This is especially the case among urban, cosmopolitan intellectuals, Jews, and humanistic professionals. On the other hand,

> as cultural distance from the therapist grows and social rank declines, individuals are less likely to seek therapy voluntarily, to be provided with therapy if they do seek it, and to receive long-term therapy from a prestigious therapist. They are, instead, more likely to receive coercive control or to be neglected completely. (p. 141)

In other words, psychopathology is available for those who are more pliable and able to pay, but only social control is available for the recalcitrant and the poor.

But psychopathology's reduction of sociopathology yields a remainder. Reduction cannot completely displace social reality. Those aspects of sociopathology which cannot be mastered as psychopathology will be then handled as problems of social deviance. This is especially revealed in the case of the double-binding of lower-class African Americans. Kleiner and Dalgard (1975) found that if there exists a black lower class culture that fosters the belief that the opportunity system is closed, then the motivational characteristics of lower class individuals will not include the traditional middle class emphasis on the success ethic; their self-esteem will be intact; the risk of mental illness will be low and the risk of delinquency will be high.

On the other hand,

to the extent that black persons reject this culture and identify with the larger white society, they will perceive a relatively open opportunity structure, have higher goal striving motivation, low self-esteem, and be a relatively high risk of mental illness. (reprinted in Mezzich and Berganza, eds., 1984, p. 268)

Class and race doubly code the bodies of lower-class African Americans. From within this double-boundary, the perception and motivation of lower-class African Americans differentiate and reconfirm for them two alternative social realities. Psychopathology is the price for integration, while social deviance is the normalizing consequence for those who do not. Both alternatives exact an excessive burden on African-American bodies.

Retrospect: The Problematic of the Body
in Late Capitalism

The body is not a subject. It is a subject-effect. There is no body in itself. It is our lived body. On the one hand, we are preoccupied with the image of our body; on the other, our bodily life is much more than what any image or representation can comprehend. In fact, these images and representations are used to manipulate our bodily life. This is the central contradiction between a visualized body and the hegemonic capitalist practices which construct our body.

We have all experienced the impact of the capitalist market economy. It infiltrates and alters every aspect of our lives in the late twentieth century. This ubiquitous experience is what Marxists call the hegemony of exchangist practices, i.e., practices dictated by capital accumulation, or what non-Marxists call the bottom line of the free market. I have argued here that the hegemony of exchangist practices in late-capitalist USA involves two fundamental changes. First, the development of all the second as well as first terms of the sign correlates which structure the terrain of production and consumption; and second, the valorization of all hitherto reciprocal, non-exchangist practices, whether in social reproduction, gender and sexuality, or psychopathology—hence the underdevelopment of bodily needs as means for late-capitalist development.

Analyzing the structure of capitalist production in the nineteenth century, Marx emphasized the development of exchange value, quantity, and the reproduction of capital, but assumed the unproblematicity of use value, quality, and the reproduction of labor. All these second terms constructed and satisfied the slow-changing needs of the human body. I have argued that these second terms referred to and depended on the non-exchangist values or "meanings" which the socially reciprocal practices in other relatively autonomous terrains generated and sustained. The seeming stability of the second terms in the terrain of production *and* the relative autonomy of non-exchangist terrains, I have argued, actually required each other.

However, the hegemony of exchangist practices in late capitalism has ended both the seemingly stable second terms, and the relative autonomy of non-exchangist terrains. The traditional Marxist concept of structure, in other words, is no longer helpful in characterizing late-capitalist exchangist practices. "Structure" is currently replaced by a "combination and recombination" of structure, discourse, cybernetic systems, and semiotics. The result is the "deterritorialization and reterritorialization" of formerly relatively autonomous terrains. Thus, postmodernist concern with the destabilization of referents is no idle academic chitchat, but refracts an inherent aspect of the new hegemony.

Capitalist development destabilizes all qualitatively distinct use values and non-exchangist terrains. Yet, the production and accumulation of exchange value requires continuing valorization and underdevelopment. Three trends are currently underway in late-capitalist USA, within the context of a much more competitive, unstable capitalist world economy. First, by means of a combination of peripheral Fordism and peripheral Taylorization, US transnational corporations and the hegemonic state, together with other transnationals and states, are developing and underdeveloping other parts of the world. Second, the development of late-capitalist production at home underdevelops human and global resources, especially women and minorities, i.e., those who have to sustain higher labor and lower wages. Third, the unequal development of valorized lifestyles, social reproduction, gender, sexuality, and psychopathology displaces and camouflages the unequal social relations of production.

Since all other others are destabilized, the body has emerged as the sole, remaining other in the monologic of late-capitalist accumulation. Capital accumulation and the body constitute the new binary opposition: the body acts as the other to late-capitalist development. The satisfactions of bodily needs are currently the means by which the end of late-capital accumulation is accomplished; bodily needs change for the sake of capital accumulation. Late-capitalist development's endless search for new means for capital accumulation will result in further exploitation of bodily needs.

But the body is not a mere other. This body is our own; it is the referent of all other referents—materially in the sense that it occupies space/time, and sociohistorically realized in the construction and satisfaction of needs. The body, a historical materiality, is neither a body-in-itself nor a body-for-itself, but always an embodied being-in-the-

world, constructed and realized within social practices to satisfy changing needs. There is no body as an entity prior to social codings and
practices. The body in late-capitalist USA is constructed and realized in
an expanded, accelerated whirlwind of exchangist practices. Yet none of
us can entirely disavow exchangist practices for an alternative, ideal community. Neither can late-capitalist accumulation dispense with us, since
accumulation must extract surplus value from laboring, consuming
bodies. Robotic, labor-less, non-human machines do not produce surplus value, since surplus value is extracted from production and consumption to satisfy bodily needs. Capital must always develop at the
expense of all bodies, all non-exchangist values, all others.

How do we resist? How can we make the satisfactions of bodily needs
an end? Not just an end in itself, but a social, human end serving all of
us? Resistance is the negation of, i.e., the active opposition to, capital.
Resistance is critical in the sense that it seeks to reverse the means/ends
relations in the late-capitalist opposition between bodily needs and capital accumulation. Since the hegemony of exchangist practices has destabilized all the other others and valorized all non-exchangist practices,
critical resistance has to be postmodern.

Everything is valorized in late capitalism; therefore everything is potentially political. Old tactics and strategies no longer work. Given their
failures, a combinative, transgressive, open-ended politics of resistance is
required against existing structural, discursive, systematic, and semiotic
practices. With bodily needs being the means for the accumulation of
exchange value, life in late-capitalist USA has gone beyond the surreal.
In resisting, we transform ourselves from being merely the passive other
to capital accumulation. Our resistance moves us from the sur- or
hyper-real to the political. The creation of new values for social, human
ends opposes the revival of old, nostalgic values in the service of capital
accumulation.

Postmodern critical resistance takes into account that we live in an age
of the politics of decoding and recoding. We cannot fall back on the body
as an individual identity, subjectivity, private self, or any other autonomous, stable, unitary entity. Such conceptualizations might have been
useful under industrial capitalism, because they presupposed the structural oppositions between public and private, work and leisure, production and social reproduction, individual and society. But the older, more
stable context no longer exists in late capitalism. Nor is temporality, i.e.,
the experience of time, linear, as it was in nineteenth-century histo-

riography; nor is it intentional, as in the phenomenology of internal time-consciousness. Temporality is also valorized, in as much as the past gets nostalgically re-imaged for the sake of the present. Nostalgic images meta-signify old values in new contexts, for new purposes. The sentimental longing for and the cynical recycling of past values have become ever more important in the development of exchangist practices. There are at present neither unitary individual subject, nor continuous time framework. With the deterritorialization and reterritorialization of the satisfaction of bodily needs, all stable identities, all values are placed in question.

To the extent that exchangist practices in late capitalism consist of the combination and recombination of structure, discourse, systems, and semiotics, resistance must be combinative and open-ended. Resistance as counter-practice must seize and recode issues of bodily needs which the hegemony of exchangist practices have provoked. It must be founded on class/gender/race differences, not because they are essential, but because capital accumulation exploits all these differentials. Resistance must be discursively coherent and plausible, yet transgressive against existing discourses, in order to mobilize different groups and sorts of peoples. It must take into account the weight of cybernetic systems, which favor the established power. And it must be semiotically sophisticated in its counter-practices. Otherwise, it can mount no effective opposition to capital's combination and recombination of structural, discursive, systematic, and semiotic practices.

The politics of resistance is intrinsically an ethical issue. Ethical concepts do not reside within a text. The deconstruction of a text yields no ethical answer. The concept of ethic has to do with personal choice and conduct; in other words, practice. It has to do with reflexive intention and social, human responsibility. Practice is more than text, discourse and language. In carrying out intended acts within the context of established, precedented practices, counter-practice is concerned with ethics. There is no "we" constituted prior to social practices. Resisting capital's marginalization of us as mere means, we create ourselves and others as ethical ends. Our resistances re-center us, by up-ending the opposition between capital accumulation and bodily needs. Undertaking resistance as counter-practices, in the very process of attempting to change the world, we change ourselves and others.

Take as an example the issue of identity politics for women and minorities in the USA. The opposing discriminatory practices that the established power sets up opens the possibility for oppressed peoples to define ourselves, and claim our self-identities, while at the same time insisting on equality. But no woman exists per se; no African American, no gay or lesbian exists as a stable unitary self. A claimed counter-identity against wasp/male definition and a disciplining of identity is vulnerable, since it is easily co-opted through the segmentation of life-style consumption. Furthermore, claimed counter identity leads to the naturalization and romanticization of origins and roots. The standpoint of critical resistance allows us to see identity politics as a struggle against discrimination. But this same standpoint reveals that the disparate identity politics of diverse, different minorities and women do not in themselves cohere as resistance against the hegemonic power. While we support identity politics in resisting the wasp-male definition of identity, we need to go beyond it and overcome the limits of identity politics. Even white men, as Gayatri Spivak pointed out, need to resist. (1990, pp. 62–3) After all, the wasp/male doesn't have a stable identity either. The construction of wasp/male identity depends upon its other, namely the marginalization of other classes, races, genders, sexes. Oppressing others, they oppress themselves. The agenda of resistance and its class/gender/race composition must therefore be enlarged; we all need to oppose the hegemony of exchangist practices.

Furthermore, resistance at the metropolitan center, be it identity politics, or social, environmental movements, must always take into account the resistances of the world's other peoples. What we attempt at the center is combinative and transgressive counter-practices against late-capitalist hegemony. Peoples in other parts of the world resist not only the transnationals, late-capitalists, and hegemonic states, but also the indigenous comprador bourgeois, feudal patriarchs, and military dictators. Their resistances are even more complex and multilayered than our own, and yet their resistances and ours are related. We need a postmodern politics to combine the resistance of the center with those in other parts of the world against the inhuman accumulation of capital for the sake of accumulation. We do not control the hegemony of exchangist practices which set a determining context for us. But we can define our resistance, our counter-practices as opposition to capital accumulation for the sake of capital accumulation, the secular Behemoth.

References

(Note: With due apology to all the authors I read over the years, too numerous to list in a bibliography, I include here only reference titles.)

Aglietta, Michael (1979), *A Theory of Capitalist Regulation*, tr. David Fernbach, London, NLB.

Altman, Dennis (1982), *The Homosexualization of America, the Americanization of the Homosexual*, New York, St. Martin's Press.

Altman, Meryl (1984), "Everything They Always Wanted You to Know: The Ideology of Popular Sex Literature," *Pleasure and Danger*, ed. Carole S. Vance, Boston, R. & K. Paul.

American Psychiatric Association, Committee on Nomenclature and Statistics (1952), *Diagnostic and Statistical Manual: Mental Disorders*, Washington, D.C.

American Psychiatric Association, Committee on Nomenclature and Statistics (1968 and 1980 eds.), *Diagnostic and Statistical Manual of Mental Disorders*, Washington, D.C.

Amin, Samir (1976), *Unequal Development*, tr. Brian Pearce, New York, Monthly Review Press.

Amsden, Alice, "Third World Industrialization: 'Global Fordism' or a New Model?" *New Left Review*, 182 (1990).

Armytage, W. H. G., R. Chester, and John Peel, eds. (1980), *Changing Patterns of Sexual Behavior*, New York, Academic Press.

Arney, William Ray, and Bernard J. Bergen (1984), *Medicine and the Management of Living*, Chicago, University of Chicago Press.

Attewell, Paul (1984), *Radical Political Economy since the Sixties*, New Brunswick, New Jersey, Rutgers University Press.

Barash, David P. (1982), *Sociobiology and Behavior*, 2d ed., New York, Elsevier.

Barlow, Tani E. (1991), "Theorizing Woman: *Funu, Guojia, Jiating*," *Gender*, 10.

Barnett, Rosalind, Lois Biener, and Grace Baruch (1987), *Gender and Stress*, New York, Free Press.

Barthes, Roland (1975), *Mythologies*, tr. Annette Lavers, New York, Hill and Wang.

Barthes, Roland (1977), *Image - Music - Text*, sel. and tr. Stephen Heath, New York, Hill and Wang.

Baudrillard, Jean (1981), *For a Critique of the Political Economy of the Sign*, tr. with introd. Charles Levin, St. Louis, Missouri, Telos Press.

Baudrillard, Jean (1983), *Simulations*, trs. Paul Foss, Paul Patton, and Philip Beitchman, New York, Semiotext(e).

Baudrillard, Jean (1987), *Forget Foucault & Forget Baudrillard*, New York, Semiotext(e).

Becker, Gary S. (1976), *The Economic Approach to Human Behavior*, Chicago, University of Chicago Press.

Beneria, Lourdes, and Catharine R. Stimpson eds. (1987), *Women, Household, and the Economy*, New Brunswick, New Jersey, Rutgers University Press.

Benjamin, Harry (1966), *The Transsexual Phenomenon*, New York, Julian Press.

Benjamin, Walter (1969), *Illuminations*, ed. with introd. Hannah Arendt, tr. Harry Zohn, New York, Schocken Books.

Birken, Lawrence (1988), *Consuming Passion*, Ithaca, New York, Cornell University Press.

Blackburn, Phil, Rod Coombs, and Kenneth Green (1985), *Technology, Economic Growth and the Labor Process*, London, Macmillan.

Blank, Robert H. (1990), *Regulating Reproduction*, New York, Columbia University Press.

Bloom, David E., and Sanders D. Korenman (March 1986), "Spending Habits of American Consumers," *American Demographics*.

Bluestone, Barry (1972), "Economic Crisis and the Law of Uneven Development," *Politics and Society*, III.

Bornstein, Kate (1994), *Gender Outlaw*, New York, Routledge.

Boston Women's Health Book Collective (1973), *Our Bodies, Ourselves*, New York, Simon & Schuster.

Bourdieu, Pierre (1977), *Outline of a Theory of Practice*, Cambridge, Cambridge University Press.

Bowles, Samuel (1982), "The Post-Keynesian Capital-Labor Stalemate," *Socialist Review*, 65.

Bowles, Samuel, David Gordon, and Thomas Weisskopf (1983), *Beyond the Waste Land*, Garden City, New York, Anchor/Doubleday.

Braverman, Harry (1974), *Labor and Monopoly Capital*, New York, Monthly Review Press.

Brown, Clair (1987), "Consumption Norms, Work Roles, and Economic Growth, 1918–80," *Gender in the Workplace*, eds. Clair Brown & Joseph A. Pechman, Washington, D.C., Brookings Institute.

Brown, P. T. (1980), "The Development of Sexual Function Therapies after Masters and Johnson," *Changing Patterns of Sexual Behavior*, eds. W. H. G. Armytage, R. Chester, and John Peel, New York, Academic Press.

Bruch, Hilde (1978), *The Golden Cage: The Enigma of Anorexia Nervosa*, Cambridge, Massachusetts, Harvard University Press.

Brumberg, Joan Jacobs (1988), *Fasting Girls: the Emergence of Anorexia Nervosa as a Modern Disease*, Cambridge, Massachusetts, Harvard University Press.

Burawoy, Michael (1985), *The Politics of Production*, London, NLB.

Butler, Judith (1990), *Gender Trouble*, New York, Routledge.

CACI Market Analysis Division (1988), *The ACORN Market Segmentation System: User's Guide*, Fairfax, Virginia.

Califia, Pat (1983), "Gender-Bending: Playing with Roles and Reversals," *The Advocate*, September 15.

Casalino, Larry (1991), "Decoding the Human Genome Project: An Interview with Evelyn Fox Keller," *Socialist Review*, XXI: 2.

Castel, Robert, Francoise Castel, and Anne Lovell (1982), *The Psychiatric Society*, tr. Arthur Goldhammer, New York, Columbia University Press.

Cavestro, William (1989), "Automation, New Technology and Work Content," *The Transformation of Work?*, ed. Stephen Wood, London, Unwin Hyman.

Collier, Jane, Michelle Z. Rosaldo, and Sylvia Yanagisako (1982), "Is There a Family? New Anthropological Views," *Rethinking the Family*, ed. Barrie Thorne with Marilyn Yalom, New York, Longman.

Collier, Jane Fishburne, and Sylvia Junko Yanagisako, eds. (1987), *Gender and Kinship*, Palo Alto, Stanford University Press.

Comfort, Alex, ed. (1972), *The Joy of Sex*, New York, Crown.

Coontz, Stephanie (1992), *The Way We Never Were*, New York, Basic Books.

Cowan, Ruth Schwartz (1983), *More Work for Mother*, New York, Basic Books.

Coward, Rosalind (1978), " 'Sexual Liberation' and the Family," *m/f*, 1.

Crimp, Douglas (1988), "AIDS: Cultural Analysis/Cultural Activism," *AIDS: Cultural Analysis/Cultural Activism*, ed. Douglas Crimp, Cambridge, Massachusetts, MIT Press.

Davis, Morris (1982), "The Impact of Workplace Heath and Safety on Black Workers," *Occupational Safety and Health*, by Frank Goldsmith and Lorin E. Kerr, New York, Human Sciences Press.

Davis, Morris E., and Andrew S. Rowland (1983), "Problems Faced by Minority Workers," *Occupational Health*, eds. Barry S. Levy and David H. Wegmen, Boston, Little, Brown.

Davis, Nanette J. (1985), *From Crime to Choice*, Westport, Connecticut, Greenwood.

Day, Richard (1986), "Social Stress and Schizophrenia," *Handbook of Schizophrenia*, Part 1: *Epidemiology, Aetiology and Clinical Features*, eds. Graham D. Burrows, Trevor R. Norman, and Gertrude Rubinstein, Amsterdam, Elsevier.

Debord, Guy (1977), *The Society of the Spectacle*, Detroit, Black & Red.

de Lauretis, Teresa (1984), *Alice Doesn't: Feminism, Semiotics, Cinema,* Bloomington, Indiana University Press.

de Lauretis, Teresa, ed. (1991), *Differences,* III: 2: "Queer Theory" issue.

Deleuze, Gilles, and Felix Guattari (1977), *Anti-Oedipus: Capitalism and Schizophrenia,* trs. Robert Hurley, Mark Seem, and Helen R. Lane, New York, Viking Press.

D'Emilio, John (1983), *Sexual Politics, Sexual Communities,* Chicago, University of Chicago Press.

de Saussure, Ferdinand (1966), *Course in General Linguistics,* Charles Bally and Albert Sechehaye, eds., in collaboration with Albert Riedlinger, tr. with introd. and notes Wade Baskin, New York, McGraw-Hill.

di Leonardo, Micaela, ed. (1991), *Gender at the Crossroads of Knowledge: Feminist Anthropology in the Postmodern Era,* Berkeley, University of California Press.

Dreifus, Claudia (1971), *Radical Lifestyles,* New York, Lancer Books.

Duden, Barbara (1987), *Repertory on Body History: An Annotated Bibliography,* Pasadena, California Institute of Technology, Division of the Humanities and Social Sciences.

Eco, Umberto (1976), *A Theory of Semiotics,* Bloomington, Indiana University Press.

Edwards, Richard C. (1979), *Contested Terrain,* New York, Basic Books.

Ehrenreich, Barbara (1989), *Fear of Falling,* New York, Harper-Collins.

Ehrenreich, Barbara, Elizabeth Hess, and Gloria Jacobs (1986), *Re-making Love; the Feminization of Sex,* New York, Anchor/Doubleday.

Ehrenreich, Barbara, and David Nasaw (May 14, 1983), "Kids as Consumers and Commodities," *Nation.*

Eisenstein, Sergei (1957), *Film Form; Essays in Film, Theory,* ed. and tr. Jay Leyda, New York, Harcourt, Brace.

Engel, George L. (1977), "The Need for a New Medical Model: A Challenge for Biomedicine," *Science,* 196.

Engelhardt, H. Tristram Jr. (1986), *The Foundations of Bioethics,* New York, Oxford University Press.

English, Deirdre, Amber Hollibaugh, and Gayle Rubin (1981), "Talking Sex," *Socialist Review,* 58.

Epstein, Julia (1991), "Transsexualism: Reflections on the Persistence of Gender and the Mutability of Sex," *Body Guards,* eds. Julia Epstein and Kristina Straub, New York, Routledge.

Epstein, Steven (1987), "Gay Politics, Ethnic Identity," *Socialist Review,* 93/94.

Escobar, Arturo (1987), *Power and Visibility: The Invention and Management of Development in the Third World,* University of California, Berkeley, Ph.D. dissertation in development philosophy, policy, and planning.

Escoffier, Jeffrey (1985), "Sexual Revolution and the Politics of Gay Identity," *Socialist Review,* 82/83.

Feher, Michel, with Ramona Naddaff and Nadia Tazi, eds. (1989), *Fragments for a History of the Human Body*, 3 parts, New York, Zone.

Feldberg, Roslyn L., and Evelyn Nakano Glenn (1983), "Effects of Office Automation on Women Clerical Workers," *Machina Ex Dea: Feminist Perspectives on Technology*, ed. Joan Rothschild, New York, Pergamon Press.

Flax, Jane (1987), "Postmodernism and Gender Relations in Feminist Theory," *Signs*, XII: 4.

Folbre, Nancy, and Heidi Hartmann (1988), "The Rhetoric of Self-Interest: Ideology of Gender in Economic Theory," *The Consequences of Economic Rhetoric*, eds. Arjo Klamer, Donald N. McCloskey, and Robert M. Solow, Cambridge, Cambridge University Press.

Forester, Tom, ed. (1981), *The Microelectronics Revolution*, Cambridge, Massachusetts, M.I.T. Press.

Foster, Hal, ed. (1984), *The Anti-Aesthetic; Essays on Postmodern Culture*, Port Townsend, Washington, Bay Press.

Foucault, Michel (1970), *The Order of Things*, New York, Random House.

Foucault, Michel (1977), *Language, Counter-Memory, Practice*, ed. with introd. Donald F. Burchard, trs. Donald F. Burchard and Sherry Simon, Ithaca, Cornell University Press.

Foucault, Michel (1978a), *Discipline and Punish*, tr. Alan Sheridan, New York, Pantheon Books.

Foucault, Michel (1978b), *The History of Sexuality*, vol. I: *An Introduction*, tr. Robert Hurley, New York, Pantheon Books.

Foucault, Michel (1981), *Power/Knowledge*, ed. Colin Gordon, trs. Colin Gordon, Leo Marshall, John Mepham, and Kate Soper, New York, Pantheon Books.

Foucault, Michel (1984), "Sex, Power and the Politics of Identity," an interview by Bob Gallagher and Alexander Wilson, *The Advocate*, August 7.

Freedman, Estelle B. (1983), "Uncontrolled Desire: The Threats of the Sexual Psychopath in America, 1935–60," paper delivered at the annual meeting of the American Historical Association, San Francisco.

Freeman, Sue J. M. (1990), *Managing Lives: Corporate Women and Social Change*, Amherst, University of Massachusetts Press.

Friedman, Milton, with Rose D. Friedman (1962), *Capitalism and Freedom*, Chicago, University of Chicago Press.

Garber, Marjorie (1991), *Vested Interests: Cross-Dressing and Cultural Anxiety*, New York, Routledge.

Garfinkel, Paul E., and David M. Garner (1982), *Anorexia Nervosa; A Multidimensional Perspective*, New York, Brunner/Mazel.

Garner, David M., and Paul E. Garfinkel, eds. (1984), *Handbook of Psychotherapy for Anorexia Nervosa and Bulimia*, New York, Guilford Press.

Gilbert, Neil (1983), *Capitalism and the Welfare State*, New Haven, Yale University Press.

Glazer, Nona Y. (1984), "Servants to Capital: Unpaid Domestic Labor and Paid Work," *Review of Radical Political Economics*, XVI.

Goldman, Benjamin, and Michael Chappelle (August 5–18, 1992), "Is HIV = AIDS Wrong?" *In These Times.*

Gordon, David M., ed. (1977), *Problems in Political Economy*, 2d ed., Lexington, Massachusetts, D. C. Heath.

Gordon, David M., Richard Edwards, and Michael Reich (1982), *Segmented Work, Divided Workers*, Cambridge, Cambridge University Press.

Grossman, Allyson Sherman (February 1982), "More than Half of All Children Having Working Mothers," *Monthly Labor Review.*

Habermas, Jurgen (1975), *Legitimation Crisis*, tr. Thomas McCarthy, Boston, Beacon Press.

Hacker, Andrew (May 3, 1979), "Goodbye to Marriage," *New York Review of Books.*

Hacker, Andrew (March 18, 1982), "Farewell to the Family," *New York Review of Books.*

Haraway, Donna J. (1984), "Class, Race, Sex, Scientific Objects of Knowledge," *Women in Scientific and Engineering Professions*, eds. Violet B. Haas and Carolyn C. Perrucci, Ann Arbor, University of Michigan Press.

Haraway, Donna J. (1985), "A Manifesto for Cyborgs," *Socialist Review*, 80.

Haraway, Donna J. (1989), "The Biopolitics of Postmodern Bodies: Determinants of Self in Immune System Discourse," *Differences*, I: 1.

Hartmann, Heidi I. (1981), "The Family as the Locus of Gender, Class, and Political Struggle," *Signs*, VI.

Hartmann, Heidi I. (1987), "Internal Labor Markets and Gender," in *Gender in the Workplace*, eds. Clair Brown and Joseph A. Pechman, Washington, D.C., Brookings Institute.

Hartsock, Nancy (1983), *Money, Sex, and Power: Toward a Feminist Historical Materialism*, New York, Longman.

Harvey, David (1982), *The Limits to Capital*, Chicago, University of Chicago Press.

Harvey, David (1989), *The Condition of Postmodernity*, Oxford, Basil Blackwell.

Haug, Wolfgang Fritz (1986), *Critique of Commodity Aesthetics*, tr. Robert Bock, introd. Stuart Hall, London, Polity Press.

Hayles, N. Katherine (1987), "Text Out of Context: Situating Postmodernism Within an Information Society," *Discourse*, 9.

Henriques, Julian, Wendy Hollway, Cathy Urwin, Couze Venn, and Valerie Walkerdine (1984), *Changing the Subject*, London, Methuen.

Herdt, Gilbert, ed. (1994), *Third Sex, Third Gender*, New York, Zone Books.

Himmelweit, Susan, and Simon Mohun (1977), "Domestic Labour and Capital," *Cambridge Journal of Economics*, I.

Holtzman, Neil A. (1989), *Proceed with Caution*, Baltimore, Johns Hopkins University Press.

hooks, bell (1984), *Feminist Theory from Margin to Center*, Boston, South End Press.

Hoos, Ida R. (1983), *Systems Analysis in Public Policy, A Critique*, rev. ed., Berkeley, University of California Press.

Horwitz, Allan V. (1982), *The Social Control of Mental Illness*, New York, Academic Press.

Howard, Robert (1985), *Brave New Workplace*, New York, Viking.

Howells, John G., ed. (1991), *The Concept of Schizophrenia*, Washington, D.C., American Psychiatric Press.

Hubbard, Ruth, Mary Sue Henifin, and Barbara Fried, eds. (1979), *Women Look at Biology Looking at Women*, Boston, G. K. Hall.

Hubbard, Ruth, and Elijah Wald (1993), *Explaining the Gene Myth*, Boston, Beacon Press.

Jameson, Fredric (1983), "Postmodernism and Consumer Society," *The Anti-Aesthetic*, ed. Hal Foster, Port Townsend, Washington, Bay Press.

Jameson, Fredric (1984), "Postmodernism, or, The Cultural Logic of Capitalism," *New Left Review*, 146.

Jencks, Christopher (1994a), "The Homeless," *New York Review of Books*, April 21.

Jencks, Christopher (1994b), "Housing the Homeless," *New York Review of Books*, May 12, 1994.

Kanter, Rosabeth Moss (1977), *Men and Women of the Corporation*, New York, Basic Books.

Kappeler, Susanne (1986), *The Pornography of Representation*, Cambridge, Polity.

Katona, George, and Eva Mueller (1968), *Consumer Responses to Income Increases*, Washington, D.C., Brookings Institute.

Katz, Jonathan (1990), "The Invention of Heterosexuality," *Socialist Review*, XX: 1.

Keller, Evelyn Fox (1985), *Reflections on Gender and Science*, New Haven, Yale University Press.

Kendall, Robert E., John E. Cooper, A. J. Gurlay, J. R. M. Copeland, Lawrence Sharpe, and Barry J. Gurland (1971), "Diagnostic Criteria of American and British Psychiatrists," *Archives of General Psychiatry*, 25.

Kessler, Suzanne J., and Wendy McKenna (1985), *Gender: An Ethnomethodological Approach*, Chicago, University of Chicago Press.

Kirk, Stuart A., and Herb Kutchins (1992), *The Selling of DSM*, Hawthorne, New York, Aldine de Gruyter.

Klamer, Arjo (1984), *Conversations with Economists*, Totowa, New Jersey, Rowman and Allanheld.

Klamer, Arjo, and David Colander (1990), *The Making of an Economist*, Boulder, Colorado, Westview.

Klamer, Arjo, Donald N. McCloskey, and Robert M. Solow, eds. (1988), *The Consequences of Economic Rhetoric,* Cambridge, Cambridge University Press.

Kleiner, Robert J., and Odd Stefan Dalgard (1975), "Social Mobility and Psychiatric Disorder: A Re-Evaluation and Interpretation," *American Journal of Psychotherapy,* 29.

Kroker, Arthur and Marilouise Kroker (1987), "Theses on the Disappearing Body in the Hyper-Modern Condition," *Body Invaders,* eds. Arthur and Marilouise Kroker, New York, St. Martin's Press.

Kuhn, Annette, and AnnMarie Wolpe, eds. (1978), *Feminism and Materialism,* London, R. & K. Paul.

Kuttner, Robert (1991), *The End of Laissez-Faire,* New York, A. A. Knopf.

Laclau, Ernesto, and Chantal Mouffe (1985), *Hegemony and Socialist Strategy,* London, Verso.

Lancaster, Kelvin (1971), *Consumer Demand: A New Approach,* New York, Columbia University Press.

Lancaster, Kelvin (1979), *Variety, Equity, and Efficiency,* New York, Columbia University Press.

Langholz-Leymore, Varda (1975), *Hidden Myth,* New York, Basic Books.

Laqueur, Thomas (1990), *Making Sex: Body and Gender from the Greeks to Freud,* Cambridge, Massachusetts, Harvard University Press.

Lefebvre, Henri ([1974] 1991), *The Production of Space,* tr. Donald Nicholson-Smith, Oxford, Blackwell.

Leggett, John C., and Claudette Cervinka (1979), "The Ideology and Methodology of Employment Statistics," *The American Working Class,* eds. Irving Louis Horowitz, John C. Leggett, and Martin Oppenheimer, New Brunswick, New Jersey, Transaction.

Leiss, William (1976), *The Limits to Satisfaction,* Toronto, University of Toronto Press.

Leiss, William, Stephen Kline, and Sut Jhally (1988), *Social Communication in Advertising,* Scarborough, Ontario, Nelson Canada.

Lerman, Paul (1982), *Deinstitutionalization and the Welfare State,* New Brunswick, New Jersey, Rutgers University Press.

Levidow, Les, and Kevin Robins, eds. (1989), *Cyborg Worlds: The Military Information Society,* London, Free Association Books.

Levin, David Michael, ed. (1987), *Pathologies of the Modern Self,* New York, New York University Press.

Levitan, Sar A., and Clifford M. Johnson (1982), *Second Thoughts on Work,* Kalamazoo, Michigan, W. E. Upjohn Institute for Employment Research.

Levy, Frank (1987), *Dollars and Dreams,* New York, Russell Sage Foundation.

Lewontin, R. C., Steve Rose, and Leon J. Kamin (1984), *Not In Our Genes; Biology, Ideology, and Human Nature,* New York, Pantheon Books.

Lipietz, Alain (1982), "Towards Global Fordism?" *New Left Review,* 132.

Lipietz, Alain (1986), "New Tendencies in the International Division of Labor: Regimes of Accumulation and Modes of Regulation," in *Production, Work, Territory,* eds. Allen J. Scott and Michael Storper, Boston, Allen & Unwin.

Lipietz, Alain (1987), *Mirages and Miracles,* London, Verso.

Lowe, Donald M. (1982), *History of Bourgeois Perception,* Chicago, University of Chicago Press.

Lyotard, Jean-Francois (1984), *The Postmodern Condition: A Report on Knowledge,* trs. Geoff Bennington and Brian Massumi, Minneapolis, University of Minnesota Press.

Macpherson, C. B. (1962), *The Political Theory of Possessive Individualism,* London, Oxford University Press.

McAdoo, Harriette Pipes, ed. (1988), *Black Families,* 2d ed., Newbury Park, California, Sage.

McCormick, Ernest J. (1970), *Human Factors Engineering,* 3d ed., New York, McGraw-Hill.

McIntosh, Mary (1968), "The Homosexual Role," *Social Problems,* XVI.

Mandel, Ernest (1975), *Late Capitalism,* tr. Joris De Bres, London, NLB.

Marable, Manning (1983), *How Capitalism Underdeveloped Black America,* Boston, South End Press.

Marcuse, Herbert (1964), *One-Dimensional Man,* Boston, Beacon Press.

"Marital Status and Living Arrangements: March 1982" (1983), Washington, D.C., U.S. Bureau of the Census.

Martin, Elmer P., and Joanne Mitchell Martin (1978), *The Black Extended Family,* Chicago, University of Chicago Press.

Marx, Karl (1906), *Capital,* vol. I: *The Process of Capitalist Production,* trs. Samuel Moore and Edward Aveling, ed. Frederick Engels, Chicago, Charles H. Kerr.

Marx, Karl (1967), *Capital,* 3 vols., ed. Frederick Engels, New York, International Publishers.

Marx, Karl (1970), "Preface" (1859) to *A Contribution to the Critique of Political Economy,* ed. with introd. Maurice Dobb, New York, International Publishers.

Marx, Karl (1972), "Theses on Feuerbach," *The Marx-Engels Reader,* ed. Robert C. Tucker, New York, W. W. Norton.

Marx, Karl (1973), *Grundrisse,* tr. with foreword Martin Nicolaus, Harmondsworth, England, Penguin Books.

Marx, Karl, and Frederick Engels (1947), *The German Ideology,* ed. with introd. R. Pascal, New York, International Publishers.

Maslach, Christina (1982), *Burnout, The Cost of Caring,* Englewood Cliffs, N.J., Prentice-Hall.

May, Elaine Tyler (1988), *Homeward Bound: American Families in the Cold War Era,* New York, Basic Books.

Mezzich, Juan E., and Carlos E. Berganza, eds. (1984), *Culture and Psychopathology*, New York, Columbia University Press.

Milkman, Ruth (1987), *Gender at Work*, Urbana, University of Illinois Press.

Mishler, Elliot G. et al. (1981), *Social Contexts of Health, Illness, and Patient Care*, Cambridge, Cambridge University Press.

Mitchell, Arnold (1983), *The Nine American Lifestyles*, New York, Warner Books.

Mollica, Richard F. (1987), "Upside-Down Psychiatry: A Genealogy of Mental Health Services," *Pathologies of the Modern Self*, ed. David Michael Levin, New York, New York University Press.

Moore, Kristin A., and Sandra L. Hofferth (1979), "Women and Their Children," *The Subtle Revolution*, ed. Ralph E. Smith, Washington, D.C., Urban Institute.

Morris, Jan (1974), *Conundrum*, New York, Harcourt Brace Jovanovich.

Mouffe, Chantal (1993), *The Return of the Political*, London, Verso.

Moulton, Ruth (1980), "Anxiety and the New Feminism," *Handbook on Stress and Anxiety*, eds. Irwin L. Kutash, Louis B. Schlesinger and Associates, San Francisco, Jossey-Bass.

National Research Council (1983), *Video Displays, Work, and Vision*, Washington, D.C., National Academy Press.

National Urban League (1983), *The State of Black America*, New York, National Urban League.

National Urban League (1986), *The State of Black America*, New York, National Urban League.

O'Connor, James (1973), *Fiscal Crisis of the State*, New York, St. Martin's Press.

O'Connor, James (1984), *Accumulation Crisis*, New York, Basil Blackwell.

Offe, Claus (1984), *Contradictions of the Welfare State*, ed. John Keane, Cambridge, Massachusetts, MIT Press.

Omi, Michael, and Howard Winant (1986), *Racial Formation in the United States*, New York, Routledge and Kegan Paul.

Ortner, Sherry, and Harriet Whitehead, eds. (1981), *Sexual Meanings: The Cultural Construction of Gender*, Cambridge, Cambridge University Press.

Page, Benjamin I. (1983), *Who Gets What from Government*, Berkeley, University of California Press.

Pawelski, Thomas J., Martin Harrow, and Linda S. Grossman (1987), "The Construct of Schizophrenia," *Clinical Research in Schizophrenia*, eds. Roy R. Grinker and Martin Harrow, Springfield, Illinois, Charles C. Thomas.

Petchesky, Rosalind Pollock (1987), "Foetal Images: the Power of Visual Culture in the Politics of Reproduction," *Reproductive Technologies*, ed. Michelle Stanworth, Cambridge, Polity Press.

Physician Task Force on Hunger in America (1985), *Hunger in America*, Middletown, Connecticut, Wesleyan University Press.

Piven, Frances Fox, and Richard A. Cloward (1982), *The New Class War*, New York, Pantheon Books.

Polanyi, Karl (1957), *The Great Transformation*, Boston, Beacon Press.

Popplestone, John A., and Marion White McPherson eds. (1988), *Dictionary of Concepts in General Psychology*, New York, Greenwood Press.

Postman, Neil (1982), *The Disappearance of Childhood*, New York, Dell/Laurel.

Pringle, Rosemary (1989), *Secretaries Talk*, London, Verso.

Radical History Review (1979), 20: special issue on "Sexuality in History."

Rapp, Rayna (1982), "Family and Class in Contemporary America," *Rethinking the Family*, ed. Barrie Thorne with Marilyn Yalom, New York, Longman.

Raymond, Janice G. (1979), *The Transsexual Empire*, Boston, Beacon Press.

Reich, Robert B. (1983), *The Next American Frontier*, New York, Times Books.

Reskin, Barbara F., and Heidi I. Hartmann (1986), *Women's Work, Men's Work: Sex Segregation on the Job*, Washington, D.C., National Academy Press.

Review of Radical Political Economics (1984), Spring: special issue on "The Political Economy of Women."

Rich, B. Ruby (1986), "Feminism and Sexuality in the 1980s - Review Essay," *Feminist Studies*, Fall.

Robinson, Paul A. (1976), *The Modernization of Sex*, New York, Harper & Row.

Roediger, David R. (1991), *The Wages of Whiteness*, London, Verso Press.

Rorty, Richard (1982), *Consequences of Pragmatism*, Minneapolis, University of Minnesota Press.

Rosenbaum, Bent, and Harly Sonne (1986), *The Language of Psychosis*, New York, New York University Press.

Ross, Ellen (1980), " 'The Love Crisis': Couples Advice Books of the Late 1970s," *Signs*, VI.

Rubin, Gayle (1984), "Thinking Sex: Notes for a Radical Theory of the Politics of Sexuality," *Pleasure and Danger*, ed. Carole S. Vance, Boston, R. & K. Paul.

Salloway, Jeffrey Colman (1982), *Health Care Delivery Systems*, Boulder, Colorado, Westview Press.

SAUS 1982–83: U.S. Bureau of the Census (1982), *Statistical Abstracts of the U.S., 1982–83*, Washington, D.C.

SAUS 1992: U.S. Bureau of the Census (1992), *Statistical Abstracts of the U.S., 1992*, Washington, D.C.

Schied, H. W. (1990), "Psychiatric Concepts and Therapy," *Schizophrenia: Concepts, Vulnerability, and Intervention*, eds. Eckart R. Straub and Kurt Hahlweg, Berlin, Springer-Verlag.

Schneider, David M. (1980), *American Kinship, A Cultural Account*, 2d ed., Chicago, University of Chicago Press.

Schor, Juliet B. (1991), *The Overworked American*, New York, Basic Books.

Schwartz, Gail Garfield, and William Neikirk (1983), *The Work Revolution*, New York, Rawson Associates.

Scull, Andrew (1977), *Decarceration: Community Treatment and the Deviant,* Englewood Cliffs, New Jersey, Prentice-Hall.

Seaman, Barbara (1972), *Free and Female,* New York, Coward-McCann & Geoghegan. *Semiotext(e)* (1981): *Polysexuality,* IV, 1.

Shaiken, Harley (1984), *Work Transformed: Automation and Labor in the Computer Age,* New York, Holt, Rinehart and Winston.

Shapiro, Jeremy I. (1972), "One-Dimensionality: The Universal Semiotic of Technological Experience," *Critical Interruptions,* ed. Paul Breines, New York, Herder and Herder.

Shapiro, Judith (1991), "Transsexualism: Reflections on the Persistence of Gender and the Mutability of Sex," *Body Guards,* eds. Julia Epstein and Kristina Straub, New York, Routledge.

Shattuck, Roger (1958), *The Banquet Years,* New York, Harcourt, Brace.

Shulman, Alix (1971), "Organs and Orgasms," *Woman in Sexist Society,* eds. Vivian Gornick and Barbara K. Moran, New York, Basic Books.

Silverman, Deborah (1986), *Selling Culture,* New York, Pantheon.

Singer, Peter, and Deane Wells (1984), *The Reproduction Revolution,* Oxford, Oxford University Press.

Smith, Ralph E. (1979), "The Movement of Women into the Labor Force," *The Subtle Revolution,* ed. Ralph E. Smith, Washington, D.C., Urban Institute.

Snitow, Ann, Christine Stansell, and Sharon Thompson, eds. (1983), *Powers of Desire,* New York, Monthly Review Press.

Soja, Edward W. (1989), *Postmodern Geographies,* London, Verso.

Sontag, Susan (1977), *On Photography,* New York, Dell.

Sorkin, Michael (1986), "Simulation: Faking It," *Watching Television,* ed. Todd Gitlin, New York, Pantheon Books.

Spivak, Gayatri Chakravorty (1990), *The Post-Colonial Critic,* ed. Sarah Harasym, New York, Routledge.

Stanworth, Michelle, ed. (1987), *Reproductive Technologies,* Cambridge, Polity Press.

Stember, Charles Herbert (1976), *Sexual Racism,* New York, Harper & Row.

Strasser, Susan (1982), *Never Done; A History of American Housework,* New York, Pantheon Books.

Straub, Eckart R., and Kurt Hahlweg, eds. (1990), *Schizophrenia: Concepts, Vulnerability, and Intervention,* Berlin, Springer-Verlag.

Strauss, Anselm, Shizuko Fagerhaugh, Barbara Suczek, and Carolyn Wiener (1985), *Social Organization of Medical Work,* Chicago, University of Chicago Press.

Suransky, Valerie Polakow (1982), *The Erosion of Childhood,* Chicago, University of Chicago Press.

Tagg, John (1988), *The Burden of Representation,* Basingstoke, England, Macmillan Education.

Terry, Jenny (1989), "The Body Invaded: Medical Surveillance of Women as Reproducer," *Socialist Review,* XIX: 3.

Thorne, Barrie, ed. with Marilyn Yalom (1982), *Rethinking the Family,* New York, Longman.

Treichler, Paula L. (1992), "AIDS, HIV, and the Cultural Construction of Reality," *The Time of AIDS,* eds. Gilbert Herdt and Shirley Lindenbaum, Newbury Park, California, Sage Publications.

"U.S. Children and Their Families," *A Report . . . of the Select Committee on Children, Youth and Families* (May 1983), Washington, D.C., U.S. House of Representatives.

Vance, Carole S., ed. (1984), *Pleasure and Danger: Exploring Female Sexuality,* Boston, R. & K. Paul.

Vestergaard, Torben, and Kim Schroeder (1985), *The Language of Advertising,* Oxford, Basil Blackwell.

Vickery, Clair (1979), "Women's Economic Contribution to the Family," *The Subtle Revolution* ed. Ralph E. Smith, Washington, D.C., Urban Institute.

Voloshinov, V. N. (1986), *Marxism and the Philosophy of Language,* trs. Ladislav Matejka and I. R. Titunik, Cambridge, Massachusetts, Harvard University Press.

Wachtel, Howard M. (1986), *The Money Mandarins,* New York, Pantheon Books.

Warner, Richard (1985), *Recovery from Schizophrenia; Psychiatry and Political Economy,* London, R. & K. Paul.

Weeks, Jeffrey (1981), *Sex, Politics and Society,* London, Longman.

Weeks, Jeffrey (1985), *Sexuality and Its Discontent,* London, R. & K. Paul.

Weinberg, Martin S., ed. (1976), *Sex Research: Studies from the Kinsey Institute,* New York, Oxford University Press.

Weir, Margaret, Ann Shola Orloff, and Theda Skocpol, eds. (1988), *The Politics of Social Policy in the United States,* Princeton, Princeton University Press.

Weir, Robert F. (1989), *Abating Treatment with Critically Ill Patients,* New York, Oxford University Press.

West, Cornel (1993), *Race Matters,* Boston, Beacon Press.

Weitzman, Lenore J. (1985), *The Divorce Revolution,* New York, Free Press.

Westbrook, Robert (1983), "Politics as Consumption," *The Culture of Consumption,* eds. Richard Wightman Fox and T. Jackson Lears, New York, Pantheon Books.

Wexler, Philip (1983), *Critical Social Psychology,* Boston, R. & K. Paul.

Williams, Christine L. (1989), *Gender Differences at Work,* Berkeley, University of California Press.

Williamson, Judith (1978), *Decoding Advertisements,* London, Marion Boyars.

Wilson, Edward O. (1978), "Introduction: What Is Sociobiology?" *Sociobiology and Human Nature,* eds. Michael S. Gregory, Anita Silvers, and Diane Sutch, San Francisco, Jossey-Bass.

Wilson, William Julius (1980), *The Declining Significance of Race,* 2d ed., Chicago, University of Chicago Press.

Wilson, William Julius (1987), *The Truly Disadvantaged,* Chicago, University of Chicago Press.

Winn, Marie (1983), *Children without Childhood,* New York, Pantheon Press.

Winograd, Terry, and Fernando Flores (1986), *Understanding Computers and Cognition: A New Foundation for Design,* Norwood, New Jersey, Ablex Publishing Corporation.

Wong, Stephen E. et al. (1986), "Behavioral Approaches to the Treatment of Schizophrenia," *Handbook of Schizophrenia,* Part 2: *Management and Research,* eds. Graham D. Burrows, Trevor R. Norman, and Gertrude Rubinstein, Amsterdam, Elsevier.

Wood, Stephen (1989), "The Transformation of Work?" *The Transformation of Work?,* ed. Stephen Wood, London, Unwin Hyman.

Yanagisako, Sylvia Junko, and Jane Fishburne Collier (1987), "Toward a Unified Analysis of Gender and Kinship," *Gender and Kinship: Essays Toward a Unified Analysis,* eds. Jane Fishburne Collier and Sylvia Junko Yanagisako, Stanford, Stanford University Press.

Young, Kate, Carol Wolkowitz, and Roslyn McCullagh, eds. (1981), *Of Marriage and the Market,* 2d ed., London, R. & K. Paul.

Xenos, Nicholas (1989), *Scarcity and Modernity,* London, Routledge.

Zettl, Herbert (1973), *Sight, Sound, Motion,* Belmont, California, Wadsworth.

Zubin, Joseph (1986), "Models for the Aetiology of Schizophrenia," *Handbook of Studies on Schizophrenia,* Part 1: *Epidemiology, Aetiology and Clinical Features,* eds. Graham D. Burrows, Trevor R. Norman, and Gertrude Rubinstein, Amsterdam, Elsevier.

Zuboff, Shoshana (1988), *In the Age of the Smart Machine,* New York, Basic Books.

Index

Donald M. Lowe is the author of *History of Bourgeois
Perception* and associate editor of *positions: east asia
cultures critique.*

Library of Congress Cataloging-in-Publication Data
The body in late-capitalist USA / Donald M. Lowe.
Includes bibliographical references and index.
ISBN 0-8223-1660-9 (alk. paper). — ISBN 0-8223-1672-2
(pbk. : alk. paper)
    1. United States—Social conditions—1980–
2. Capitalism—United States.   3. Body, Human—
Social aspects.   4. Family—United States.   5. Sex
role—United States.   6. Mental health—United
States.   I. Title.
HN59.2.L69   1995
306.4—dc20   95-9237 CIP